FINGEST:
STONY GROUND

John Holborow

MINERVA PRESS

ATLANTA LONDON SYDNEY

FINGEST: STONY GROUND
Copyright © John Holborow 1999

All Rights Reserved

ISBN 0 75410 602 0

First Published 1999 by
MINERVA PRESS
315–317 Regent Street
London W1R 7YB

Printed in Great Britain for Minerva Press

FINGEST:
STONY GROUND

Fig. 1: Church of St Bartholomew, Fingest. Copy of a pen and ink sketch made in 1902 by W.A. Forsyth.

Chapter I
Looking for a Parish's Past

The prospect of the church from the parsonage house (The Old Rectory) – a view my family and I daily enjoyed during the years we lived there – is pictured on the postcards for sale in its nave. Architecturally plain and simple as it seems to the casual eye of the passing winter traveller or summer visitor, Fingest church is nonetheless unique among the small village churches of Buckinghamshire (it seats barely a hundred) for the explicit authority of its massive foursquare Norman tower, quite overshadowing the humbler dimensions of its nave and chancel (Fig. 1).

How a church so confidently expressing ecclesiastical rank came to be built many centuries ago in a then remote Chiltern valley is a confusing question and one that generates others. Was there a pre-Conquest church? If there was, why here? Was there a manor first? If so, who were its earliest lords? Did they found the church? *This* church? Why is the church so eccentrically sited in the extreme south-western corner of the old parish, hardly a stone's throw from Turville's? There is a churchyard, but no village green; so where is, or was it? Where did the parson and his parishioners of earlier times live? What sort of people were they? To what extent – if at all – have parish life and customs over the centuries reflected the turmoil and tumult of the nation's history?

And added to these is another question which, for me at any rate, has proved dishearteningly unanswerable. Why have the parishioners of Fingest – not to mention the local clergy – over the space of a few years, without a breath of public consultation, allowed traditional Anglican worship with its beautiful liturgy to wither as precipitately as Jonah's gourd?

Such questions – topographical, historical, ecclesiastical and (heaven defend us!) semiotical and sociological – can hardly be avoided when the past of any old parish in England is turned over and scrutinised in historical perspective. As you and I, dear reader, shall be seeing, they are no less relevant when we deal with Fingest.

The Challenge Facing a Local Historiographer

The first thing to come to terms with is how large and seemingly irreducible are the gaps in Fingest's recorded local history, in Roman times to begin with, and then the long void of the Dark and early Middle Ages. Things improve marginally as we reach the later Middle Ages, and a bit more as we come to the Reformation, the Commonwealth (or Great Rebellion as a past Fingest curate put it) and the Glorious Revolution. As we move through the eighteenth century there is a surprising amount recorded about what by then, to the wider world, seemed no more than a forgotten Chiltern village.

With so patchy a background, it is a ticklish task at best to piece together such fragments as may decently cover the origins and history of church, manor and parish – let alone map their fortunes through diocesan and secular changes of nine centuries. As for me, an innocent tyro in this field, the first consideration was whether my role was to be that of antiquary, chronicler or, God willing, historian.

Arnaldo Momigliano (*Studies In Historiography*, London, Weidenfeld & Nicolson, 1996, p.3) suggests shrewd definitions of these different attitudes:

Antiquary suggests the notion of a student of the past who is not quite a historian because 1) historians write in chronological order; antiquarians write in a systematic order; 2) historians produce those facts which serve to illustrate or explain a certain situation; antiquaries collect all the items that are connected with a certain subject, whether they help to solve a problem or not. The subject matter contributes to the distinction between historians and antiquaries only in so far as certain subjects (such as political institutions, religion, private life) have traditionally been considered more suitable for systematic description than for a chronological account. When a man writes in chronological order, but without explaining the facts, we call him a chronicler; when a man collects all the facts available to him but does not order them systematically, we set him aside as muddle-headed.

That the role of antiquary was already more than a century ago failing to win top echelon approval was made clear by R.W. Dixon in his *History of the Church In England* (London, 1878, vol. II, p.354) where he had this to say about the sixteenth century antiquary John Leland:

This unhappy man […] one of that inexplicable race who haunt old libraries, crawl around mouldering walls, dwell among tombs, and for no earthly advantage lose their youth, their eyes, their nerves in poring over the various relics of departed ages […]

I'm afraid, like Leland, I have been of an unmistakably antiquarian mind in collecting (indeed poring over) my material; and I've unashamedly enjoyed doing so. I must confess, too, that in writing it down (or writing it up) I have had to struggle hard to escape the comfortable role of chronicler, let alone a muddle-headed one.

What follows, reader, is my meagre attempt to knit together a patchwork of local history, however ragged, seeking to show where it shadows the patterns of a millennium of national history.

Chapter II
Making a Start

Deficiencies accepted, I will begin by just looking round to see what truly (that is, historically) lies within the village and parish and what does not. The first thing to notice is that the length of the south wall of the churchyard marks, as it has for centuries, the southern boundary of the ecclesiastical parish of Fingest; a boundary demarcated by Fingest Lane, running east and west in front of The Chequers, and separating Fingest from Hambleden parish to the south.

People who live here today will find what follows familiar and obvious. For others, a map will help. Fig. 2 shows the extent of the few dozen acres that now comprise the ecclesiastical parish as defined by an *Order in Council* (*London Gazette*, 17th September, 1976), and compares it with the thirteen hundred or so acres it covered for centuries, until in 1852 Cadmore End seceded as a chapelry (*Victorian County History of Buckinghamshire*, vol. iii, p.42). (A reminder here that civil parish boundaries, both past and present, have differed and still differ markedly from ecclesiastical.)

The Present Village and Parish

The buildings clustered round the church are quite few in number (Figs. 3, 4). It follows from what we have just

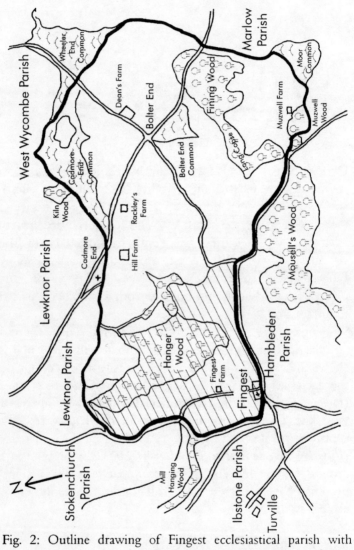

Fig. 2: Outline drawing of Fingest ecclesiastical parish with adjoining parishes, based on the Tithe Apportionment map of 1838. The shaded area is the present ecclesiastical parish defined by a 1976 order in council.

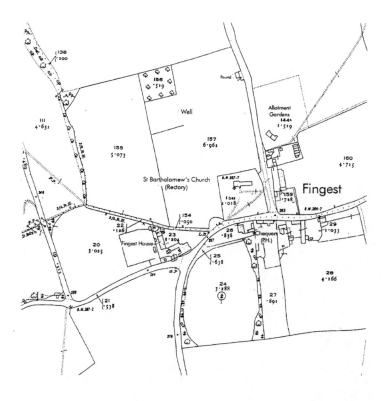

Figs. 3 & 4: Buildings around the church as shown in Ordnance Surveys of 1922 and 1984. In Fig. 3 a line of dots along the lane south of the churchyard marks the Fingest–Hambleden boundary; continuing north-west along Mill Hanging Wood it marks the Fingest–Ibstone boundary. It also shows the site of the manor's ancient well, and that nothing remains remains of the old manor house to its east. In Fig. 4 the new manor house of the 1930s is west of the well.

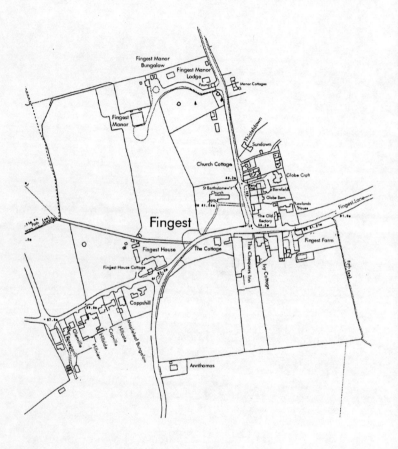

Fingest

Fig. 4

seen that those south of Fingest Lane and the footpath to Mill Hanging Wood are, and have always been, in the ecclesiastical parish of Hambleden, not Fingest. This is also true of a number of houses traditionally (that is, in recent memory) thought of as being 'Fingest houses'; these are Mousells (along Fingest Lane), Fingest Farm, Ivy Cottage, The Chequers public house, The Cottage; and, moving back across Fingest Lane to join the footpath to Mill Hanging Wood, Fingest House, the row of bungalows and houses opposite it on the road to Turville, and the houses on the first part of the road to Skirmett.

The present-day (1976) ecclesiastical parish now includes Fingest Manor with its outbuildings, and The Lodge; and, across Chequers Lane, Manor Farm and its outbuildings, Manor Cottages, the two semi-detached houses 'Thistledown' and 'Sundawn', Church Cottage, the Chequers Lane Cottages, the pair of semi-detached houses Nos. 1 and 2 Chequers Lane, Glebe Croft, the two cottages Barn End and Barnsfield, Glebe Barn, The Old Rectory, Lowlands House, Long Hanger and Hanger Farm Cottages (along Fingest Lane). Nine Acres is excluded, though it was once within the old parish boundary.

The new parish boundary extends northward only as far as Gravesend in Chequers Lane, and then leaves the lane and follows the north margin of Hanger Wood; thence it runs south along the Cadmore End track and skirts three fields (pastures known formerly as Great Hayne, Little Hayne and Flealands) down to Luxter's Cross – a perimeter of barely five miles. We shall see later that the old parish was much bigger, reaching into Cadmore End Common and Wheeler End Common, with Bolter End, and taking in Lane End schoolhouse, but still with the church and manor in its extreme south-west corner.

14

The Church

Next, the church itself – by far the oldest surviving building in the village. We shall be looking at its architecture and furnishings later, but some external features immediately strike the eye. We have already remarked the unique character of the lofty Norman tower, dwarfing the nave by thirty feet. At first sight it looks as though it was first built alone; but the nave walls are of identical construction, and on entering the church through the south porch we see that the tower's big round internal arch, opening eastwards (Fig. 10, section E–F), can only have been formed during the initial building.

The present chancel, a twelfth century addition, more or less continues the lines of the nave. Apart from the porch, there are no external structural additions, nor reason to think that any such were later pulled down. What we see now (save for some windows inserted, the double-gabled roof of the tower, the restored porch, and some Victorian buttressing) is the outline of the church familiar to the people of Fingest when Edward I was King.

That the church still has much the same appearance as it had seven centuries ago speaks of the lack of local gentry and/or wealth in Fingest after the early mediaeval building phase. It boasts no chantry chapels or architectural embellishments and the population of the parish seems never to have swelled enough to warrant even the addition of an aisle.

The Benefice – A Chequered History

This centuries-long ebbing of ecclesiastical importance mirrors the changes that overtook the patronage of the benefice. These, and the vexed questions of whether the manor, the church, or both existed before the Conquest (and if they did who owned them) I shall discuss later. But, to tickle the inquiring reader's palate, here is the briefest of summaries of what lies in store.

I shall be arguing later (Chapter IX) that at the time of the Conquest a parish already existed, under the pastoral mandate of St Albans monastery. By the middle of the twelfth century the benefice had passed by royal settlement to the see of Lincoln, the abbot of St Albans relinquishing the lordship of the manor in favour of the Bishop of Lincoln. Thus throughout the Middle Ages the lords of Fingest Manor were mighty (but for the most part absentee) ecclesiastical dignitaries of exalted rank.

The sixteenth century saw the lordship transferred to the Duke of Somerset, who, in turn, licenced a grant of the manor of Fingest to a prebendary of Wells cathedral. It was a lease by a successor of this prebendary to a yeoman of Great Marlow at the end of the sixteenth century that for the first time established a local lord in the manor of Fingest. The Wells prebendaries exercised the power of advowson of the benefice, though the rector was still collated by Lincoln. Several members of the new lord's family, the Ferrers, were buried in the chancel of the church, but did not improve the church building.

I will later discuss in more detail the patronage of the benefice, and the church's outward appearance. To enter the building is to leave the mediaeval and to come upon a typical restoration of Victorian times, carried out by the popular Victorian architect George Edmund Street. Street exercised a degree of restraint that earns some gratitude, though I myself think he might well have exercised a bit more. I shall be dealing with other changes in another chapter and only reiterate here the evidence of past parish poverty presented by the virtual absence of memorial slabs, tablets and brasses, save for one or two commemorating restorations of the last century.

Getting in Deeper

The visitor entering through the south porch finds for sale on the chest by the blocked up north door a pile of printed pamphlets which briefly describe the building and give an outline of the parish's history. The pamphlet carries a good, accurate sketch of the church as it appeared in 1902 when seen from the south-west of the churchyard (Fig. 1). This was drawn by W.A. Forsyth, an architect of Great Marlborough Street, London, and used as one of the illustrations in a detailed description of the church's architecture he contributed to Records of Buckinghamshire, (*Church of St Bartholomew, Fingest*, 1902, vol. viii, p.457–462). The first edition of the pamphlet appeared in 1932. It was compiled by Mrs Harriet Montefiore, then peoples' warden and living at The Old Rectory. Bernard William Mackie of Ibstone had the year before been inducted as rector of Fingest-with-Ibstone. By 1965, when Mr Mackie died, the pamphlet had been reprinted numerous times and had undergone several revisions. A 1978 version introduced the inclusion of St Bartholomew's in the Hambleden valley group of churches, dropped some detail of doubtful authenticity, and gained much by the substitution of Forsyth's drawing for the indifferent photographs of the church which had adorned the covers of earlier editions. Any further revision may see fit to take account of the present work.

Old churches usually offer the visitor such potted history sheets, their sale generating a pittance. The information they provide may be too little for some, and too much or too boring for others, but at Fingest, at any rate, the way the pile on the chest disappears all through the summer months suggests that people like to read about the church and its history. For me, the Fingest pamphlet was one of the sparks that kindled an ardour to discover more.

At a later date, when I became a churchwarden and inherited a box of church papers, added sparks were struck by the happy fact that these included a reprint not only of Forsyth's above mentioned article, but also a paper on *Delafield's Manuscript Notes on Fingest* (J. Parker, Rec. Bucks, 1902 vol. viii, p.463–475). Delafield was curate at Fingest in the second quarter of the eighteenth century, and wrote a considerable number of manuscripts (never published) on a variety of subjects, most of them now in the Gough collection in the Bodleian library, where Parker came across the manuscripts in question.

And Deeper...

Parker's paper on Delafield was the bait that led me to Duke Humfrey's library in the Bodleian Library, Oxford, where my reader's ticket proved an 'open sesame' to an undreamed-of treasure trove of relevant manuscripts and reference books (and, for that matter, of much idle, adventitious and irrelevant reading). Among the crowning jewels for me in this hoard were the Delafield manuscripts, as much for the glimpses they give into the mind of an honourable and simple country parson as for the lineaments of rural parsonical life in the eighteenth century they depict.

Delafield's antiquarian efforts, centring as they do on a handful of local parishes, seem to have awakened little interest in his lettered neighbours. He did, however, occasionally correspond with Browne Willis, a contemporary savant of Whaddon Hall, near Winslow, who became well known for his voluminous collections of ecclesiastical and related antiquariana, no less than for his eccentric garb and behaviour. For my purposes, the numerous Willis manuscripts in the Bodleian, especially those on Buckinghamshire, yielded an unhoped-for abundance of eighteenth century information about bishoprics, deaneries, rectories, vicarages and the clergy that graced them over the centuries.

In addition to the Bodleian material, of special local interest are scattered surviving surveys, glebe terriers, tithe apportionment maps and schedules of houses and land in the manor and parish which show, some clearly, some dimly, how such things once related, if they relate no longer, to ecclesiastical and manorial matters. I am indeed grateful to archivists at a number of different records offices and libraries – Lincoln, Kew, Aylesbury, Oxford, Taunton, and Wells cathedral among many others – for their help in finding for me an astonishing number of such manuscripts, details of which are given as they are mentioned in the pages that follow.

Still on the subject of manuscripts, I am especially lucky to have had opportunity for ample access to both originals and transcripts (the latter through the kind labours of the late Mr J.W. Brooks of Maidenhead) of those most truly local of all records – the Fingest parish registers of baptism, marriages and burials, for the most part complete from 1608. In addition, I have had sight of the churchwardens' minute books (really their church account books) from 1799, and of the Fingest church trust and charity trust accounts entry book, begun in 1848 as directed by the venerable archdeacon of Bucks, the legally constituted authority.

All this was required reading and having looked at most of it, and studied a good deal of it closely, I attempt now to fashion what I have retrieved into a running (and if possible readable) account of local matters spread over the centuries from before the Conquest until now showing, if I can, how memorable events in national history have left discernible imprints on the unfolding ribbon of local history.

To start with some quotations from the writings of Delafield, here are some paragraphs from the beginning of his manuscript mentioned above (Bodleian Library, *MS Gough, Bucks 2*), written in 1746. It is headed:

An Essay towards an Account of Fingherst in the County of Bucks, Both with respect to its Antient and Present State, whether Civil or Ecclesiastical. By Thomas Delafield, Curate there.

It begins, in true schoolmasterly style, with quotations, from Cicero and Caesar:

Quis est, quem non moveat clarissimis monumentis testata consignataque Antiquitas? Cic. Div, 1.1.c.40. (Who can but be moved by the famous monuments and recorded witness of Antiquity?)
Vicus positus in Valle, non magna adjecta planitie, altissimus montibus undique continetur. Caes. Bel. Gal, lib 3 (A hamlet in a valley, encircled by no wide surrounding plain but by high mountains.)

(Fingest folk will smile, no doubt, at Delafield's putting it on a bit with his talk of high mountains.) He then launches into a long preface I feel bound to quote at some length, expressing as it does, more gracefully than I can, thoughts and doubts about why venial histories such as this are written:

Before I fall professedly to my subject, it may not be improper, in order to reconcile it to some kind of People, to endeavour to justifye my self from the imputation of applying a good deal of time, study and pains in (as it may be thought) obscure, difficult and unnecessary matters; and which do not deserve so much Attention. This is one of the great faults of Men's misapplying their literate parts, censured by Tully;

Est vitiam, quod quidam nimis magnum studium multamque operam in res obscuras, atque difficiles conferunt, easdemque non necessarias. (Cicer. offic. lib.i, cap.6 p.496.)

It must be acknowledged, that the study of Antiquities, will engage a man in obscure and difficult matters; and which will therefore require a proportionate share of Labour, and continued, re-peated applications to bring them to light, and place them in an advantageous view. But them I cannot allow, that all these pains are unnecessaryly laid out. Or that it is even an indifferent matter to mankind, whether such things be known, or suffered to subside for ever in the current of Time. I think I may offer in favour of them, Instruction, Interest, pleasure and in some sense the necessity of them to keep up a re-membrance of what otherwise would be for ever lost, as may be observed in several instances as I go along.

For a Man to be ignorant of the Transactions of former times (and Actions are the true notation of time, without the consideration of which it is but a base and empty Duration) is, saith Tully, always to be a child. It is to be destitute of a material branch of instruction.

Affert vetustas omnibus in rebus longinqua observatione incredibilem scientiam. (Cic. de divin, lib.i, cap 499, p.451.)

Times past, and Persons that have long since made their Exit off the stage of the World, are the subject of History. And never any Reasonable Man questioned the usefulness of that Noble Science.

Historia est Testis Temporum, Lux Veritas, Vita Memoriae, Magistra vitae, et Nuncia Veritatis. (Cic. de orat, lib. 2, p.105.)

These are advantages that are incontestible. Nor is there less to be said for the pleasure of it; especially to Persons that have any Notice of acquaintance with, or relation to, the Places that are the Subject of such Disquisitions.

A man cannot but be pleased to find an Account of Persons, that have long since possessed the Places where he now resideth. And, as is the case of this Particular place, to find it first in the immediate Demesne of the Antient Kings of this land. Then part of the Possessions of one of the most noted Abbies of England. Next to have been the Scite of a Palace for the Residence of a long Series of Bishops, and its Manour and Lordship their Freehold. And lastly to be made the Establishment of a Prebend of the Church to which it is at present annexed. From these Alterations in the Supreme Possessors of our place, we shall come to such a succession of Splendid and illustrious Lay Personages, of devout Religious, of learned and reverend Bishops and Dignitaries, as a Parish near it so distinguished will hardly be found.

To lay down these things in Order, I shall therefore betake myself, not doubting but the candid and curious will favour the Attempt: which if it be not perfect in its Self, hath however pointed out the way to those that are more happily furnished to compleat it.

Alas! Antiquary, chronicler or historian, I feel not more, but much less happily furnished than Thomas Delafield to attempt, let alone complete, such an account; not least, perhaps, because I so sadly lack his ability to embellish my text at will with elegantly apposite quotations from the ancients. But nevertheless... here, goes! Read on...

Chapter III
Pre-Conquest Antecedents: Any Clues?

Hope of fleshing out the wraith of pre-Conquest Fingest is all but dashed at the outset for lack of knowledge of how much these Chiltern lands, thickly afforested and wild, had already been settled. There are mentions in the Domesday Book of local land holdings in the hundred of Desborough which name Turville, Hambleden, Medmenham and Fawley, but nothing about Fingest. This does not, however, imply that it did not then exist; several local villages by then established likewise escape Domesday mention, as we'll see later.

The earliest history of most villages soon becomes the history of their churches; but since churches are not mentioned systematically in the Domesday Book, the first thing we have to do is to look for any indication elsewhere of there being churches, or church lands, here in the south-western Chilterns in Anglo-Saxon times. If there were, the question is which monasteries or minsters owned them, and by what rights of charter or writ from which kings, all lands then being royal appurtenances.

A question relevant to Fingest in particular, pre-Conquest or post-Conquest, is whether ecologically or ecclesiastically it looked north-west over the Chilterns towards Watlington and the vale of Aylesbury; or north-east, on its own side of the hills, towards, say, St Albans? Or was it from the first a village of the Hambleden valley, looking south towards the Fawley reach of the River Thames? Whatever the case, and remembering that early mediaeval villagers seldom strayed more than a few miles from their land, we need to discover when there was first a manor here (or its Anglo-Saxon counterpart, a hall, the term 'manor' having come in only with the Conqueror).

On another tack, we would like to know, too, when and how Fingest and neighbouring settlements came to be thought of as being in the county of Buckinghamshire; and looking further back, how villages in these southern hundreds of what came to be Bucks county fared between the warring English kingdoms of the Dark Ages, and the Danish incursions that followed.

And for good measure, what about the Romans?

Roman Fingest: A Faint Shadow?

A paragraph from one of Delafield's manuscripts, and a note in an antiquary journal are enough to whet our interest. In the Dark Ages and before, the Chilterns were covered by an extensive forest north of the Thames that reached eastward into Essex. In his 1746 essay *Towards an Account of Fingherst* Delafield puts his finger on the local implications:

> In what condition this place was in very antient times cannot (I presume) be averred. Unless we may suppose in the general that it was a very wilderness, full of woods, impenetrable thickets, Moors, heaths and all kinds of, forlorn and desolate places.

After further remarks about the likelihood that:

[…] the aboriginal Britains [sic] partly cleared […] these parts of the original entanglement of Brakes and Bushes, of trees and shrubs which afforded both food and shelter for wild Beasts, to dispose them for a proper Habitation for Man […]

Delafield goes on to say:

[…] which the Romans, who always aimed at softning the native fierceness of their subjects, as well as establishing their conquest, might very much assist. By directing, if not compelling the Britains, in their Labour of making the country accessible, by destroying the fastnesses, opening of woods, and laying out high roads and passages, for the greater Ease and Security of travelling; as well as for the readier approach to keep them in order […]

In a note in *The Antiquaries Journal* (1948), E.C. Rouse describes a Roman cremation burial at Fingest discovered in 1937 when a garden was being prepared for the new Fingest Manor which had just been built near the site of the old manor house (reputedly the old Bishop's Palace). At a depth of only eighteen inches a broken urn was dug up, containing a smaller vessel, some fragments of calcined human bones (probably female) and a considerable number of iron hobnails. Expert opinion on this find was that it dated from the middle of the third century, a time when the prevalent pagan burial rite had already changed from cremation to inhumation. In Roman Fingest the older custom of cremation had evidently continued, although the body had nevertheless been cast on the fire wearing the hobnailed sandals customary for inhumation. The hobnails had been collected from the pyre with fragments of bone and committed with them to the urn.

Fig. 5: Aerial view of the paddock north of the church showing footings of early manor outbuildings. (Photograph: Mr Noble Graham).

Apart from furnishing early evidence of the legendary Fingest opposition to change, this find shows that this small area was inhabited, or at any rate near human habitation, in Roman times. There is known to have been an extensive first century Romano-British settlement on the Yewden Manor site, three miles down the valley from Fingest (*Archaeologica*, 1922, vol. 71, p.141). Whether this burial was at an inhabited site, we cannot know; but the find at least suggests that the location was not then as impenetrably wooded as Delafield assumes.

Passing mention now of a more shadowy relic of past habitation. Certain features of the terrain of Fingest Manor arouse suspicion that early settlement long preceded the manorial development of the site. Careful inspection of the contour of the meadow west of the church that was in the last century called The Lawn and in this, until recently, the cricket field, shows that it includes what seems to be a segment of a low, wide circular bank and ditch – possibly an earthwork. It would need some well-planned and expensive digging to discover whether this is truly a marker of very early settlement but that the Roman burial was here suggests that it is.

Traces of a low bank are also to be seen on the south and east edges of the paddock that lies immediately north of the church. This though, with a number of right-angled and linear patterns visible on aerial photography of the same paddock (Fig. 5), may be no more than boundaries and footings of early manor yards and buildings.

The Dark Ages and Early Christian Times

As for the history of Christian Anglo-Saxon times, I am tempted to lay upon you, dear reader, the burden of deducing answers to some of the questions posed above by putting before you a conspectus of the history of the early

Church and kingdoms of Britain in all its melodramatic detail (see J.R. Green, *A Short History of the English People*, London, J.M. Dent & Sons, 1915, vol. 1) – and letting you puzzle out its pertinence. But I spare you the task, for the conclusion you would in the end come to, as I did, is that little emerges from surviving Anglo-Saxon records or, rarer, buildings that is of relevance to determining the antecedents of settlement in this neighbourhood.

To take, for example, the seventh century struggle for ascendancy in England between St Patrick's Celtic Church owing allegiance to the Abbot of Iona, and the Church of Rome obedient to the see of Canterbury. This historic contest left no mark now discernible here or hereabouts. The sealing of the authority of Rome at the Synod of Whitby was achieved in the year AD 664, and the same century saw the piecemeal merging of the many kingdoms and tribes of the old Britain into the three chief Christian kingdoms of Mercia, Wessex and Northumbria. The monarchical and ecclesiastical development that followed, which included the laying down by Archbishop Theodore in AD 672 of the first basic canons for church government in England, has left no observable imprints here.

This provoking lack of primary evidence leaves us, searching as we are for scanty clues, with no other choice but to scan the patchy chronicle of recorded events in the middle Thames region in Anglo-Saxon times for events that seen likeliest to have influenced people, however indirectly, in such pockets of land settlement as were in existence in the south-west Chilterns during the seventh, eighth and ninth centuries.

One such event, the significance of which to our purpose cannot be doubted, was the advent of Roman Christianity.

Dorchester and St Birinus

In AD 635 Birinus arrived at Dorchester-on-Thames in pagan Wessex, twelve miles west of Fingest. He was a monk of the Order of St Benedict, sent as a missionary bishop by Pope Honorius I to continue the Roman evangelisation of Britain begun by Augustine at the turn of the century. Birinus's apostolate in Wessex was greatly helped by Oswald, the pagan king of Northumbria newly converted to the Celtic Church. Oswald wanted to marry the daughter of the Wessex king, Cynegils, thus extending southward Northumbrian rule (though not in the event Celtic influence). His missionary zeal emboldened by royal favour, Birinus baptised Cynegils and his family, including his daughter, thereby neatly ensuring both the Christian nature of the proposed royal marriage and the local acceptance thereafter of the Roman church.

Bishop Birinus established the see of Dorchester-on-Thames with the Pope's grateful blessing. During his fifteen-year apostolate he built many churches in his vast diocese of Wessex; sadly, none survived the Danish incursions of the ninth century, with the possible exception of the famous Saxon church at Wing, which although mostly of tenth century construction, has an impressively doughty crypt of indeterminably earlier date.

In the Britain of the times, despite the missionary eagerness of the Northumbrian church to spread its faith to the other kingdoms of Britain, the Celtic church had failed to establish itself even as far south as the Midlands. The relevance of Birinus so far as we are concerned is that he found Wessex incontestably pagan; so pagan, in fact, that he abandoned his original intention of evangelising the Midlands and centred his mission in Dorchester-on-Thames.

Thus the Church in Wessex was from the first Roman in its allegiance; and in fact it was Oswald's successor, his brother Oswy, who, although likewise originally an Irish-trained Celtic Christian, at the Synod of Whitby thirty years later made the celebrated declaration that as between St Peter and St Columba he would obey St Peter, 'to whom the keys of heaven had been granted', putting the stamp on the Roman Church's general authority in Britain.

Whether at these times the inhabitants, if any, of these valleys would have thought themselves subjects of the king of Wessex or of Mercia is a moot point. Much later, after the Conquest, William I moved the seat of the bishopric of Dorchester to Lincoln, but Bishops of Lincoln nevertheless, as patrons, continued until 1837 to collate rectors to the office and benefice of Fingest. It appears that Fingest, in whatever form it existed before the Conquest, can hardly be thought to have escaped inclusion in the diocese of Dorchester. The question again presents itself: was there a church, however primitive, founded here for Christian worship at any time during the two or three centuries before the Norman Conquest?

Before we can begin to find an answer, we have to consider what is generally known about the circumstances governing the building of small country churches in Anglo-Saxon times.

Minster Churches and Lesser Churches

The Celtic tradition of St Columba saw the position of the Church very clearly as alternative to, not part of, society. This meant that Celtic religion centred in remote monasteries of strict monkish rule and was not 'in the world' of secular priests and local church-building. After the Synod of Whitby the opposite Roman view, that of St Augustine, prevailed – that the Church both embraces and reflects society. Theodore's policy of diocesan rationalisation and creation of new sees led to the founding of new monastic houses, seats of the new bishops and served by monks of the strict Benedictine order. But at the same time it was clearly seen that such monasteries should also provide for the active spreading of Christianity more widely among a backward people. Within a century after Birinus the English word for monastery ('mynster') was being used to cover not only 'head minsters' or cathedrals (that is, bishops' seats) but also their newly developed off-shoots, 'ordinary' minsters. These were served by small groups of collegiate priests who, while still members of a bishop's *familia*, had begun to look upon themselves as missionary deputies of the strict monks with a duty to travel about wide areas around their minsters, preaching to and converting the peasantry.

The mission stations from which such pastoral work was first carried out were called 'old minsters', and regarded as mother churches. The parishioners of such a minster owed it their tithes, and were obliged to bring their children to it for baptism, and their dead for burial. Tithe duty was perhaps based on existing tax assessments, many head minsters having been originally sited at royal houses. At any rate, a means of permanent endowment was found in the annual gift for Church purposes of a tenth of the produce of the soil, a revival in fact of the old Jewish system.

'Lesser Churches'

According to Sir Frank Stenton, the most ancient of such minsters in the middle Thames country were at Aylesbury, Reading (St Mary's), Sonning, Bampton and Lambourn – the first three less than twenty miles from Fingest. Many ancient parish churches of today represent old minsters whose monastic links in later times disappeared without trace, only their parochial functions persisting. But we know nothing now of how near missionary zeal brought any of these five to this Chiltern valley.

By the eighth century, missionary spread from old minsters was bringing into existence a third class of church. These were the 'lesser churches' – lesser, but like the minsters having graveyards. By the end of the century most of the churches in the country were of this class. Every founding of such a local church led to the creation of a parish, with the consequent withdrawal of a tract from the area formerly served by a minster, so that by the time of the Conquest many minsters had lost much of their practical function.

Lesser churches were founded not by kings or bishops but by lay noblemen and landowners. Such a church was the founder's private property; he was its patron and had authority to present a priest to the living. When a priest arriving as a missionary from a minster was thus authorised to settle in the household of an Anglo-Saxon thegn who had converted to the Christian faith, he became in effect the latter's chaplain and the lord's estate became his parish. A variation not uncommon in Anglo-Saxon times was for the bishop to ordain as deacon the thegn himself, who thus acquired the benefice, and received a portion of the tithes due to the mother church. As deacon he did not have spiritual charge of the parish ('cure of souls'), but as patron he had power to appoint and pay a man holding the full order of priesthood to administer those sacraments which as deacon were beyond his power. This priest was the lord's servant, but a freeman, not a serf, and also owed obedience to the bishop. He was settled with his own land – the glebe; his only duty to the community apart from his spiritual functions (in contemporary documents he is called the

Mass or Altar priest) was that he usually kept the bull and boar that served his parishioners' beasts.

Early Anglo-Saxon Church-Building

On most estates there was at first no separate church building, the priest being content to preach or administer the rites either in the open with a cross raised on high, or in the lord's hall. This use of halls as churches was originally common; but as the conversion of the people working on the estate – the villeins, bordars and serfs – progressed, it was natural that the lord would feel the need to build a church separate from his own hall, both for general use and to reflect his own position as patron.

The halls of all but the wealthiest thegns were built mostly of wood, and the first Saxon parish churches likewise. Among churches that have survived with fabric of Anglo-Saxon origin, only one, at Greenstead in Essex, has kept any of its original wooden structure above ground.

Rebuilding of wooden churches in stone nearer the time of the Conquest accounts for the survivors, some of which we shall look at shortly.

The earlier Saxon churches often had the character of both dwellings and churches, with sometimes rooms in their wooden towers or above their naves or chancels. It is likely, indeed, that the Anglo-Saxon nave and chancel was modelled on the hall and chamber of a thegn's house. In later stone churches where the original Saxon plan in part survives, the chancel is clearly divided from the nave by a wall pierced by only a narrow opening. Thus perhaps was foreshadowed what later centuries came to regard as the customary responsibility of the people for the fabric of the nave, and of the parson or rector for the chancel.

Faced with irksome silence in Anglo-Saxon history on the subject of our local churches, we may well begin to wonder whether a disquisition on early church-building has much relevance to Fingest. Are there any grounds for thinking that a pre-Conquest church, or for that matter parish, in fact existed here? The patient reader will find the argument set out in the next chapters, with due consideration of whether the present fabric of the church, or part of it, is of pre-Conquest Saxon provenance.

The even more important question of who owned the lands in this part of the Chilterns seems to meet the same baffling muteness in recorded history. We have to listen hard and long to hear the whispers of inference, at length achieving audibility in a later chapter.

Shifting our ground a little for the moment, we may then stand back and wonder whether there are *any* surviving churches in the neighbourhood that have undeniably pre-Conquest features? Happily, this is a question that there are some satisfactory answers to.

Chapter IV
Surviving Pre-Conquest Chiltern Churches

A current Ordnance Survey (*Britain Before the Norman Conquest*) covering the period from the accession of Alfred in AD 871 to the Norman Conquest shows bishops' seats, monasteries and minsters, and maps the three hundred and sixty-seven churches now surviving in England which have pre-Conquest features. In many, of course, the features in question constitute only fragments of their present structure.

Of the three hundred and sixty-seven churches mapped, forty-one were probably founded in AD 600–800, and only eleven during 800–950, the period of the Viking stormclouds; the great majority, three hundred and fifteen churches, date their foundation to between 950 and 1100. For about ten per cent of the latter there is nothing to show whether they were built shortly before or after the Conquest, despite having definite Anglo-Saxon characteristics. These figures are quoted from the Ordnance Survey accompanying text by H.M. and J. Taylor, based on their extensive 1965 survey (*Anglo-Saxon Architecture*, Cambridge University Press, 1965). Fingest church is excluded from the 950–1100 list, although two noted authorities, A.W. Clapham and Nikolaus Pevsner, have described its architecture as an outstanding example of Saxon–Norman overlap. Clapham, in fact, compared

Fingest's tower with those in known pre-Conquest churches which seem to have served as naves (*English Romanesque Architecture*; Oxford, 1936, vol. ii, p.105).

Scanning the range of the Chiltern hills on this 'pre-Conquest' Ordnance map, we find a dearth of recognised pre-Conquest sites of any sort. It is true that within a twenty mile radius of Fingest there are four such 'lesser' churches mapped, one at Hardwick just north of Aylesbury, another at Waterperry a few miles east of Oxford on the River Thame, a third at Oxford itself, and the fourth at Iver north-east of Windsor. All four, however, lie well clear of Chiltern territory.

A smaller circle of a ten mile radius around Fingest, taking in the south-western part of the Chilterns, includes no surviving pre-Conquest churches of 'lesser' type; but it does just embrace the sites of four minster churches of the period. These are Bensington (now Benson), Cookham, White Waltham and Sonning.

In the zone between the ten and twenty mile radius circles we find the sites of the minsters of Oxford, Headington, Aylesbury and Haddenham (the last two in Bucks). Also, the bishop's seat at Dorchester-on-Thames, the monasteries at Abingdon, Cholsey and Reading, and, for good measure, the royal residence at Old Windsor. To complete the picture, twenty-five miles to the north-east of Fingest, and on the same south-eastern side of the Chiltern hills, lay the ancient monastery of St Albans.

Two inferences can be drawn. Before the Conquest the south-western Chiltern tracts were clearly not popular as founding sites for churches, or at any rate as church rebuilding sites after Danish onslaughts. On the other hand, there undoubtedly is, or was, a considerable number of minsters and monasteries in the neighbourhood (and even the possibility of a local royal interest) that might have had claims of one sort or another on these Chiltern lands.

Arguments over which of these foundations is likeliest to have shaped Fingest will be developed later. But first, we ought to consider what effects the pre-Conquest intrusions of the Danes, which wrought such marked change on so much of Britain, may have had on settlements like ours in the Chiltern valleys.

The Vikings, The Danelaw – and Fingest

In the fifth century the Anglo-Saxons were pagan invaders fighting Christian defenders; by the ninth, they were Christian defenders fighting pagan Danish intruders. By the time Alfred succeeded as King of the West Saxons in AD 871, the aggressive thrust of the Danish Great Army had already achieved the overthrow of Northumbria, East Anglia and Mercia, and a powerful force was driving far into the West Country. Alfred's famous victory over the Danes at Edington in 878 at the last moment saved the Christian independence of his kingdom of Wessex. At the solemn peace of Wedmore, Alfred and the Danish King Guthrum agreed a boundary between what had admittedly become Danish territory to the east and north – later to be known as the Danelaw – and Alfred's kingdom to the south and west. The Ordnance Survey map of pre-Conquest England shows this Danelaw boundary running some way east of Fingest, at its nearest passing through Luton twenty-five miles away.

The Chilterns then lay geographically in the kingdom of Mercia, and before Alfred's victory they had been cruelly overrun in the Danish push from Mercia into Wessex. After Alfred's death in 899 the Danes breached the boundary to extend the Danelaw south-westwards again. It was the combined heroic efforts of Alfred's son Edward the Elder and his sister Aethelflaed that in the early tenth century drove the Danish armies back northwards and east, eventually to the Humber.

During this reconquest of the Danelaw, Edward the Elder in 914 first fortified Buckingham as a permanent stronghold on the river Ouse, and then in 917 from a fortified Towcester forced submission on the whole Danish army at Northampton. In the territories thus rescued from the ravages of Danish occupation, Edward named 'contributory hidages', taxed for contribution to the support and defence of his newly established strongholds of Buckingham and Northampton. These hidages were land holdings in local hundreds which later formed parts of the framework of shires recognised thereafter as Buckinghamshire and Northamptonshire.

The next century, which saw the rise to national power of the West Saxon kingdom and then its fall, ended with the renewal of Danish incursions under Swein. Between 1009 and 1012 the future history of England was decided – and much of the physical evidence of Anglo-Saxon culture in England was destroyed. The extent of this destruction is laconically described in the twelfth century *Chronicon ex Chronicis* of Florence of Worcester:

> The aforesaid Danish arm quitted their ships in the month of January, marched to Oxford through the wood called Chiltern, and plundered it and burnt it; then they returned, pillaging both sides of the Thames.

By the spring of the same year, 1010, the Danes had defeated an army of East Anglians and Cambridgeshire men near Thetford. The way into Mercia was now open and they spent the next three months raiding south and west. To quote Florence of Worcester again:

East Anglia, East Saxony (Wessex), Middle Saxony, Hertfordshire, Buckinghamshire, Oxfordshire, Bedfordshire, Cambridgeshire, half Huntingdonshire, a greater part of Northamptonshire, and on the south side of the Thames, Kent, Surrey, South Wessex, Southamptonshire, Wiltshire and Berkshire being by the aforesaid Danish army utterly wasted with fire and sword.

So we see that in the tenth and eleventh centuries – in 914 and 917 in Edward the Elder's time, in 1010 during Swein's invasion and campaign of plunder, and again in 1016 during Cnut's defeat of Aethelred's son Edmund Ironside – the county of Buckinghamshire was ravaged, as Florence of Worcester records, at least four times.

Despite this sequence of Danish incursions, earlier English place names in Bucks remained mostly unchanged. However, according to A. Mawer and F.M. Stenton (*The Place Names of Buckinghamshire*, Cambridge University Press, 1969, p.xvii), evidence of Scandinavian influence appears in the names of Fingest and of Skirmett, half a mile away. 'Skirmett', they claim, descends from the Old English 'scir-gemot', the 'scir' being a group of hundreds with a common court. For the mediaeval form of this Old English place name to have retained so permanently its initial 'sk' sound, local Scandinavian influence must have been strong. Mawer and Stenton derive the place name 'Fingest' from an earlier 'Thing-hurst', and indeed many entries in the rolls of the thirteenth and fourteenth century Bishops of Lincoln write it thus. The word 'thing', which occurs in many local names in the northern Danelaw, is the Anglo-Scandinavian for an assembly. 'It is a safe assumption,' say Mawer and Stenton, 'that the "thing" which gave its name to Fingest was identical with the "scir-gemot" which is the origin of the name Skirmett.' They go on to assert that the first element in the name 'Turville' is the Scandinavian personal name 'Thyri', and note that as late as the twelfth century Scandinavian names were still being used in the south of Buckinghamshire. We shall be seeing later, though, that A.H.J. Baines draws a different conclusion from his dissection of the name 'Turville'.

By 1019 King Cnut had succeeded his elder brother Harold as king of the great Scandinavian empire. He abruptly reformed the hitherto barbaric character of his court and took pains to assume a wise and temperate mien, seeing himself, moreover, as a rightful English King and Protector of an ancient and learned English Church. But the damage to Anglo-Saxon culture had become irreparable by the end of three decades of Danish rule and the restoration of the Saxon monarchy with the accession of Aethelred's son, Edward the Confessor, could do nothing to remedy the loss.

Nevertheless it must be admitted that, for our present purpose, it would be less than honest to conceal the fact that, Florence of Worcester's account and Mawer and Stenton's Scandinavian attribution of the pronunciation of Skirmett notwithstanding, hard evidence that Danish damage explains the lack of remnants of Anglo-Saxon culture in this neck of the woods is woefully scanty. Pre-Conquest churches hereabouts were conspicuously absent.

Chapter V
The Mediaeval Chiltern Terrain

So far, then, it seems that history, local or otherwise, rather conspicuously fails to find reason to mention Chiltern lands and people as participating significantly in the unfolding of pre-Conquest events. A more credible explanation of this muteness than the effects of Danish pillage and plunder is to be found in the nature of the south-west Chiltern hill country – exceptionally thickly wooded and unwelcoming to agricultural settlement, and from earliest Anglo-Saxon times a principal haunt of fugitives and wild beasts. Even by 1086 there was vastly more Chiltern woodland than there is today, capable, as the Domesday Book records, of providing pannage (beech-mast and acorns) for a quite exceptionally large number of swine. The Chilterns and the Weald apart, only fifteen per cent of all the land surveyed in the Domesday Book was so heavily wooded.

The Chiltern escarpment divides south Buckinghamshire into two parts. Morley Davies's description in 1909 (*The Ancient Hundreds of Buckinghamshire*, Rec. Bucks, vol. ix, p.104), save for its mention of thatch, still holds today:

> To the N.W. lies the great clay-bottomed plain, where for mile after mile the pastures with their plough-rippled surface repeat with almost wearisome monotony the story of past agricultural revolutions,

and where every old cottage roof is thatched. To the S.E. is the beech-wooded Chiltern plateau, deeply scored by valleys which are either dry or occupied by inappropriately small streams, and descending by terraces to the Thames. Here we look in vain for signs of ancient ploughlands turned to grass, and tiles take the place of thatch on the cottage roofs.

Romano-British and early Anglo-Saxon settlements in the Chilterns were mostly confined to the lower levels of these valleys, in which the gravelly soils permitted farming of a sort. Between the valleys stretched the wooded upland tracts, covered with clay and flints, and unfavourable for even the most toilsome agricultural working.

The Hambleden Valley and its Tributary Branches

From Mill End in the winding valley of the Thames, the Hambleden valley runs northwards into the Chilterns for about four miles before it is divided easterly and westerly by the Ibstone upland. Fingest lies just within the eastern branch which continues nearly to Stokenchurch, while Turville village lies a little way into the westerly branch which spreads further towards Northend and Wormsley Park. No part of the Chiltern countryside is as well-favoured as this unique system of valleys enfolding the villages of Hambleden, Skirmett, Fingest and Turville.

'Inappropriately watered,' as Morley Davies says, the Hambleden valley carries only the little Hamble brook, which springs from sparse local sources including the mere trickle in Skirmett which gives Watery Lane its name. Sometimes in dry years (especially since 1989) the brook altogether ceases to flow. It appears never to have been thought capable of powering even the smallest mill – unlike the river Rye in the Wycombe valley to the east, which at one time served several paper and other mills along its course.

Watering must have precisely determined the siting of many ancient villages in S. Bucks. Most of them lie either in the Wycombe gap in the Chilterns or, like Marlow, Medmenham and Fawley are essentially riparian, with access to the Thames. Turville and Fingest, though as old, do not fit this pattern. Fingest, Turville and Hambleden, in their separate valleys, are sited on what are known as the younger river gravels, which were deposited as terraces of a proto-Thames and join the Hambleden valley to merge with the wide gravel bands that lie on either side of the present river. The rainfall water that drains through the upper and middle chalk crops of the neighbouring hills and runs out into the younger river gravels in the valleys, as for example at Watery Lane, is readily tapped in all three villages and several wells either survive or their sites are known. In contrast the wells at Ibstone, on its clay hilltops, must be deeper.

Population

When the Domesday Book place names are plotted on a map of the South-East of England, the Chiltern plateau, unlike the plain north-west of it, is one of the emptiest areas. In their book *The Domesday Geography of S.E. England* (Cambridge, 1962), H.C. Darby and E.M.J. Campbell show that the population density of the S. Bucks hundreds of Desborough, Burnham and Stoke was no more than a quarter that of Risborough or other more northerly Bucks hundreds. Further, there was an average of only one plough-team at work for each square mile of these three southern hundreds, whilst northern hundreds customarily fielded three or four times as many. Clearly the nature of the terrain contributed largely to this difference. Nevertheless woodland, though not inhabitable, was exploited as an additional means of livelihood in adjoining valleys.

How Ancient Woodlands Were Used

There is no better guide to this subject than Oliver Rackham's *Trees and Woodland in the British Landscape* (*Archaeology in the Field*, London, 1981) from which I have brought together the following, I hope not too inaccurate, outline.

Prehistoric forests, the 'wildwood', which covered the whole of England, were a mosaic of oakwoods, hazelwoods, ashwoods, elmwoods and, especially in the south, lime-woods – and presumably beechwoods, though Rackham does not mention beech. Woodland management began with Neolithic settlers of 4000 BC who destroyed wildwood to create farmland and moorland. Native wildwood, Rackham says with truth, is no longer even remembered.

Woods are the result of woodmanship. They yield a regular supply of timber and underwood. Underwood makes use of the property of coppicing. Coppiced stools produce a succession of poles or rods; scattered among the stools are standard trees, usually oaks, eventually yielding timber for beams or planks.

Ancient woods have sharply defined edges, bounded by irregular perimeters, not straight lines. Early maps show many wood outlines to be exactly the same as they are now. It is certainly true that in the case of Fingest woods, the outlines of Great Hanger Wood and Long Coppice shown on the official 1838 map of the parish (which was drawn to define the agreed apportionment of rent charges in lieu of tithes) correspond closely with the outlines of Hanger Wood and Long Copse shown on the 1981 Ordnance map (Pathfinder Series). Such ancient woods as these two have rounded woodbanks and an outer ditch to keep grazing animals out. Other woods that surround Fingest – Mill Hanging Wood, Goddard's Wood, Fingest Wood and Mousell's Wood – have the same features.

Wood-pastures were, and are, used both for trees and for grazing sheep, cattle or deer. These two functions are opposed, the shade of the trees being bad for the pasture, and the livestock eating the regrowth of the trees. The latter hazard was (and still is, where appropriate) avoided by pollarding, i.e. cutting the trees several feet above ground.

Wood-pasture had three variants: wooded commons, where the grazing and sometimes the trees belonged to persons having common rights; parks, private wood-pastures in which the owner kept deer, confined by a park pale; and wooded forests, a kind of wood-pasture in which the king, or some other magnate, had the right to keep deer protected by special by-laws. (A 'forest' was a place of deer, not of trees; some were wooded, some not.)

Wooded commons were the only wood-pasture known to the Anglo-Saxons and were probably of prehistoric origin. Cattle and sheep were turned loose to make a precarious living, sometimes in competition with native red deer and roe deer.

Parks were introduced by the Normans, who were in-terested in deer husbandry as an alternative to agriculture on poor-quality land. Looking forward two hundred and fifty years after the Domesday survey, we find that the Bishop of Lincoln in 1330 was licensed to impark his wood at Fingest with three hundred acres of land adjoining. This encroachment on the common land was the cause of much complaint at the time, and we shall hear more later of what happened to the Bishop and his park.

What is relevant here is that the common land of Fingest, as of most of the Chilterns, continued into the fourteenth century to be well-wooded. It looks therefore as if much of the land farmed here at the time of the

Conquest was, at best, wood-pasture, and as such later regarded by the Bishop's bailiff as more suitable for parkland for deer. The grubbing up of trees and scrub (a process known as assarting) to push back the woodland boundaries and extend the arable land in the valleys was not widely practised until the thirteenth century.

Rackham (convincingly, one must agree) recognises two sorts of countryside in the English landscape. Ancient countryside, according to Rackham, is 'the England of hamlets and lonely mediaeval farmsteads, of winding lanes, dark hollow-ways, and intricate footpaths, of thick mixed hedges and many small woods – a land of surprises and still a land of mystery'. 'Planned countryside' is 'the England of large regular fields with flimsy hawthorn hedges, of few, often straight roads, of clumps of trees in the corners of fields, of Georgian farmsteads, and of a large village every two miles – a land of predictability and of straight lines'. There is no difficulty, I think, in identifying the Chiltern lands around Fingest as ancient countryside.

Chapter VI

Fingest Manor:
Pre-Conquest – Or Not?

Having now some idea of the sort of countryside that clothed the Chiltern plateau and its deeply scored valleys in the eleventh century, we can begin to put together a picture of contemporary Fingest in such a setting.

A prime difficulty we run into, however, is that, until after the Conquest, there is a provoking lack of named reference to Fingest in surviving records of the time. No contemporary scribe tells us, even sketchily, who was the local landowner or who lived on the land. Equally thwarting is that we are not told whether there was a church of any sort here already when the Conqueror was skirting the Chilterns on his way to Berkhamsted to receive the oath of fealty from the vanquished English who had abandoned the defence of London. So we have to fall back on inference from less relevant documents that *have* survived – not always an easy exercise.

Manors in the Domesday Book

When was there first a recognisable manor in Fingest? Well, as every schoolboy knows, the place to look for names of manors in Norman England is the Domesday Book. For Desborough (Dustenberg), the hundred in which Fingest lies, we find fifteen Buckinghamshire manors noted therein, including Fawley (Falelie), Hambleden (Hambledene), Medmenham (Medemeham), Ibstone (Hibestanes) and Turville (Tilleberie); but no entry for Fingest, under this or any other name. Omitted also from mention in the Domesday Book are thirty-two other Bucks parishes of similar antiquity, as the Lysons in their *Magna Britannica* (published in 1806) point out, while at least forty churches or chapels in Buckinghamshire bear traces of Norman building. The weakness of the Domesday Book as a guide to settlement, as P.H. Sawyer observes in his book *From Roman Britain to Norman England* (Methuen & Co., London, 1978, p.138):

> [...] is not surprising, for it was not intended for that purpose. It was, in fact, compiled [...] to record the possible yield of estates to their lords through rents, renders, services and direct exploitation, and [...] what dues, including taxation, were owed to the king. The compilers were therefore interested only in places through which such payments of tax or rent were made; hamlets, farms and even sizeable settlements that rendered their taxes or seigneurial dues through some other estate might well not be named.

We might reasonably argue, then, that even had there been a Fingest Manor in 1086, its fiscal value may well have been too low to merit separate assessment. But this, of course, raises the question of which neighbouring estate it could have made its inconsiderable payment through – and why. Or, more intriguingly, whether it may have been immune from payment altogether?

'Manor' was a word unfamiliar in England until the arrival of the Conqueror. In its origin (Latin *manerium*) it is but one more name for a house, or what in Anglo-Saxon was called a 'heal' or hall. As used in the Norman sense in the Domesday Book, 'manor' has a wider, more technical meaning. It is not my purpose here to expound the minutiae of interpreting Domesday entries. We need to recognise, however, that the Domesday compilers used the word 'manor' to mean not just a given hall, nor even just the land (or 'demesne') that the owner (or tenant) of the hall occupied and cultivated for himself; but also all other land and houses that he held and were occupied by his villeins. The description 'manor' thus covered estates both large and very small. Manors so identified differed enormously in character, some being a single village, hamlet or even a farm, and others comprising a large number of properties, often at a distance from the one from which the manor took its name. Again, the meaning of the word to the Normans differed markedly from that of the Anglo-Saxon 'hall' in that it was the land unit William used for assessing in detail his newly conquered country's resources.

Until the Conquest, little was known and less written about the true extent of these. Taxation by the Anglo-Danish crown, and liability for certain common burdens such as the upkeep of roads and bridges, and of course, military service had for long been based not on the actual capabilities of estates, but on a unit known as the 'hide'. A hide was originally conceived of as the average agricultural holding of a peasant family, supposedly one hundred and twenty acres. As an accounting unit for taxation, however, it frequently represented a different, often smaller acreage – sometimes less than half this. The land-tax of the Anglo-Saxon and Anglo-Danish kings, or 'geld', was variously levied at two to six shillings a hide, forming a portion of the annual royal revenue used to maintain an armed force, or when arms failed, to buy off invading armies.

One of the tasks of those who conducted the Domesday survey was to ensure that the full liability of estates was recorded, while taking due account of special immunities claimed by lands belonging to the King or to the Church. As well as this, it was felt to be important, with so much land having changed hands since 1066 at the Conqueror's decree, to ensure that by 1086, when the survey took place, the land in each estate was held by good title. For each estate, the occupants of the soil are classified, usually in detail. For example, entries for the Ely survey for the Domesday Book (transcribed by F.W. Maitland from a twelfth century document) were couched in the following terms:

> The King's barons inquired by the oath of the sheriff of the shire and of all the barons and of their Frenchmen and of the whole hundred, the priest, reeve and six villani of every vill, how the mansion (*mansio*) is called, who held it in the time of King Edward, who holds it now, how many hides, how many ploughteams on the demesne, how many plough-teams of the men, how many *villani*, how many *cotarii*, how many *servi*, how many *liberi homines*, how many *sochemanni*, how much wood, how much meadow, how much pasture, how many mills, how many fisheries, how much has been taken away therefrom, how much added thereto, and how much there is now, how much each *liber homo* and *sochemannus* had and has: All this thrice over, to wit as regards the time of King Edward, the time when King William gave it, and the present time, and whether more can be had thence than is had now.

The Domesday entries for Hambleden and Turville are set down using the same terms.

Fingest Manor: the First Mention

Not specified in the Domesday survey, Fingest is first
mentioned as a manor by Matthew Paris, writing in the
middle of the thirteenth century. His *Chronica Majora* was
included by Thomas Walsingham in his history of the
abbots of the monastery of St Albans (*Gesta Abbatum
Monasterii Sancti Albani*) compiled in Richard II's reign. This
first Fingest entry is to be found in *The Rolls Series* (vol. i,
p.155). According to Matthew Paris, Richard de Albini
(Albensio, anglicised as 'Daubeny') a Norman of noble
birth who succeeded as fifteenth Abbot of St Albans in
1097, was a friend of both William Rufus and Henry I.
From them he procured for the abbey ownership of the
church of St Mary Wymondham in Norfolk, the church of
Hatfield Peverel in Essex and the church of Millbrook in
Bedfordshire. What's more, and very much to our point,
other grants made to St Albans with royal approval included
'the manor of Tingehurste, with the church and tithes'.
The account in Paris is this:

> *Reddita sunt etiam huic ecclesiae [Sti.Albani] manerium
> vocatum Tingehurste, et ecclesia cum decimis omnibus ad
> eam pertinentibus et ad manerium adjacentibus.*

Having quoted Paris, Delafield in his *Account of Fingest* goes
on to say:

> Here we have our place (as if well known) called by
> its old name of Tingehurste; and are assured that it
> was then a Manour, doubtless of very long standing;
> and had a Parochial Church endowed with the tithes
> of the Parish and of the whole Manour adjoyning.
> This (whether Grant or Restoration) was confirmed

by King Henry the first; who began 1100, in the 4th
year of the Presidence of our Abbot Richard.

Dugdale, in his *Monasticum Anglicanum*, published 1655–
1673, tells the same story, but with an important addition,
as we shall be seeing in Chapter VII.

Sadly, contemporary documentation of this grant of
Fingest Manor and church to St Albans in the early twelfth
century has disappeared with nearly all other original
documents of mediaeval St Albans (Rodney Thomson,
Manuscripts from St Albans Abbey, University of Tasmania,
1982). But we may reasonably conclude that Matthew
Paris, a monk and reputable historian of St Albans, had had
sight of the monastery's cartularies of the century preceding
his own, and reports what he knew at first hand.

Richard Daubeny died in 1119. It was during his abbacy,
Delafield tells us, that St Albans, having been freed from
the jurisdiction of the Archbishops of Canterbury,
professed subjection and obedience to the see of Lincoln:

> Abbot Richard receiving the blessing from the bishop
> of that see that he might the more strictly govern his
> Monks. Which we shall find hereafter to be the
> occasion of very great Dissension between the two
> Bodies, and which will highly affect our Lordship of
> Fingherst.

Of this dissension and its outcome we shall be hearing
more in due course. The questions that face us now are:
how and when did the manor that clearly existed as a
negotiable entity in the early twelfth century originally take
shape; and when was the church founded that equally
clearly formed part of the manor, and received tithes from
it?

We may postpone consideration of what can be deduced about the likely date of the church from architectural study for the moment. As to the origins of Fingest Manor, nothing remains now of either the old house itself, or of written evidence of its original extent. Lacking both, we perhaps find the first pertinent question to be: was it part of a larger manor – perhaps Hambleden manor?

If this had been the case and assuming that Hambleden already had its own church, the church at Fingest would have been a chapel-of-ease – a rarity until the thirteenth century. However then it would not have had its own graveyard as indeed the church at Frieth, built in the nineteenth century as a chapelry of Hambleden, still has none. Furthermore, lying as it does to the south of the church and occupying the land between the church and Fingest Lane (which marks the old Hambleden–Fingest parish boundary), the Fingest churchyard is clearly integral with the mediaeval layout of the church and parsonage within Fingest Manor lands.

Another contributory crumb of information is to be found in an account of the churchyard 'mounds' (that is, boundaries) in one of the seventeenth century Fingest parish registers (see Chapter XVIII). This describes a gate in the east fence of the churchyard, but none in the fence on the South or Hambleden side. This implies that, in the seventeenth century at least, churchgoers to Fingest did not arrive from the Skirmett direction. And a final point against Fingest being originally a part of Hambleden parish is that no part of Hambleden church can claim to be of earlier date than Fingest's tower and nave, and there is no evidence that a prior Saxon church existed in Hambleden.

Adjacent Manors and Parishes

We come back, then, to the question of Fingest as a separate manor in the eleventh century: did it exist, and if so who held it?

The tithe apportionment map of 1838 (Fig. 2) shows the parishes skirting the parish of Fingest. It gives what is very likely a realistic picture of the relationships of manors adjacent to each other and to Fingest at the time of the Domesday survey, where the respective manors, often coterminous with their parishes, are nearly all mentioned by name, together with the names of the men (or women) who held them before and after the Conquest.

The maps in Figs. 2 and 15 may help the reader follow the parish topography. To the south of Fingest is Hambleden which, with Marlow, was held before the conquest by Algar, Earl of Mercia. William took them both from Algar's son and gave them to no less a person than his own wife, Queen Matilda.

On the west, Turville (not directly contiguous, being separated from Fingest by a southward spur of Ibstone parish) had two manors. Turville Court Manor (in the Domesday Book, 'Tilleberie') which was held before the Conquest by Turbert, 'a man' of the same Algar. Afterwards, it came into the hands of the Norman baron, Nigel de Albini (Daubeny) of the same family as the fifteenth abbot of St Albans who later with royal approval accepted Fingest as a gift. Nigel de Albini held directly from William the barony-in-chief of Cainhoe castle in Hertfordshire, Turville Court being but a minor outlying manor of the same fief. By about 1200, Turville Court Manor had passed into the tenancy of the Marston family, one of whom, Niel de Marston, as its lord, gave its church to the Abbey of St Albans.

The second manor, known as Turville St Albans, had reputedly been acquired by St Albans Abbey from King Ecgfrith in the eighth century; we shall hear more of Ecgfrith and Turville shortly.

The next parish Ibstone, now lying wholly in Buckinghamshire, was at the Conquest partly in Buckinghamshire and partly in Oxfordshire. The part in Bucks (two hides known as Hibestanes) was held before the Conquest by Tovi, a thane of King Edward. In Oxfordshire there were two other parts, Ebestan (one hide) held by Ulf, and Ypestan, also one hide (and apparently geld-free) the name of whose pre-Conquest holder is not known. By 1086, King William's legate or messenger, by name Hervey, held the whole four hides.

Also on the west (then in Oxon, though in 1896 transferred to Bucks) is Stokenchurch which, like Fingest, gets no mention in the Domesday Book, perhaps because it was subsumed into the Oxfordshire land in Aston Rowant held by the Norman Miles Crispin from the Honour of Wallingford. By the thirteenth century however, three manors had become established: Stokenchurch Manor, Mallet's or Mallard's Court Manor, and Exchequers or Chequers Manor. Chequers Manor was held by a member of another Norman family, the Scaccarios, whose history was bound up with another neighbour of Fingest parish, lying on its north-west. This was a detached portion of the Oxfordshire parish of Lewknor, identified by Morley Davies (Rec. Bucks, 1949, vol. 15(3), p.166) with the 'lost' hamlet of Abefeld (Fig. 15) and still marked as 'Lewknor parish' on the Fingest tithe apportionment map of 1838 (Fig. 2). Morley Davies identifies as Abefeld a piece of land mentioned in the Domesday Book and the relationship this may have had with Fingest will be discussed later.

Completing the list of parishes adjoining Fingest are West Wycombe (in the Domesday Book, 'Wicumbe') on the north-east and Marlow ('Merlaue'). West Wycombe was held before the Conquest by Stigand, the usurping Archbishop of Canterbury promoted by Harold until he was deposed in 1070. At the time of the Domesday survey it was held by the Bishop of Winchester, and as before the Conquest supplied the monks of the church of Winchester. Marlow, as we have seen, was held by Earl Algar before, and by Queen Matilda after the Conquest.

Thus, from in a fairly complete list, we find nothing, in the Domesday account of any of these neighbouring manors to suggest that its assessment included that of Fingest. And as for a Fingest manorial landholder there is definitely no record in the Domesday Book.

King's or Church Demesne?

The proximity to Fingest of a number of minsters and monasteries has been noted in previous chapters. A possibility we have to consider then is that Fingest, whether simply as land or as a manorial estate, was initially a property of the Church.

It seems that in Saxon times most of the Chilterns lay within the great diocese of Dorchester. This, with its bishop's seat in the Benedictine abbey church founded by St Birinus in the village of Dorchester-on-Thames, extended north as far as the Humber. After the Conquest King William, who disapproved of bishops' sees being sited in country villages, laid it down that they should be established where the seats of military power were, in a principal town in each diocese. He saw to it, moreover, that they were appropriately re-sited without delay, and in 1072 the see of Dorchester was removed to Lincoln with Remigius, almoner of the Norman Abbey of Fécamp, as its first bishop.

We know from the foundation charter of the new cathedral of St Mary at Lincoln (quoted in Dugdale's *Monasticon*) that it was endowed with the churches of Buckingham and Aylesbury, and the manor of Wooburn. The two churches had been part of the endowment of the old see of Dorchester, but the manor of Wooburn was in a different category, being part of King Harold's forfeited property. In his invaluable *Domesday Book and Beyond*, (Cambridge University Press, 1897) F.W. Maitland notes that manors held before the Conquest by the house of Godwine (Harold's family), were in Domesday sometimes described as 'comital manors' to distinguish them from manors held by the Confessor, which were 'the king's demesne which belongs to the kingdom'. Since only three or four decades later Fingest Manor, as we know, passed with royal approval into the hands of St Albans Abbey, it is tempting to propose that it, like Wooburn, was a comital manor forfeited from Harold to William, and thus joined that 'private' part of the royal demesne which was not regarded as 'belonging to the kingdom'. If this had indeed been the case, it would explain the omission of Fingest Manor's assessment from the Domesday survey as due to its 'private' royal lordship – at least until William's death in 1087. After this, as we shall see, the Albini family seem to have had their eye on it increasingly.

Manors in Buckinghamshire were indeed then mostly in the hands of lay lords, there being no religious houses in the county until the twelfth century. True, the sees of Canterbury and Winchester both held endowments in Bucks before the conquest including, as named in the Survey, lands in Monk's Risborough, Haddenham, Cuddington and West Wycombe; but none of this episcopal property included Fingest. Also ruled out are the nearer abbeys of Reading and Cholsey, which had both been destroyed and their property alienated in 1006 when the Danes burnt Wallingford.

Thomas Delafield had little doubt about the origins of Fingest Manor. In his *Account of Fingest* he begins a chapter entitled *Dominium Regale* with the following:

> The first Hint of the condition of our place of Fingherst, that it had relation to the Kings of England, as their antient demains, was in a Presentment of the Homage in a Court there held 18 Eliz. 1576 viz. *Praesentant Homaginum quod Tenentes hujus Manerii tenent Terras suas per Antiquum Dominicum.* And again 23 Eliz. Apr. 4 *Juratores praesentant quod Tenentes manerii praedicti tenent Terras suas per copiam et antiquum Dominum secundum consuetudinem Manerii de Fingest.*
>
> Antient Demesnes (as our writers tell us) are such Lands or Manors as were in the hands of Edward the Confessor before the Conquest or of King William the Conqueror. And the Tenants in ancient demesne had this priviledge, that they could not be sued out of the Lord's Court.

In a marginal note Delafield, writes a reference, 'chartul p.23'. Which cartulary he meant we do not know, but there is no reason to doubt that he is here quoting verbatim.

Delafield thus clearly favours Fingest Manor as being 'king's demesne'. As to which king's the idea is worth pursuing further that in King Edward's time Fingest, like Wooburn, was indeed a comital manor in the hands of the house of Godwine. Godwine's earldom by 1051 embraced all England south of the Thames, and in addition his son Swein had been awarded a contiguous earldom, carved out of West Saxon and Mercian shires, which might well have included the south-west Chilterns and their valleys. When

Godwine died in 1053 his elder son Harold succeeded to his earldom.

Both Harold and his notorious brother were alike untouched by the religious movement that Edward strongly favoured, so it is hardly surprising that, as we have noted already, Buckinghamshire saw no flowering of monasticism, let alone of church-building, before the Conquest. At all events, we may justifiably speculate that the House of Earl Godwine, the first English statesman who was neither king nor priest, once held sway in these Chiltern valleys; if in this context Fingest 'Manor' had by then taken shape, it could only have passed to William at the Conquest, thus acquiring its rights as 'antient desmesne'. We shall be looking into this again in Chapter IX.

Chapter VII
St Albans, Fingest and Turville

Notwithstanding the speculations just aired about 'king's demesne', there remain good reasons for hesitating to exclude summarily the possibility of much earlier pre-Conquest ownership by the Church of lands at least neighbouring Fingest.

In his *Additions to Dugdale's Monasticon* (1793) Stevens prints a supposedly verbatim, copy of a charter of Ecgfrith, King of the Mercians, in 796 granting to St Albans monastery ten 'manentes' at Thyrefeld (Turville, as we shall see later). However, Mawer and Stenton in *Place Names of Buckinghamshire* and M. Gelling in *Early Charters of the Thames Valley* (1979) say that this charter, like so many produced in mediaeval times to support monastic claims to lands, is a forgery. Dr Gelling adds, however, that as the name Turville appears in its Old English spelling (Thyrefeld) the forgery may have made use of a pre-Conquest record.

In a paper entitled *'Turville, Radenore and the Chiltern Feld'* (Rec. Bucks, 1981, vol. xxii(4)) Dr A.H.J. Baines argues that though this cartulary text is indeed very likely not genuine as it stands, it is reliable in substance. Although doubtless corrupted to support the Abbey's claims, the list of its signatories is chronologically consistent. He further points out that the new abbey church of St Albans had been finished in 795, the year before Ecgfrith's father, Offa, died, so it is likely that Ecgfrith was fulfilling Offa's intention in making a territorial gift to the abbey his famous father had founded. The 'manentes' specified were likely to have been potential rather than actual households, the prospective taxable capacity of which (and the extent of their royal immunity therefrom) could be estimated even then.

If Baines is right about the validity of St Albans's claim to manorial land in Turville long before the Conquest then this, with Delafield's hint that the grant of Fingest Manor and church to St Albans was a restoration of a right, encourages a closer look at the relationships of both Turville and Fingest to the Abbey, and a comparison of the two parishes for similarities.

Let us first take stock of what can reasonably be deduced about the extent, lordships and ecclesiastical ties of the manors of Turville before and after the Conquest – and here Baines's paper is an invaluable help.

To begin with, what can be learnt about pre-Conquest Turville by dissecting its name? If the charter of Ecgfrith in which it is written 'Thyrefeld' has an authentic basis, then Baines suggests Mawer and Stenton are amiss in identifying the 'Tur' element with the Old Danish name 'Thyri', since the date of the charter (796) precedes the Viking invasions. Baines thinks it derives instead from the Old English 'thyrre' (sometimes written 'thyre') meaning 'dry, lacking water or moisture'. The 'feld' part, Baines argues, is like the Afrikaans 'veldt' – Afrikaans, he reminds us, is a Germanic tongue – and means 'open country'. So 'Thyrefeld' means 'tract of dry open country' – clearly inapplicable to the present Turville village which lies in a valley in surroundings that are still remarkably well-wooded. Further, the Turville valley gravel (see Chapter V) seems to indicate that the present village once stood on a winter-bourne, a stream flowing only in winter. The name Thyrefeld, on the other hand, is wholly appropriate to Turville Heath and the dry commons north and south of it.

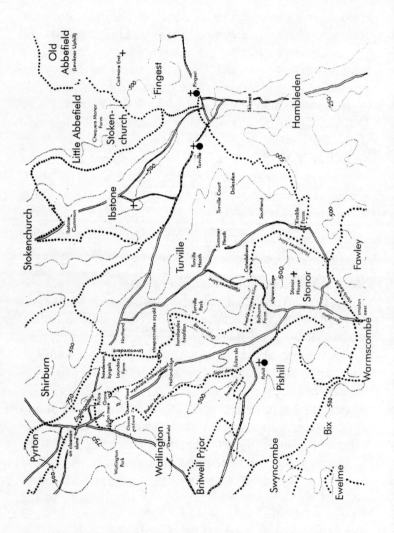

Fig. 6: Map from A.H.J. Baines's paper *Turville, Radenore and the Chiltern 'Feld'*. Note neck of heathland between Pyrton and Stonor connecting Watlington with Turville. Names in Old English mark the bounds of the Radenore estate.

Baines goes on (though it may seem for the moment not strictly relevant here) to submit that in the sixth or early seventh century Turville (Thyrefeld) belonged to a larger Oxfordshire land unit, Watlington-with-Turville.

This, he proposes, was an Anglian enclave; Anglian, because Watlington appears to be the 'tun' of the Waeclingas, the middle Anglian people in possession of the Roman city of Verulamium in the seventh century. Baines envisages this group of Anglian settlers as having migrated to and established themselves within the local, primarily Saxon, society of the 'Cilternsaetan', but still remembering their provenance in what was to become the founding city of St Albans monastery. By the mid-seventh century the Waeclingas were paying tribute to the King of Mercia, as the *Tribal Hidage* records. (The reader who is puzzled as to how Watlington, in the plain, linked with Turville in the Chilterns, will find helpful the map (Fig. 6) in Baines's paper which shows the narrow neck of heathland between Pyrton and Stonor which connected them.)

If we accept his main argument so far, it is reasonable to go on to suggest, as Baines does, that the name 'Thyrefeld' – 'dry, open country' – was originally applied to the tract of land comprising the chain of commons from North End through Turville Heath and Summer Heath to South End. Under Offa, the name of this already royal estate came to include land in the Idlecombe (Wormsley–Turville) valley and in the Dolesden valley up to Kimble Farm. Although it did not originally relate to it, it may well have also taken in Turville valley and village where they border with Ibstone parish. The remembered tribal origins in Verulamium of its Anglian people may well explain why 'Thyrefeld' was granted by a Mercian king to St Albans Abbey; Watlington itself remained in the hands of the Mercian crown until 887.

To pursue Baines's line of reasoning further, in 774 or thereabouts, Offa granted Worcester Abbey 40 hides from a large estate known then as 'Readanora' (later 'Radenore') comprising Pyrton, Pishill and Stonor. While the charter recording this grant has also been thought a forgery, it carries a later and very likely legitimate addition giving in detail the bounds of the land in question, which match those in a later version dating from 1070. From a critical comparison of the two versions Baines concludes that the eastern boundary of the piece of Radenore which is the subject of the grant is both the western boundary of 'Thyrefeld', and the Oxon-Bucks county border in this region. This gives us the boundary of 'Thyrefeld-Turville' as it stood before the Conquest, with its ancient commitment to St Albans.

We are left with a need to explain the apparent inconsistency of the Domesday account of 'Tilleberie', which runs as follows:

Nigel de Albini holds Tilleberie. It is assessed at 5 hides. There is land for 11 ploughs. On the demesne are 3; and 13 villeins with 1 bordar have 7 ploughs and there could be an eighth. There is woodland [to feed] 20 swine. In all it is worth 7 pounds; when received 100 shillings; T.R.E.7 pounds. This manor Turbert a man of Earl Algar held and could sell.

If indeed Thyrefeld was anciently St Albans's property, the fact that the Domesday survey says Tilleberie was held before the Conquest by 'a man of Earl Algar' begets serious doubt whether the meaning of 'Tilleberie' has been correctly construed. The more so since, as Baines points out, 'Tilleberie' is entered as having woodland to feed only 20 swine, is not accredited with meadow, and is assessed at only 5 hides. This does not sound like a description of the

'Thyrefeld' we have identified above, with its 10 manentes, equivalent to as much as 10 hides (*V.C.H. Herts*, iv. 368, p.14).

The implication of Baines's interesting research is that the name 'Thyrefeld' did not originally relate to the village site in the valley. He suggests that the name given to the village in the Domesday Book – Tilleberie – took origin as Tilla's 'burh'. The sequence of pre-Conquest events he proposes is that

> St Albans lost the estate [Thyrefeld] during the Danish wars or the troubles which followed Edgar's death in 975, and recovered only half of it – not the better half – leaving the new village to Tilla's successors. The resulting two manors are represented today by Turville Park, the manor house of Turville St Albans, and Turville Court, nearer the church and village.

Admittedly this account of events lacks corroborative detail, but it goes some way towards explaining the coexistence in Turville of two manors separate and independent at the time of the Conquest.

The Albini Family, Turville and Fingest

In the Domesday survey Nigel de Albini is named as the holder of the manor of Tilleberie (or Turville Court Manor as it became). The reader will recall another de Albini, Richard Daubeny, Abbot of St Albans monastery when Fingest was appropriated early in the twelfth century.

The Albinis were originally Norsemen who invaded and during the ninth century eventually settled in northern France. The name seems to have become attached to more than one family, at least in England after the Conquest.

Before, they were connected with the dukedom of Normandy and with the lords of Cotentin and the Channel Isles. By 1045, one Nigel with his son William had settled in Aubigny in Brittany, thus acquiring the family name de Albini. Another William d'Albini, who held the court office of butler to William of Normandy and attended him in his invasion of England, was the first Albini known to have appropriated an English church to St Albans, in the shape of Tallington in Lincolnshire.

How the Nigel de Albini of the Tilleberie entry in the Domesday survey was related to these other Albinis is by no means clear. He was an important holder of land however, and a tenant-in-chief of the Conqueror. His fief comprised twenty-five knight's fees centred, as we have seen, on the barony of D'Aubigny of Cainhoe in Bedfordshire. He brought with him to England a namesake, Nigel de Wast from Cotentin, who became tenant of Cainhoe castle, and granted Millbrook priory to St Albans during the abbacy of Richard Daubeny. It is clear that St Albans enjoyed the favours of the barons of d'Aubigny, at any rate after the death of William I.

Another William de Aubigny (probably the younger son of the same Nigel, and the holder of fees in Norfolk and Derbyshire) is named in a charter of St Albans (No.4; *MS Cotton Nero D vii, fol. 91b*) which Dugdale reproduces in his *Monasticum Anglicanum*. It records cells founded under the rule of Abbot Paul and includes the following:

Willelmus de Albeneio, pincera regis, simili ductus affectu, penes locum istium dedit Santo Albano cellam de Wymundeham, et manerium de Tyngehurst, quod donationem filius eius Willelmus de Albeneio confirmavit.

This cartulary text extract, if genuine, appears to establish that Fingest Manor, like Turville-Tilleberie, was in the hands of the Albini family before the end of the eleventh century, if not earlier. Who its pre-Conquest owner was, curious reader, persuasive argument will identify in the next chapter.

Richard Daubeny's abbacy was a profitable one for the fortunes of his abbey, though he had critics who, perhaps unjustly, accused him of using his influence to favour his relatives. He was a man of wide education who, to quote Delafield again:

> governed the Abbey magnificently for Twenty Two years: by reforming religion within and enlarging it without: in founding new Cells, and procuring Lands, Possessions, Churches and many other valuable things to it [...] He was also in good Esteem with Pope Urban the 2d. and Anselm ArchBishop of Canterbury, which gained him the acquaintance and Friendship of the whole court.
>
> But besides these outward advantages of Birth, and the Friendship of the great and powerful, he was endewed with a natural industry, and a flow of eloquence, and a proper sense of Religion, that highly improved them. The effect of all which qualifications thus united was the favour of the ruling powers, and by that means great acquisitions gained to the convent where he presided.

Delafield's ideas on how St Albans acquired Fingest I have already mentioned. He goes on:

> Besides this (for I shall just take notice of places in these parts) was granted to the Convent of St Albans, Lands of thirty shillings yearly value in Wallingford: [...] And an Acre of land in Woodstock for the Entertainment of the Abbot [...] I need not stand to

mention the noble repositories he made for the Relicks of the saints belonging to St Albans [...] Nor yet his being cured of a withered arm, in return for the assistance he once gave to the Body of St Cuthbert in preventing its dropping to pieces on occasion of its being translated from one place to another.

We shall presently come across a passage in Delafield that makes clear why it was Richard Daubeny worked so hard to procure possessions for his Abbey, using what influence he had with his relatives to this end.

First, however we go back to Delafield on the turmoil of local pre- and post-Conquest events in the Chilterns. In 1047 Leofstan, a Saxon 'also called Plumstan [...] a friend, confessor and counsellor of King Edward and his queen Editha', became abbot of St Albans. As Dugdale (*Monasticon*, vol. ii, p.181 et seq.) describes it, Leofstan promised

to render the approaches to the monastery safe and commodious to travellers, caused the woods which extended from the edge of the Chiltern, southward, between that part of the country and London, along the course of the Roman road called Watling street, to be cut down; and the more effectively to clear this tract from the depredation of robbers who had infested it, granted the manor of Flamstead [Flamstead is near Harpenden] to a valiant knight called Thurnot [...] who covenanted to protect [...] the western district from the incursions of robbers and beasts of prey [and] complied until the time of King William, when [on his] refusal of submission to the Norman yoke [he was] deprived of Flamstead [which was] given to Roger de Thoni.

Four years after the Conquest Frederic, a member of the old Saxon nobility and a kinsman of King Cnut, was appointed abbot. Dugdale continues:

> in these turbulent times the woods between St Albans and London were again infested with robbers. Frederic leased the manor of Aldenham [near Bushey] to the abbat of Westminster for 20 years upon condition he should protect the roads in the neighbourhood.

At the time of the Conquest Frederic had given refuge to refractory nobles opposing King William, and had cut down trees on the roadside to impede the Conqueror's march. When at Berkhamsted he came face-to-face with William he curtly explained that he was only doing his duty. Moreover, he extracted from William an oath to observe inviolate the ancient laws of the realm. On the attempted countrywide uprising in 1069 William disregarded his oath, crushing and oppressing the patriotic party. He replaced Stigand as Archbishop with Lanfranc from Normandy, and Englishmen by Normans as senior ecclesiastics and administrators. The story goes that William taunted Frederic with the English being so easily conquered; Frederic said that William owed the ease of his conquest to the Church, which by gift of former kings held so much of the land but produced no knights therefrom. William replied: 'Out of your own mouth I judge you, and I begin with you, resuming the possessions with which you are so abundantly supplied, that knights may be provided from them for the defence of the realm.'

The outcome for St Albans of this confrontation between its defiant Anglo-Danish abbot and the victorious William is succinctly described by Paris:

Rex [...] Frederic Abbatis Sancti Albani maneria, praedia, domos, et possessiones devastavit.

The historian and antiquary Nathaniel Salmon likewise, in his *History of Hertfordshire* (published in 1728) says:

In short, there is of the Lands hereabouts [formerly appropriated to St Albans] a disorderly account; there has been chopping and changing, and the Confusion, I imagine, is owing to the Conqueror's dispossessing the Abbots of St Albans of their lands, upon the grudge he owed to the brave Frederick, that opposed his being King, and crammed the Oath, to observe the Confessor's establishment, down his Throat.

In the interests of truthfulness, however, I have to say that in the same passage Salmon says:

There is in the Grants to the Monastery of St Albans Mention made of a Place called Tinghurst, with the church and all the Tythes belonging to it, confirmed by Henry I.

This agrees precisely with what Paris and Delafield say. But Salmon goes on:

And in a Statute of the 4th of Queen Mary, several Manors are annexed to the Dutchy of Lancaster, as Eastwick, Hunsdon, Milkly and others, and Tinghurst, which I take to be [...] Titterberst, or rather part of it.

Under a separate heading 'Theobald's-street' Salmon says the name of this village in Domesday is written 'Titterberst' and 'Titterbersth' and it is divided into five parcels etc. So far, I have been unable to trace the statute in question. Further, we shall see in a later chapter that in 1551, two years before Queen Mary's accession, the archives of Wells cathedral record the grant of the manor of Tingherst to a prebendary called Thynne of Wells; so what the Duchy of Lancaster annexed in the shape of Tinghurst remains a mystery. (Salmon's contention that 'Titterberst' is to be construed as 'Tinghurst' I leave to the reader's judgement.)

In 1077 Frederic died (he had fled to Ely, near Hereward the Wake's last stronghold). He was succeeded as Abbot by Paul of Caen, a Norman, and a relative of Langfranc, with whom William had soon replaced Stigand as Archbishop of Canterbury. By 1085 there were only two Englishmen to twenty-four Frenchmen among the free tenants of St Albans abbey.

It was Abbot Paul who began the building of the new church replacing Offa's old cathedral at St Albans. On his death in 1093 the abbacy remained vacant for four years, William Rufus appropriating its revenues while controversy persisted whether the next abbot should be English or Norman. The choice fell on Richard Daubeny.

To take up Delafield's account of events at St Albans, he goes on:

What is more worthy of remark, and of greater certainly, is that in the year of our Lord 1115 He [Abbot Richard] caused to be dedicated the conventual church of St Albans, which his Predecessor Paul had built; the solemnity of which was performed by Geoffrey, Bishop of Roan [Rouen], Richard de Belmeis, Bp. of London, Ralph Flambard, Bp. of London [a clerical slip – he means Durham] Robert Blouet, Bp. of Lincoln and Roger Bp. of Salisbury, assisted by many Abbots, in the presence of King Henry, Maud his first Queen, Daughter of Malcolm,

King of Scotland and of many Earls, Barons and
Nobles and a numberless attendance of other
Persons on Tuesday 28th December, 16 Hen. I.

And all becomes plain...

The exasperated reader may now, at last, be able to make
sense of the lengthy diversion I have felt it necessary to
make into the affairs of Turville.

In brief, as a result of Abbot Frederic's intransigence
William had dispossessed his abbey of much of its land. We
do not know exactly how much, but it looks as if it was the
opportunity for Nigel de Albini to acquire the
Hertfordshire manors in the neighbourhood of Cainhoe.
Among other outlying manors he also acquired the part of
Thyrefeld that the Domesday Book calls Tilleberie, taking
it from the English 'Earl Algar's man, Turbert'. Thyrefeld,
including Tilleberie (if Dr Baines is right, as I believe he is),
had from the eighth century been St Albans property, and
the Abbey after the Conquest seems to have been able to
retain most of it, though shorn of Tilleberie.

Richard Daubeny saw that, with the building of the new
conventual church being completed during his abbacy,
there would be a grand and solemn service of dedication to
be prepared for. With William I dead, and he himself on
good terms first with William Rufus and then Henry I, the
time must have seemed ripe to reclaim – with the king's
approval, and using the influence of the Albini family –
lands (and churches) to which St Albans Abbey had
historical claims. It looks very much as if William d'Aubeny
recognised Fingest as among the latter. After William I's
death his personal rights to Fingest Manor soon withered,
and Nigel D'Aubeny and after him his son William pressed
the favourable opportunity to subsume its lordship under
their feudal tenancy of Tilleberie. This had the double

advantage of reviving recognition of Fingest's benefice (then still the sole benefice locally) as having been collated by St Albans from Earl Algar's times, and at the same time halting further topographical encroachment on the parish by Hambleden under the heirs of Queen Matilda. William d'Aubeny now added the gift of the manor to the advowson already in the Abbey's hands, with the encouragement (to say the least) of Abbot Richard.

Chapter VIII
The Church of St Bartholomew

The prime cause arousing interest in Fingest's origins is the manifest antiquity of its church. Given the pattern of early church building in this country, several questions pose themselves. Why, how, and when did this building of such unique cast come to be raised in this very spot over eight centuries ago, a small seemingly remote spur at the head of what we now call 'the Hambleden valley'?

No useful answers being forthcoming from the very scanty writings discoverable on the subject, we probably do best to start by using our eyes and looking hard at the church as it now stands. There follows the result of my efforts at deducing the sequence of stages in the church's building, dating them, and then attempting to match findings with the changing monastic and diocesan lordships that overtook the manor and church from before the Conquest to Henry VII's accession in 1485; that is during 'the Middle Ages'.

Assured of the breadth of interest of the reader who has got thus far, I may add that the more searching our scrutiny of local ecclesiological and ecclesiastical matters, the more likely we are to get some inkling of the lives of priests and people in the small world encompassed by this Chiltern parish in mediaeval times. What happened to local life in Tudor times and afterwards, which is no less interesting, we shall try to piece together later.

St Bartholomew

Before looking at the church building itself, we might first consider its dedication to the apostle Bartholomew. Among apostolic dedicatees of ancient churches the relatively obscure Bartholomew is surprisingly favoured. In his *Dedications and Patron Saints of English Churches* (O.U.P. 1914) Francis Bond ranks Bartholomew fifth (one hundred and sixty-five churches) among the apostles in order of pre-nineteenth century popularity in this respect. Peter (one thousand one hundred and forty churches), Andrew (six hundred and thirty-seven), James the Greater (four hundred and fourteen) and John (one hundred and eighty-one) outstrip Bartholomew. In a monumental three-volume work *Studies in Church Dedications* published in 1899, Frances Arnold-Foster found one hundred and forty-seven 'ancient' (that is, pre-Reformation) English churches dedicated to St Bartholomew, with only three in the eighteenth century, and thirty-four in the nineteenth.

The reason for St Bartholomew's high ranking in early times is probably to be found in the many strange tales that were then current of the miraculous preservation of this apostle's remains. Bartholomew (generally identified with Nathaniel) is, according to the Roman Martyrology attributed with an apostolate in India and in Armenia, where at Derbend on the Caspian sea he was said to have been flayed alive before being beheaded, hence his iconographic emblem of a flaying-knife (David Hugh Farmer, *Oxford Dictionary of Saints*, 1978). His relics were supposed to have been translated to the island of Lipari, then to Benevento, and lastly to Rome, where St Bartholomew's church on the Tiber still claims them. The mode of his martyrdom made him the patron saint of tanners, and all who work with skins.

In Buckinghamshire, out of the one hundred and eighty-one ancient churches she identified in the county, Frances Arnold-Foster found Fingest to be the only one dedicated to Bartholomew. In this she confirms Browne Willis's note that among the many churches he visited in Buckinghamshire hundreds during the first half of the eighteenth century, only Fingest's was thus dedicated (Bodleian Library, *Willis MS*, vol. xxv, pp.v, vi, vii).

Touching relics of the saint, we ought especially to note (why, I shall shortly explain) that an arm of St Bartholomew (lacking its integument, presumably) is said to have been given to Canterbury in the early eleventh century by Cnut's wife, Queen Emma. Arnold-Foster however, quoting from Baring-Gould's *Lives of the Saints*, says the donor was Anselm, who succeeded Lanfranc as Archbishop in 1093. The sensational acquisition of this prized apostolic relic by Canterbury (or tales of it) led to wide contemporary diffusion of the cult of Bartholomew in England, which no doubt explains his adoption as patron saint by so many of the churches then newly built or rebuilt. If the Queen Emma tale were true, it would argue a pre-Conquest dedication to Bartholomew of a church in Fingest, most likely a wooden one, since the most that can be reasonably claimed for the existing stone tower and nave is Saxo-Norman overlap. If on the other hand Anselm was in fact the donor of the holy relic in question, this would argue that the dedication to Bartholomew was only of the stone church soon after the Conquest.

It was mooted in the previous chapter that after Harold's demise, Fingest being a comital manor became the personal property of the king, the king in question being of course William I. Although this was a time when St Bartholomew's popularity in England as a dedicatee would shortly reach (Anselm), or had already reached (Queen Emma), a peak, newly built churches in the south-west

Chilterns, till then Earl Godwine's family territory, were a rarity. A check on the dates of foundation attributed to other ancient parish churches in these local hundreds shows that Fingest's was very likely the earliest stone church to be built in south Buckinghamshire.

Was it, then, contemporary apostolic popularity that settled the question of Fingest's dedication? The structural dating of the oldest parts of the church's stone fabric certainly seems to fit with Anselm's consecration at Canterbury in 1093. All the same, one cannot help wondering whether there may have been some earlier reason, now long forgotten, for venerating Bartholomew at Fingest. Perhaps some tale of another relic? Or of a somehow associated burial? Or, more practically perhaps, a local tannery skill in this deer-forest region? We are unlikely ever to discover.

Whatever its reason Fingest's dedication may have had wider significance later by bringing the church to the notice of Richard Daubeny, fifteenth abbot of St Albans. The reader will recall Delafield saying that Daubeny had recovered from a withering of his arm as a result, so he believed, of the intercession of St Cuthbert. This being so, it is perhaps not too speculative to suggest that the name of St Bartholomew brought to Abbot Richard's mind not skins or tannery but a personally and anatomically pertinent image of the relic itself. Fingest's manor, with its church's apposite dedication, must therefore have seemed an especially apt addition to the church property which he was everywhere reacquiring to celebrate the completion and consecration of his great new conventual church of St Alban.

At any rate, Matthew Paris, writing in the thirteenth century, reiterates in his *Chronica Majora* that Henry I granted 'Tingehurste, with manor, church and tithes', to St Albans during Daubeny's abbacy. This is substantiated by

Ground Plan

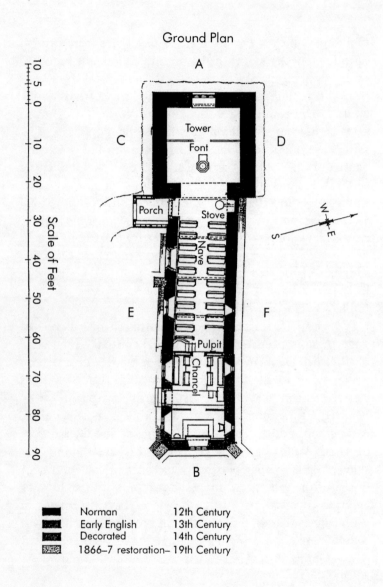

A

Tower

Font

C   D

Porch   Stove

Nave

E   F

Pulpit

Chancel

B

Scale of Feet

- **Norman** — 12th Century
- **Early English** — 13th Century
- **Decorated** — 14th Century
- **1866–7 restoration** — 19th Century

Fig. 7: Ground Plan of St Bartholomew's, drawn and measured by W.A. Forsyth (Rec. Bucks. viii, 458, 1902)

an entry among the papal registers of 1219 recording a grant by Pope Honorius III to another William, a later abbot of St Albans, of protection and confirmation of possessions and privileges in accordance with a series of previous papal bulls. The grant names 'Tinghurste' along with numerous other possessions of the Abbot which are particularised in the bulls (*Calendar of Entries In the Papal Registers relating to Gt. Britain and Ireland: Papal Letters*, vol. i, p.63).

The Church Building

Accepting the difficulties with primary dating – that is dating based upon historical or archaeological evidence – we may look at the building in two different ways. Firstly, making a ground plan (Fig. 7) and then measuring, drawing and describing the building as it stands, identifying so far as we can features that on evidence from other churches we may take as characteristic of this or that architectural period. This process is known as 'secondary dating'.

Having assigned dates, however approximate, to the different parts of the building, we come to the second way of looking at it – involving conjecture, not to say imagination. How far can we marry the parts of the building we identify as truly original, and those which are clearly additions or alterations, with historical events that we know had bearing on the contemporary standing of the church and manor? Or in other words, relate the ecclesiological to the ecclesiastical?

As to the first approach, we are unlikely to better the accuracy of the account that Forsyth published in 1902 (Rec. Bucks, vol. viii, p.456) and I make no attempt to improve on his description. Today's observer will find that the general features of the building differ little from what Forsyth saw. Guided by him, we may select what seems

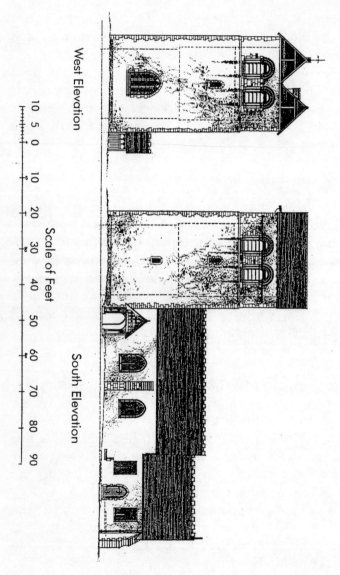

West Elevation

South Elevation

10 5 0   10   20   30   40   50   60   70   80   90

Scale of Feet

Fig. 8: West and south elevations. (W. A. Forsyth, Rec. Bucks, viii, 458, 1902)

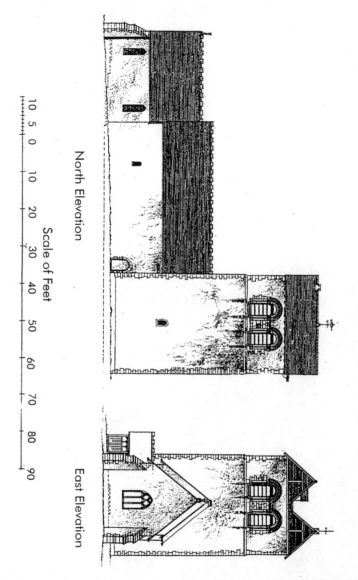

North Elevation

Scale of Feet

East Elevation

Fig. 9: East and north elevations. (W. A. Forsyth, Rec. Bucks,. viii, 458, 1902)

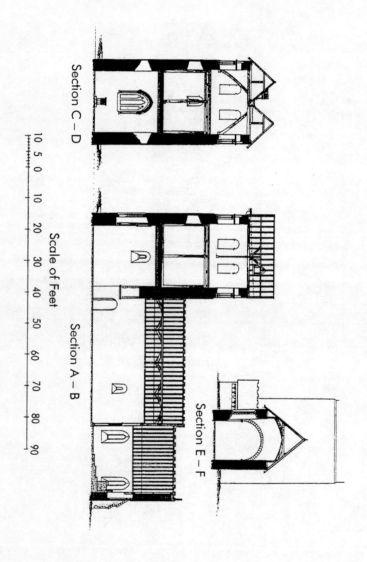

Fig. 10: Sections of church: A, B, C, D, E, F. See also Fig. 7. (W. A. Forsyth, Rec. Bucks, viii, 458, 1902)

Fig. 11 & 12: Romanesque openings in tower's top storey. North face: western and eastern arched openings; roll-moulding of different orders. (Photographed by Mr Brian Redmond).

Fig. 13: South face: champfered abaci carried across between openings and continued as string courses to outer corners. Original small second storey window shaped in crudely worked stones. (Photographed by Mr Brian Redmond).

likeliest to help us answer the questions posed at the beginning of this chapter – when, how and why?

THE TOWER (FIGS. 1, 8, 9)

Forsyth remarks that of the churches of the Desborough hundred, that at Fingest:

> Is perhaps the most remarkable in the matter of proportions, possessing a dignity and grandeur seldom seen in churches of the village type. The feature which produces this particular character and so compels our attention is the Norman Tower; not only by reason of its unusually large scale in relation to the Nave, but also by its actual design in which latter respect it is perhaps unique.

Since Forsyth, no writer has disagreed that the tower and nave are both Norman; indeed, as I shall be arguing later, they are late eleventh century.

A look at the tower from outside sees it rising sixty feet above the ground, and measuring eight feet wider and thirty feet higher than the nave. Its walls are of flint set in rubble rendered with mortar, and finished with very numerous stone quoins of small size set flush with the mortar face.

The tower is very truly and soundly built. Its inside diagonal measurements at ground level are exactly equal (27ft 4½in). Little or no settlement has taken place, and the walls stand as true and vertical as when they were first built. Around its base on the south, west and north sides is a sloping-sided ditch three–five feet wide and one–two feet deep, the bottom of which very likely corresponds to the original ground level.

The tower is arranged in three storeys (Fig. 10). There is no external access and, moreover, a complete lack of any indication of there having ever been a west or other ground floor door in the tower. At the top, the twin tiled gables are a famous feature, giving an unmistakable silhouette to the first glimpse of the church that comes into the view of the traveller descending to Fingest from The Peacock or Cadmore End. The top storey is the centre of interest; in each of the four sides is a pair of Romanesque openings or windows set in ashlar limestone coursing, and enriched with roll-moulded arches of two orders set on cushion caps, columns and bases, the detail of which is typical of the best work of the period (Figs. 11, 12). Chamfered abaci are carried across between the windows, and on the south side are continued as a string course to the outer corners of the tower (Fig. 13). The whole of this upper storey is set back slightly, with a splayed offset.

In marked contrast are the starkly unornamented lower two storeys, which have but two small round arched windows set high in the north and south faces of the first storey, and a similar pair in the west and south sides of the second storey. Where these earliest windows have escaped the repairs of the last century, their original small external openings are seen to be shaped of crudely worked stones (Fig. 13). All four are deeply splayed inside, maximising the little light they transmit. A drawing by Charlotte Piggott of the church in the 1840s shows the lower small south window blocked up (Rec. Bucks, 1993, vol. xxxiii, p.72).

The tower's ground storey has two major features. First is the large round stone arch in the thickness of its east face, opening into and corresponding in width with the nave (Fig. 10). The dressed stones (*voussoirs*) shaping the arch's west and east sides are on the same small scale as the tower's quoins outside, a characteristic of building stones used for angles and arches at the earliest period of Norman building in England. In Anglo-Saxon arches the *voussoirs* are usually single large through-stones. The massive shafts of the arch, the abaci (now partly restored) supporting the arch, and the dressed stones of the arch itself are, like the tower's first two storeys outside, totally unornamented – no mouldings, engaged columns, carved capitals or motifs. This can only mean that there were no skilled Norman masons to hand when the church's first stage was being completed; the builders had to rely on Saxon stoneworkers used only to plain arches and massive impost blocks. Conditions were clearly different when it came to building the tower's top storey, an addition explained in a later chapter.

The other major feature of the tower's first storey is the three-light early English west window (Fig. 10), 'in clunch of the best thirteenth century building' as Forsyth describes it. It is a window of plate tracery, the earliest form that such windows took before the development of more elaborate rib frameworks. It has three trefoiled lights with a quatrefoil over each side-light, the central light rising to the apex. The opening inside is in the form of a single pointed arch, beautifully moulded, having a label with carved terminals, delicately carved caps and moulded shafts and bases.

THE NAVE

The nave is unarguably contemporary with the first two storeys of the tower, and has similar walls, only slightly less thick, of field flints and rubble rendered with lime mortar. At its junction with the tower the original Norman inner arches of its north and south doors can still be made out, though hidden under cement rendering and, like the *voussoirs* of the main arch, under coats of emulsion paint that were applied throughout, in direct contravention of expert architectural advice solicited but then ignored during the unhappy renovations of 1967.

The outer arch of the north door (now blocked) is again pointed work of the thirteenth century (Fig. 9). The south door's outer arch, with the porch, is part of the Victorian restoration.

At the easternmost end of the nave's north wall is a single small deeply-splayed round-arched window, identical to those in the tower (Figs. 9, 10). In the south wall opposite, probably replacing one similar, is a Decorated two-light window of the fourteenth century (Fig. 8). A second westerly window in the south wall is – according to Forsyth again – a very poor nineteenth century copy (Fig. 8); this was put in in 1845, and a contemporary entry in the churchwardens' minute book shows that for the stonework Thos. Knapp was paid £7.17s.0d, while for the glazing D. Davis got £1.6s.0d and for the ironwork H. Carpenter £1.7s.0d.

The nave's south wall has developed over the centuries a slight outward lean from bottom to top, which a Victorian buttress has done little to arrest. Inside, it is substantially thicker in its bottom three or four feet, which gives a bulged appearance below the sills of its two windows. At the Victorian restoration a stone pulpit was keyed into this wall's eastern end. When this was removed in 1990, it was seen that at this end at any rate the bulge in the south wall under its plaster surface is composed of courses of bricks. The part of the wall revealed by removal of the pulpit was of ancient flint, rubble and lime mortar, like much of the rest of the church's fabric. The band of post-mediaeval brickwork was probably intended to strengthen or stabilise the wall. A report from a visitation of 1637, under the direction of Bishop Williams of Lincoln investigating the state of Buckinghamshire churches, mentions 'Fingestre. Church and chancel In decay In the foundations' (Robert Gibbs, Rec. Bucks, vol. vi, p.154).

An especially pleasing feature of the nave is the timber of its open oak roof (Fig. 10). Until well into the present century the timbers of both the nave and chancel roofs were hidden by plaster ceilings; these are mentioned in a description of the church by T. Hugh Bryant in *The Reading Mercury, Oxford Gazette, Newbury Herald and Berks County Paper* of 16th July, 1898. Moreover, the 1637 report of Bishop Williams says that 'the chancel wants tiling and ceiling, as the church is ceiled'. Clearly, to deliberately expose even roof timbers such as these is a relatively modern preference.

Forsyth, dating the roof framing as thirteenth or fourteenth century, describes it 'as of steep pitch [...] with five sets of principal rafters having tie beams stiffened with curved struts to carry the purlins, which are also assisted by shaped struts from the principals'. The hand-shaping of its constituent timbers, the details of its fine mediaeval construction, and its still perfect condition, are best seen at noon on a fine summer day when the sun shines through the south windows.

THE CHANCEL

Both unexpected and unusual is the absence of a chancel arch. There is nothing to suggest that the Victorian pitch-pine screen between the nave and chancel replaces an earlier stone arch; in fact it merely adjoins the massive 12 x 8 inch tie-beam above which carries the end timbers of the nave roof (Fig. 14). We shall come to the likeliest reason for the absence of a structural chancel arch later.

When repairs to the nineteenth century tiling and battening of the gable end of the nave roof were being carried out in 1986, it was possible to climb the scaffolding and get a closer look at the mediaeval roof framing, especially the oak tie-beam and end timbers (Fig. 14), all still in perfect condition and iron-hard.

The ground plan of the church (Fig. 7) shows that its axis is irregular, inclining somewhat to the south in the nave and chancel, though in general south-east by east. The

Fig. 14: Mediaeval timber framing at east end of nave roof, exposed during re-tiling; note oaken end timbers and heavy tie-beam instead of chancel arch.

chancel is over a foot wider than the nave, largely because the south wall of the nave itself veers little by little southward as it runs east; but the greater width of the chancel produces a slight break in the morth wall of the church (Fig. 7).

The two early English lancet windows in its north wall (Figs 9, 10) are the only remaining evidence that the chancel is thirteenth century work. The 1637 visitation report says that one of them was then 'partly dammed up'; at some later date, it appears, both were blocked up, for a brass plate on the sill of the westerly one one says that both windows were re-opened in 1849 'by the poor of the District aided by the bereaved family' of Emily Gowland 'the friend of the poor'. (Her gravestone lies outside, near the chancel door).

On the same brass plate Geo. A. Baker, M.A., Rector and Thomas Sewell, M.A., Curate record that also in 1849 the chancel was renovated. This seems to have amounted to putting the windows in order, including the east window with its painted Crucifixion. It is likely that the timbers and tiling of the chancel roof were renewed at the same time. (The graves of the Rev. Baker and the Rev. Sewell, like Emily Gowland's, lie outside the chancel door).

In the south wall of the chancel are a pair of decorated or transitional windows (Fig. 8) of the late fourteenth century (according to Forsyth) or fifteenth century (according to the Royal Commission on Historical Monuments, Bucks, 1912). Each is of two trefoiled ogee lights under a square head with pierced spandrels. Forsyth percipiently notes that 'the main O-gee of the tracery is not a flowing line, but has a slight break or distortion, giving it an individual character'. The upper part of the southwall of the chancel appears to have been rebuilt, probably when these windows were inserted (*VCH Bucks*, vol. iii, p.44). These windows were likewise restored (through to what extent is not clear) during the 1849 renovations 'to the revered memory of Emily Gowland by the Revd Thos. Sewell, his wife and children' as another brass plate records.

Outside, where the south wall of the chancel meets the south wall of the nave, there are still visible a few dressed stones, fitted together vertically and projecting somewhat. As they look now, embedded in the pebble-dash cement rendering applied in 1967, they seem to have no explanation. However, in his 1902 paper Forsyth includes a drawing of the south elevation of the church (Fig. 8) which clearly shows in this position part of the lintel and east jamb of an otherwise vanished window, overlapping the south chancel wall; the present few vertical stones are its last visible remains. Descriptions in the *VCH Bucks* (vol. iii, p.44) written in 1925, and in the *RCHM Bucks* (1912 ed., p.157) agree with Forsyth's sketch, the former mentioning 'the sill and lower portion of the east jamb of an original "low-side" window', the latter saying 'in the outer surface of the wall, low down, the sill and part of one jamb of a thirteenth century lancet'. The surviving visible dressed stones of the jamb in fact exactly match in moulding, shape and size those in the outside jambs of the thirteenth century lancet windows in the chancel's north wall. It seems certain that a 'low-side' window was part of the design of the chancel added to replace the apse in the thirteenth century. More of 'low-side' windows later, reader; this one was evidently in place for the whole of the thirteenth and most of the fourteenth century until it was blocked out with the rebuilding of the south chancel wall with its two windows.

The early fifteenth century stone framing of the east window (Fig. 9) has three trefoiled lights and tracery in a two-centred head. Its central Crucifixion was designed and painted by Francis Philip Baraud. I am grateful to an expert on the work of G.E. Street, Paul Joyce, for the information that Baraud (1824–1900) was one of the artists used by

Powell's of Whitefriars, London, who supplied the glass and quarry pattern for both this and the south chancel windows. Powell's *Patent Glass Index* for 1849 lists the Crucifixion design, so it looks as if Baraud's glass was put in during the 1849 renovations of Baker and Sewell. The earlier stained glass in the chancel windows had by then evidently been lost; but we know what it depicted from Browne Willis's account of his visit to Fingest in 1715 or thereabouts (*Willis MS,* vol. x, p.20):

> In the East Window of the Chancel and South of the Church the portraiture of the Virgin Mary. In a South Window of the Chancel the portraiture of St Bartholomew and another saint under this.

And Browne Willis adds:

> In another window *Fecit istam Fenestram Mosewell.*

The Restoration of 1868–69

In 1852 Fingest and Ibstone rectories became subsumed under a new benefice, Fingest-with-Ibstone, created when Cadmore End seceded from Fingest as a consolidated chapelry. The parish priest George Augustus Baker, initially curate officiating at both Ibstone and Fingest, was appointed rector of Fingest in 1841, and then of the newly formed Fingest-with-Ibstone in 1852, with his parsonage at Ibstone. This dual arrangement of the benefice, part in Oxfordshire and part in Buckinghamshire, with two different patrons, persisted until 1976 when Fingest was reinstated as a separate benefice but of much reduced area (Fig. 2).

Two years after Baker's death in 1866, restoration of the church began under the pastorate of the new incumbent

Richard Philip Goldsworthy Tiddeman, rector from 1866 to 1878. The cost of the restoration was seven hundred pounds (*MS Dioc. Papers c.2210*, Oxford County Hall Archives). Baker's sister Georgiana played a part in raising a fund to pay for the work, collecting one hundred and thirty-five pounds and herself contributing one hundred pounds, as she writes in a letter of 3rd January, 1868, to the diocesan fund agent, saying that the fund then stood at five hundred and fifty-two pounds, 'but there is still a good deal to be raised if Mr Street's plans are to be carried out'. Another letter from her in May 1869 complains that twenty pounds promised by the Diocesan Church Building Society has still not been received (Bodleian Library, *MSS Top, Bucks, c.6, 393, 398; VCH Bucks,* vol. iii, p.44). Paul Joyce's notes, which he kindly showed me, give the date of the restoration as 1866–67, but Georgiana Baker's letters seem to establish that it was 1868–69.

George Edmund Street was Oxford diocesan architect from 1850 until his death in 1881. In 1866 he had competed successfully for the design of the new Law Courts in the Strand, and thereafter his advice was sought in restoring a large number of churches in Bucks and in other parts of the country.

At Fingest, Street's restoration added a buttress to the south nave wall and two equally unnecessary, though then fashionable, angle buttresses at the east corners of the chancel (Figs. 7, 8, 9). He 'renewed' the south nave windows by framing them outside in concrete and presumably reglazing them, although the new westerly one could not have needed much attention. He re-battened and re-tiled the nave roof, put a stone cross on the east gable, and rebuilt the south porch in pitch-pine, giving it a new door with wrought-iron hinges. The stone of the outer arch of the south doorway into the nave and of the priest's doorway in the chancel he replaced, and provided a new door to match the south door. As we have seen, the inner arches of the Norman south and north doors survived but, sadly, were hidden under cement coverings, and the same is true of the jambs and round or pointed heads of all the splayed mediaeval windows. This makes it impossible to tell now whether their reveals and/or jambs were originally laid in dressed stone or merely in rubble.

Inside, Street completely refitted the church, imprinting his Victorian stamp throughout. He laid new tiled floors, and reseated the nave and chancel. In the nave he put pew benches of heavy pine, and in the chancel priests' and choir stalls of fine oak joinery. Mistakenly, in my opinion, these handsome oak choir stalls were removed from the chancel at the 1967 'restoration' and relegated to the back of the church.

Street replaced the old chancel screen (for a note on this see Lipscomb below) with a new screen and arch of heavy pitch-pine; he also put in another pine screen to enclose a vestry area under the tower. Mediaeval builders made no separate provision for a clergy vesting room; it was customary for the people to watch the priest vesting publicly before the altar, donning alb, chasuble, amice, stole and maniple. Such vestments were kept in a chest under the stone altar. Some Anglican clergy still put on the chasuble during the eucharist, taking it from the altar rail before the prayer of consecration.

Another typically Victorian addition of Street's was a bulky semi-octagonal stone pulpit built in front of the south panels of his new chancel screen; what, if anything, had served as pulpit from Reformation times and after we do not know. He also installed a new base to the old font and placed it where it now stands under the tower. Behind the altar he devised a low frieze-type carved reredos of dressed stone decorated with a continuous row of

94

quatrefoiled circular panels, and an east wall dado area covered with tiles; the stone reredos and dado tiles were removed in 1967, and the stone pulpit, which massively obscured the south side of the chancel, was taken down in 1990.

In his 1902 paper, Forsyth notes that at Street's restoration:

> An eighteenth century carved altarpiece, the altar rails, the screen between nave and chancel, and a south porch appear to have been removed and were replaced by similar fittings of a 'Gothic revival' character.

Forsyth further makes critical mention of the raising of the chancel, sanctuary and altar by a succession of steps

> For the intended benefit of the service at the expense of the internal proportions of the fabric: from the fact of the chancel windows being considerably lower than those of the nave, the effect of these rising levels is much felt.

He goes on to compare Fingest's rising step levels unfavourably with the charm of a uniform floor level throughout, like that which has unusually survived in Radnage church. Anyone who knows Radnage may be hard put to disagree.

The wooden altar table is also attributed to Street. Doubtless the broad wooden gothic arching of its oaken front and side panels is his, but the table itself is obviously older, being made up of smooth, polished thick elm boards, with occasional flaws replaced by meticulously shaped good elm inserts. On its underside the rough untreated boarding has what seem to be four shallow mortices, perhaps made during Commonwealth years to receive legs to make a 'Lord's table' to stand in the chancel.

One untoward effect of Street's activities was that the new rising steps in the chancel were laid over at least three graves. The inscriptions on two of these we know from Browne Willis's record of his visit (*Willis MS*, vol. x, p.21). Willis writes in his own hand:

> Under the South wall of the Chancel within the Altar Rails on an Ordinary Stone a brass plate thereon this Inscription
>
> > *Here lyes Christopher Edwards of ffingest who lived there 40 yeares peaceably with his neighbours a benefactor both to the parsonage House and Chancell he dyed the 10 Day of July 1647.*

Browne Willis continues:

> On a black Marble under the North Window this Engraved
> > *Here lyeth interred the Body of Mr Thomas Ferrers alias Turner Gent. who married the daughter of Mr Bernard who had by her two sons Thomas and John and 4 Daughters Mary Elizabeth Nathany and Deborah he departed this life the 11 of March 1646 being the Lord of Fingest Manor who was very Godly and truely loving to his Wife and Children.*
> >
> > *I know that my Redeemer liveth Job 19, 25*
> >
> > *Altho' my Body laid now to sleep, within the Grave. Yet afterwards In Glorious State more Beauty it shall have When Death hath held it down awhile anon it shall arise With Christ to Reign forever more above the Starry Skies*

> *Them that sleep in Jesus will God bring with Him 1*
> *Thes. 4, 14*

A third grave in the chancel is mentioned in the parish register:

> The Rev. Howell Powell died at Turville, Decr. 15th and was buried under the Communion Table at Fingest Decr. 18th 1793. Aged 56 years. He was 23 years Vicar of Turville and 30 years Curate of Fingest, where he was buried at his own Request.

We shall later hear more of parson Christopher Edwards and of the Ferrers family.

Before leaving the chancel, we may take note of a 1932 edition of the church guide, which says that the oak floor casing in the sanctuary was put in then to cover part of the Victorian tiling, which the rector and churchwardens thought to be 'entirely out of keeping with the rest of the Church'. This was an addition which, in fact, compounded the disproportion introduced in Victorian times with the stepped raising of the chancel floor. It apparently also included the removal of Street's altar rails and their replacement by the present arrangement.

The Twin Gables on the Tower

To turn now to this best-known feature of the church. Again, Forsyth's description cannot be bettered:

> The twin gables seen in the roof form a most satisfactory finish to the whole; the oak construction is of an interesting kind, dating probably from the early part of the 14th century, now in a very good state of preservation, and from the method of

framing and scantlings of the timber, resembles the spirit of similar work in the neighbourhood.

(Scantlings are the measurements or sizes of the timbers.)

Forsyth also thought that the red brick filling between the timbers of the gable ends was part of the Victorian restoration; more recent repair is noted in an architect's report under the diocesan scheme for inspection of churches, which states that the tower gables were virtually rebuilt in 1966 under the direction of its writer, W.S. Corbett, FRIBA.

Contradicting Forsyth, the report of the *Royal Commission for Historical Monuments*, 1912, in its volume on Bucks, quoted in the Department of the Environment's most recently published updating of local listed buildings, dates the gabled roofs as eighteenth or nineteenth century. This surely is erroneous, unless it refers merely to repair. To climb up into the belfry and inspect the framing timbers of the gables is to leave no doubt in the climber's mind that Forsyth's mediaeval dating is nearer the mark. What's more, the antiquarian Browne Willis, describing the church as he saw it in about 1715 (*Willis MS,* vol. x, p.20) says:

At the west end is a handsome large tower well wrought of free stone it seems to have been of a good height it has been taken down at Top and is covered with two tiled ridges supported by some Brick Work.

This sounds as if the tiled ridges were nothing new at the beginning of the eighteenth century. Willis's remark reminds us that whether they were added in the fourteenth century or later, they very likely replaced the original finishing, crenellated or otherwise, at the top of the tower, no doubt weatherproofed with lead when it was completed in the early twelfth century.

What Became of the Fingest Bells?

The tower's top storey, with its pairs of round-arched moulded openings and its strong stone-built appearance, was clearly added as a practical belfry and an impressive one at that. It's disappointing to find it now with but a single bell. In his authoritative tome *Church Bells of Buckinghamshire*, published in 1897, A.H. Cocks thought little of this bell, cast in 1830 by an ironfounder of Lane End, J. Hobbs, probably as his sole attempt at bellfounding.

Browne Willis says that the tower once:

Contained doubtless a large ring of Bells as the People have a Tradition that they are all taken away together with the Frame except one small modern Bell [perhaps that re-cast in 1830?].

In a marginal he adds:

The bells supposed to be taken down and sold tempore Edw. 6.

Such an order for the removal of church bells was indeed made in 1549, under Reformation legislation putting down popery.

Cocks elaborates further:

There exists a widely-known tradition that the bells which the tower formerly contained were removed to Hambleden; the most generally received version, at least here, [that is, in Fingest] is that Fingest parish was involved in debt, and that Hambleden paid off the debt on condition that the bells should be transferred to that tower.

He continues:

> All round the bell chamber of this fine early Norman
> tower are to be seen, or at least were to be seen be-
> fore the tower underwent restoration in 1885 (I have
> not seen the interior since), marks on the walls which
> seem clearly to indicate where the frame of a ring of
> bells was fixed. The existing frame is older than the
> bell, and consists of two cages, and the empty one has
> been in use. Unfortunately in the indenture made in
> 1552 concerning Thingest, the list is gone.

Cooks also notes having seen other records, viz. '14 Aug.
1637 Fingest 1 Bell' and '1714 Fingherst 1 Bell'.

That by Thomas Delafield's time Fingest had but one
bell is corroborated by his remark in his *Account of Fingherst*:

> I must not omit one thing that the Three principal
> sides of the Hills that enclose Fingherst, according to
> the Scituation of the wind, and weather, give a
> double, and sometimes a treble echo to the sound of
> the Church Bell: As I have often observed behind the
> Rectory House.

The most likely explanation of what became of the bells,
Cocks concludes:

> Though pure conjecture, however – seems to be that
> Fingest had at one time a ring of bells (three or four,
> larger numbers being rare anciently) which disap-
> peared previous to 1637 – perhaps sacriligiously sold
> at the time of the Reformation – leaving only a single
> bell; that this bell, shortly after 1714 gave place to
> two, hung in a new frame; and that within the next
> ten years one (or both) of these went to Hambleden.

Consonant with the idea of a full bell-frame originally is the fact that to this day the floor of the tower belfry is very strongly supported by oak uprights from the floor below.

We may incidentally note that Cocks's reference to restoration of the tower in 1885 agrees with entries in the churchwardens' minute book. These show that in August 1897 Mrs Mary Ann Plumridge was repaid a loan (at 4%) of £100 'contracted toward paying the Restoration of the Church Tower, June 24th 1885', and the minutes also acknowledge receipt of £78.5s.8d 'from the Charity Commissioners, the amount which had been paid into the Bank of England toward the Loan of £100, contracted in part payment on the Restoration of Fingest Church Tower June 24th 1885, by instalments from time to time (Vide Expenditure on former pages) and the compound interest which was paid on the same.'

Finally, on the subject of Fingest's bells, I cannot resist adding Cocks's remarks about them under the entry in his book on Hambleden church's bells. He says:

> There is a tradition that some of the bells came from Fingest; the most generally accepted version here [that is, in Hambleden] being that once upon a time, in the good old days, the Rectors of the two parishes played cards together for high stakes. Eventually the Rector of Fingest, having lost all his available cash, staked the bells of his parish church, and again losing, the bells were transferred to Hambleden tower.

He goes on to say that the treble, dated 1724, may represent a bell from Fingest, recast; but since no charge for this appears in the contemporary churchwarden's accounts, it is possible that while two bells came from Fingest, the surplus of metal paid for the recasting of one. I myself have difficulty in accepting this dating of Cocks's. After all, Delafield became curate at Fingest in 1726 and it is hard to picture any of the immediately preceding rectors (whom we shall be meeting later) as inveterate gamblers. Alternatively, did the lean times of the Reformation for church maintenance perforce make reluctant gamblers of the rectors of these two neighbouring parishes? It is not impossible, but we would still need to explain why recasting Fingest bell metal for Hambleden was put off for one hundred and seventy-five years.

The Font

The Fingest font is typical late fifteenth century – octagonal, and decorated with a trefoiled sunk panel on each of its sides. The bowl is relatively small and designed to be raised on a pedestal, baptism by then being confined to the newborn.

After the Reformation fonts were regarded in many churches as part of the superstitious equipment of the ritual imposed by the Bishop of Rome, and were deliberately damaged or simply neglected. The Fingest font is clearly damaged, but by its appearance as much by non-ecclesiastical use as by malice. This suggests that it spent a good deal of time outside, possibly as a water butt or trough. If this were indeed the case, there is no way of telling whether this resulted from Reformation ideas or those of later Puritan times, when clergy scoffed at the notion that baptism needed hallowed water. This was a long way from mediaeval belief, which attributed almost magical properties to the holy water in the font; as late as the fifteenth century Church authority instructed clergy to keep fonts covered and locked against sorcerers and pilferers stealing holy water for their own sinister ends. The rim of this font still carries an iron hasp let into the stone for this purpose.

That the font eventually found its way back into the church may have been a gesture acknowledging receipt by the parish in 1793 of Queen Anne's bounty, for roughly incised in the stone on its eastern side are the letters 'AR'. The new stone base was acquired during Street's restoration.

What Else was Lost in the Victorian Restoration?

When Street was commissioned to carry out work on a church his initial report usually included a description of the building as he found it, and especially of the features he proposed to modify. A letter he wrote in 1858 to the relevant authority setting out his proposals for the enlargement of Hambleden church contains such a detailed description (Bodleian Library, *MSS Top, Bucks, c.6*). I have been unable to find any trace of a similar description of Fingest church before he set about restoring it. This is a great pity, since it deprives us of any clear picture of what had already been done by Baker and Sewell in their 'renovation' of the chancel two decades earlier. More regrettably still, it deprives us of the glimpse we might otherwise have had of what survived of the mediaeval appearance of the nave and ground storey of the tower before the nineteenth century restorations were put in hand.

A report by E. Clive Rouse, the mediaeval archaeologist, who was commissioned before the 1967 restoration to inspect the church's interior walls for evidence of remains of wall paintings, shows how drastic the Victorian restorers were. He said:

The whole of the interior walls are covered with a very rough cement plaster, including all the window splays and reveals, which is probably of late 19th century date. An area was selected just east of the blocked north doorway, where one might anticipate a painting of St Christopher to have existed in mediaeval times, for testing the plaster. The Victorian surface existed right down to the original 12th century flint rubble backing without any sign of an intermediate ancient surface [...]

The ancient plaster surface was probably in bad condition and at a 19th century restoration it was decided to abandon the whole of it. This was pulled off and the present surface substituted. It is a tragic loss, for in a church with such a very large expanse of plain wall, there must have been very extensive painting in mediaeval times. The original surface was probably very uneven as flints were exposed in the characteristically yellow 12th century mortar and in two places tiles had been used in Victorian times to level up the surface. It was not possible to reach the area high up above the chancel arch where the plaster appeared to have a slightly more uneven surface, and Instructions were given to the workmen to take care when this area comes to be prepared.

Rouse goes on to emphasise one or two points of principle to be observed in the proposed further restoration, namely:

1. The architect is presumed to have given precise instructions to the builders for the use only of a lime and sand mortar in any plaster repairs inside the church that may be necessary; no patent, quick, hard-drying gypsum plasters should be used.

2. To leave exposed all stonework of arches and windows after thorough cleaning with plain water and a bristle not a wire brush.

3. When the surfaces come to be redecorated, only a lime wash to be used, toned, if toned at all, with umber rather than ochre.

One need only glance around the interior today to see that the decorator who did the 1967 work, let alone the churchwardens then responsible for the fabric of the church, completely ignored these clear instructions from a national authority on mediaeval church architecture. The decorator's quotation, which was unbelievably accepted *in toto* and put into effect, speaks of cleaning down and stopping up ceilings and walls generally, with no mention of intention to use lime and sand mortar or lime wash as expertly advised; and of applying one coat of emulsion to ceiling panels and two coats to walls – which in the event included the stones and imposts of the tower-nave arch and the whole of the graceful stonework of the west window. We may thankfully note that at least the stonework of the windows of the south nave and chancel and of the east window managed to escape this treatment. What's more the decorator, apparently also bidden to hack off and make good the external rendering of the east and south elevations of the chancel and nave, dubbed out the exposed flint in cement mortar and rendered the resulting surface in two coats with pebble dash finish, a manoeuvre falling sadly short, as any visitor can see, of the declared intention to match the old mortar rendering on the tower.

The Royal Arms in the Nave

The canvas painted with Queen Anne's Arms, now on the nave wall, was recovered in 1935 from the vestry where it had been lying unnoticed in a very poor state of repair. Mrs Harriet Montefiore, churchwarden at the time, had it repaired and restored in 1939 by William Dyer and Sons of Grosvenor Place, London, and it was rehung in the church where it now is. Writing to Mrs Montefiore from his office, Mr Dyer said in a letter:

Whilst you were here you made the remark that the church had no pictures and you were looking at the Crucifixion over our fireplace. We wonder if you would care to accept this picture for hanging in the church?

The picture was thought to be Italian of the eighteenth century, and for the next thirty-five years looked well on the wall between the two south nave windows, until in these sacrilegious times it was lost by theft. The thief also found the safe key and took a fine silver Charles I chalice with baluster stem.

Earlier Writings on the Church's Appearance

The antiquarian writers of the eighteenth century dealt more with monuments, memorials and the lives and ancestry of local big-wigs past and present than with the impression such a church as Fingest's might have made on an eighteenth century visitor standing for the first time in its nave; Browne Willis and Delafield, for all their scribes-manship, are no exception. Nineteenth century writers viewing the church before its renovations and restorations are more helpful. J.J. Sheahan's description of Fingest parish in his *History and Topography of Buckinghamshire* (1861, p.883) includes a note that in the floor of the porch there was a large coffin-shaped slab. Not mentioned elsewhere, and covered over soon after with Victorian tiling, this piece of memorial stone keeps its intriguing secret. The Victorian porch replaced an earlier one and in Norman times there was probably no porch.

As well as remarking that the roof beams were then hidden by plaster ceilings, Sheahan also notes that 'The piscina remains'. Unfortunately, he does not say where. *Piscinas* used for washing remaining consecrated bread and wine from communion vessels were often in the south wall of chancels, near the altar; but there is now no trace of what Sheahan saw. Fingest's *piscina* seems to have been lost in the 1868–69 restoration.

Although I can find no hint of its existence elsewhere, the Fingest churchwardens' minute book shows that the church used to have a gallery. In their listing of the payments made in May 1818, churchwardens C.L. Hayward and Edwd. Pheby entered 'paid Thos. Bartlett as for Bill for Gallery £5-10-0'; and in July 1822 another pair of churchwardens, Thomas Tyler and Daniel Sawyer, record the payment of four shillings and sixpence for 'Repair of seats of gallery, new book board in desk'. No trace of where the gallery was remains, except that a hole bored low in the reveal of the right-hand jamb of the west window may perhaps have held a handrail of steps up to it. Many village churches had wooden galleries fronting a west window, which accommodated the musicians accompanying the singing at services before organs or harmoniums became available, or at any rate affordable.

In *The History and Antiquities of the County of Buckingham* (1847, vol. iii, p.566) George Lipscomb notes:

In the south side of the chancel are two windows; and there is another on the north side, lancet-shaped, but long since closed. The screen or altar-piece is of wood, carved, with a pediment supported by Corinthian pilasters. Between the nave and the chancel is an open screen, with three arches; on the north side, is one small window, and another on the south.

As we have seen, Street saw fit to replace this open screen with his pitch-pine one; and in place of the carved wooden altarpiece he put a decorated stone reredos that was removed in 1967.

Nave – or Chancel?

The *RCHM* (1912) in its account of Fingest church makes the claim that:

> Part, at least, of the nave originally served as the chancel, the tower being used as the nave.

This was an idea perhaps taken from A.W. Clapham, who, discussing unusual types of parish church in his *English Romanesque Architecture* (vol. ii, p.105) says that:

> The extraordinary tower at Fingest, 27ft. square externally, evidently served as the nave of the church, and may be compared to a few pre-Conquest towers which seem to have served a similar purpose, and to the hexagonal towers of the Saxon churches of Ozleworth and Swindon which clearly did.

If it is indeed true that the base of the tower originally served as a nave, several questions arise. What could have been the need for so relatively large a chancel as the present nave's space provides, along with an apse? Whatever the reason, the nave-as-chancel theory is consistent with the absence of an arched opening at its east end which would otherwise have defined the apse as a separate chancel.

Further, it appears that the south and north doors have always been the only means of access to the tower 'nave'. It seems likely then, as the *RCHM* account suggests, that the original chancel was formed by a part, probably a major part, of the nave, together with the apse. It follows that the lay parishioner entering at the south door to reach the 'tower nave' would have found on his right a screen dividing the lay nave from the presbytery chancel. Clergy coming from the manor would enter by the north door and reach the nave-chancel through a priest's door in the screen's north end.

This screen of carved wood openwork would have depended from a rood beam above, supported on corbels built into the walls. Rood beams spanning the entry to the chancel were almost universal in mediaeval parish churches big or small, and bore a carved and often coloured crucifix or rood – a cross with the image of Christ affixed. The question at Fingest is precisely where the rood was placed. The nave walls now show no traces of corbels, nor for that matter of stairs or steps to the rood loft customarily used by the officiating priest to intone part of the liturgy of the Mass.

The natural lighting in the original nave or nave-chancel would have come from the small single-splayed window that still survives at the east end of its north wall, and from its fellow opposite. As Forsyth accepted on the suggestion of Mr W.H. St John Hope, the east end of the church was originally apsidal. Such an apse would have had a half-circle stone wall matching the nave walls in height and supplying much needed further light from one or more similarly small inwardly splayed windows. The original main roof of the church continued in semi-circular form to cover the apse, eventually to be pulled down when the thirteenth century new chancel was added.

To ask why a chancel of these dimensions was needed, and what its uses were, is to pose again our first questions. We have to resist the temptation to people the chancel with a gorgeous mediaeval hierarchy of clerics in Romish orders bent on liturgical orthodoxy. We do better, you will agree, wise reader, to keep our feet on the ground. We need to match our various structural datings with the changing administrative, theological and liturgical demands of the prelates who, as lords of this manor, had reason from time to time to celebrate Mass within its church's walls – or to delegate subordinates to do so. This takes us to the next chapter.

Chapter IX
Post-Conquest:
The First Hundred Years

Before venturing to unravel the mystery of how this church and its parish come to be where they are, I preface this next chapter with an epitome of the last; a harvest as it were for the hungry, seeking sustenance against the demands next to be made on credulity.

So, to recapitulate…

In harmony with learned opinion about Saxo-Norman overlap, we are taking it as agreed that well before the year 1100, under Norman direction, Saxon masons and Saxon labour built the stone church, with a solid two-storey tower and in the Saxon fashion a narrower easterly chancel (very likely with a rounded apse). The walls of flint, rubble and mortar are mostly as they were built then, give or take some patchy re-rendering, as are some of the few small, high and deeply splayed original windows. A decade or two into the twelfth century, skilful Norman masons heightened the tower grandly to sixty feet or more, adding a felicitously devised belfry of dressed stonework, with fine Romanesque openings to broadcast far and wide the summons of newly hung bells to the faithful.

Then, early in the thirteenth century, a new chancel with the long narrow lancet windows of the period replaced the apse, and a 'low-side' south window of similar lancet style was constructed at the junction of the new chancel and the old. Possible reasons for 'low-side' windows are discussed in Chapter X. The provision of a pitched roof for the new chancel led to the re-roofing of the old chancel-nave with the fine oak timbers we see today.

During the next two and a half centuries, larger traceried windows took the places of some of the small splayed ones and also of the narrow lancet windows in the added chancel's south wall when this was rebuilt (a process which did away with the low-side window). The two lancet windows in the chancel's north wall remained, though at times were blocked up. Also, a stone font was installed.

Its uncertain when, but it was probably earlier rather than later that the tower's leaded flat roof was repaired by capping with twin tiled gables, initiating the long battle between decay and repair which the parson and the people have intermittently joined since. In 1845 a second traceried nave window was added, and in 1849 some reopening and/or repair of windows in the chancel and repairs to its roof were carried out. Then in 1868–69 a major Victorian restoration and reorganisation, which permanently masked the mediaeval cast of the interior.

To Beginnings

So now, from the available fragments of fact, we have to piece together an explanation of how and why this church came to be built in this valley in the first place. Why on a site in an extreme corner of what later became its defined parish?

When informed guesswork suggests answers, we are still left to explain what prompted the changes to the original stone building that we have identified. (No easy problem this, reader; for all our modern knowledge, the distant past shows us for Fingest an insubstantial pageant.)

We do know that in early times lesser churches with graveyards – and Fingest's clearly qualifies as such – were almost always founded by landholders who were then the owners of the resulting places of worship. Dealing as we are with beginnings, it helps in uncovering the origins of the church, and the original extent of the accompanying parish, if we go further back to see how from pagan custom there developed, in Saxon times and after, a pattern of ecclesiastical patronage in Christian England.

Patrons and Advowsons

A pertinent entry under 'Parish' in *The Dictionary of English Church History* (ed. Ollard & Crosse, 1919) provides us with a start. It points out that a pagan Anglo-Saxon landlord in his religious capacity had by Teutonic custom the right and duty to provide worship for the benefit of his family and for dependents holding land under him, and accordingly delegated a priest to perform this. Such a lord, as owner, was patron of the place of worship, the temple, and master of his agent, the priest. Beyond what he gave the latter or allowed him to accept from worshippers, he made a profit for himself out of temple receipts.

When Christianity came to Saxon England, it proved impossible to root out this Teutonic concept of the relationship between patron (or lord) and priest. The church fabric was without question the property of the landlord, and he gave it as a benefice to what man he would. The Ollard and Crosse entry goes on to say, however, that the Church strove to ensure that the man beneficed should not be a serf, for his dependence upon his patron would then have been absolute. So although the priest was bound to perform his duties and accept the offered stipend, he had to be formally presented to the bishop for ordination, being ordained on the title of his benefice. Bishops initially played only this small part in the founding of new churches.

Local worship was maintained by permission of the lord as patron exercising the right – the advowson – of nominating the incumbent and presenting him to the bishop. As had been the case under pagan conditions of grant and tenure, the priest appointed normally held the benefice till his death.

Before the institution of compulsory tithe (which followed as the authority of bishops over parishes increased), the chief revenue for the priest was from the glebe land which the patron, if he was to obtain a priest's services, included as part of the benefice. The glebe of an English benefice was often two yard-lands, that is twice as much land as was usually held from their lord by the members of a village community.

Looking for a profit, the owner saw to it that the church had a congregation whose fees and offerings would form much of the revenue to be divided between himself and the priest. Church attendance was a compulsory duty on the part of those dependent on the lord for livelihood, in the same way as they had no choice but to grind their corn at his mill. So the extent of the lord's land, or at least its populated extent, defined the extent of the parish.

The First Fingest Benefice

Before we can get to grips with the question of how far early Fingest – church or parish – was fitted to this pattern of patronage we have to remind ourselves of the chronological and patronal constraints which limit the likelihood of explanations we may offer.

Firstly, although it is pretty clear from what we have already said that most opinion is against the idea that the first stone building was 'a Saxon church', its 'Saxon-

Norman overlap' appearance leaves doubt whether we date its building shortly before or just after the Conquest.

Secondly, given that there is no contemporary record of the initial patronage of the Fingest benefice, the strongest hint that it may have already been in existence at or about the time of the Conquest is the fact that half a century later Richard Daubeny, the fifteenth abbot of St Albans, won for his abbey from the king a carefully chosen series of ecclesiastical claims including a specific grant of the manor and church of 'Tingehurste'. This particular group of claims looks to have been unusual in that it specified manors, priories and churches – among them Fingest – not newly claimed for the abbey, but rather regarded as to be won back. Thomas Delafield clearly considered this probable – 'our Manour and Church which were then given (if not restored) to that monastery' (Bodleian Library, *Gough MS, Bucks* 2, p.132).

I shall deal further with this in a moment, but first we need to get some idea into our heads of what the terrain of 'early Fingest' might have encompassed before the building of a stone church, or any church, was thought of. Just a settled clearing in woodland or waste where two or three wooded Chiltern valleys met? A clearing especially favourable to settlement? Perhaps providing enough arable land to supplement otherwise barely adequate subsistence from swine-pasturing in the beech-woods around? Even a clearing connected in some significant way with another older settlement? Developing this last possibility, could 'Fingest' have been an outlying hamlet of the extensive first century Roman estate which we know centred on the Yewden Manor site? Whatever the case, the best of the arable land, as often in the Chilterns, was in the valley.

Seeking a thread to guide us through this conjectural labyrinth, we clutch first at a slender filament that links two village names.

Early Fingest, early Skirmett and the Hambleden Valley

Mawer and Stenton concluded, as we have seen, that Fingest and Skirmett are very likely different local names for the same Anglo-Saxon or Anglo-Scandinavian meeting place, based on the argument that the name Fingest derives from the Anglo-Scandinavian 'thing hurst' or 'assembly hill'. (Some think that 'hurst' in village names speaks to their origins as settlements in hollows or valleys in wooded hills.) Skirmett, on the other hand, derives from Old English 'scir-gemot' ('shire-moot') but with a hard Danish 'k'. While the apparent implication is that Skirmett was a meeting place of the shire courts, this seems to make far too important a mountain of Skirmett's molehill. In *The Pre-Conquest Church in England* (1961) Margaret Deansley notes that an Old English term for the parish of a church is 'shrift shire'. Is the truth of the matter that the open-air meeting place for local parish services before Fingest had a church was Skirmett? This would explain the evident linguistic identity of the two village names. Further, it would imply that the 'parish' in question included Skirmett with Fingest. To put it another way, Fingest's 'heal' or manor – perhaps as we have hinted a 'comital' manor – originally included the part of the Hambleden valley we now identify as Skirmett.

At any rate, where are these vernacular clues leading us? Well, King Cnut's Danish army had ravaged Buckinghamshire for the last time in 1016, on its way to the final defeat of Edmund Ironside in Wessex. By 1042 Edward the Confessor's accession had seen the end of Danish kings in England. By then many areas outside the Danelaw had become settled in husbandry by Danes; the persistence of Danish vernacular traits in their village names identifies as such Fingest and Skirmett. That Danish settlement hereabouts persisted after the Mercian earldom fell to Godwine is not surprising, for since Cnut's time the House of Godwine had favoured the Danish cause.

What in this densely wooded south-west Chilterns country enabled Anglo-Danish husbandry to establish itself successfully in the Hambleden valley? The Roman findings at Yewden Manor, the third century burial on the site of what centuries later became Fingest Manor, and the hint of an even earlier earthwork contour at the same spot are inklings of a long though doubtless much interrupted history of habitation along the valley's whole length. The generations who for two hundred years or more populated the Romano-British hamlet at Yewden must have productively farmed the fertile valley soil, no doubt extending the arable land by widespread assarting in order to maintain their self-sufficiency over such a period. The wealth of potsherds recovered from the Yewden site includes ware like that later found intact in the Fingest burial. It is clearly arguable that from Roman times there has been farming along the valley's whole length. How scrappily or intermittently this may have gone on through the Dark Ages and after the Saxon invasion we do not know, but evidently Anglo-Danish farmers had little difficulty in making themselves a useful living in the valley fields.

The Danes of the warring times were no church-builders, in the Chilterns or elsewhere. It therefore appears unlikely that a parish, let alone a church building of any sort, took shape here until well after 1016. But Danish attitudes softened. Cnut, by conquest monarch of the whole kingdom, and then the baptised Christian King, sought the friendship of the Saxon Church, giving it land, building churches and founding abbeys and monasteries. Matthew Paris tells us that he became 'a great favourer of the monastery of St Albans'. By 1042, when with the death of Cnut's second son the throne passed to Edward the Confessor, many Danes, having abandoned paganism for the Christian life favoured by the royal house, were already settled in the extensive lands of the monastery, (*Cotton MS, Nero D,* vol. vii).

St Albans – Fingest's First Patron?

St Albans monastery held foremost rank among English Benedictine houses in the Middle Ages because it possessed the remains of Alban, the third century protomartyr of England. Alban's canonisation by pope Adrian I had brought the abbey special privileges at Rome well before the Norman conquest. The Saxon abbot appointed in 1047, Leofstan (as we saw in an earlier chapter, a close friend and counsellor of King Edward) through his court interest obtained numerous grants of land to the monastery from the nobility and more recent settlers, especially wealthy Danes (*VCH Hertfordshire,* vol. iv, p.371).

By Edward's time it had become usual for smallholders to enjoy personal independence as freemen or 'sokemen'. Freemen who acquired as book-land or loan-land estates of a few hides (in Buckinghamshire, five hides were about one thousand one hundred acres on average) had the status of thegns, with the power of choosing their lord at will. With the religious renewal of the times, such thegns were planning churches to serve their estates, and simple church buildings were springing up everywhere within the old minster *parochiae*, so much so that the founding of such new local parishes deprived the old minsters of much of their *raison d'être*.

Earl Algar's extensive Mercian land holdings in S. Bucks included the two large estates of Marlow and Hambleden. Tilleberie, adjoining Hambleden, was before the Conquest held by Algar's man, Thorbert, according to the Domesday survey. To have merited such mention, Thorbert was likely to have been a man of some rank, a thegn under Algar's lordship. Whether he himself was Anglo-Danish we do not know, but as we have seen, Fingest and Skirmett settlers preponderantly were. The open-air church services held in their common parish must also have been attended by Thorbert's Tilleberie tenancy.

The ebbing of pastoral care from the old minsters of Aylesbury, Reading and Sonning left both Thorbert's people and the freemen of Harold's comital manor of Fingest/Skirmett with a need for a local church with a graveyard, and a resident priest to hear confessions, baptise children and bury the dead. Such a church, moreover, would provide profitable rights for its patron, for example burial rights, rights to celebrate marriages, baptismal rights and rights to take tithe and other church taxes.

Bearing all this in mind, dear reader, you will not find the following unreasonable, I trust, as the likeliest developments taking place hereabouts during the few decades before and after the Conquest.

Hows and Whys Answered

St Albans already had supposedly historical claims by charter to 'manentes' in Tyrefeld, and Thorbert must have known this. In hope of turning sacerdotal eyes from his adjoining Tilleberie with its Danish history, he doubtless encouraged the Anglo-Danish freemen of Fingest to seek Harold's assent to long-settled land in his comital manor being dedicated to a church and benefice under the patronage of the venerated monastery less than twenty-five miles away. The rights of advowson they agreed to bestow upon the abbot; but the rectorial right to the temporalities of the benefice to be retained. Such an arrangement, by which the abbey presented its own clerks-in-orders as rectors to a benefice, was not impossible under Saxon canon law.

Whatever the detail of the arrangement, the advantage to the abbey persuaded Abbot Leofstan to favour founding a church at the already-established Fingest Manor. The initial church was doubtless a wooden one, like most lesser churches of pre-Conquest times, and the necessary glebe was readily available from common waste in the upper Hambleden valley. Accepting this scenario, we may think of this first church in S. Bucks as standing more or less centrally in a Fingest parish that included Turville and Skirmett and extended a good way down the valley.

Such a relationship with St Albans before the Conquest, not to mention the favour that Fingest church enjoyed after it from Nigel his kinsman would neatly explain why Abbot Richard Daubeny in the next century felt it nothing but appropriate to add Fingest Manor, with its church and parish, to the lands he persuaded Henry I to restore to his abbey. We noted earlier, and further elaborate below, that soon after the Conquest Turville Court Manor came into the hands of another Nigel, again a member of the Norman Albini family who were still traditionally favourers of St Albans. Browne Willis's remark about Fingest (*Willis MS,* vol. x, p.22) 'the Advowson of the church and manor was soon after the Conquest given to the Abby of St Albans', may well refer to Daubeny's claim as the restoration of a right, not a new claim.

Nothing however now remains to prove the existence, let alone the manner of founding, of a church in this Chiltern valley in the Confessor's time. In face of this I only reiterate, as persuasively as the foregoing merits, the historical likelihood that a simple wooden church indeed then stood where the church stands today, serving the pastoral mandate of St Albans.

And then came the Conquest...

The Anglo-Saxon to Norman Upheaval

As we know, before the Conquest the 'manor' (as the Normans saw it) of Hambleden was in the possession of Algar, the Saxon earl of Mercia, while Thorbert, a 'man of Algar's', held Tilleburie 'manor'. Hambleden had at no time, then or thereafter, any pastoral connection with St Albans, unlike Turville (Thyrefeld) with its ancient link. The reasons for not regarding 'Thyrefeld' and 'Tilleburie' as topographically identical, I have discussed earlier.

St Albans, it seems, had before the Conquest recovered from the Danes much of the Thyrefeld land, though not the part that included Tilleburie (later Turville Court Manor). As we saw in Chapter VII, this was the part (we now know it as Turville village) which at the Conquest Nigel de Albini acquired, ousting Thorbert.

Tilleburie, but a small outlying manor of Nigel's barony-in-chief of Cainhoe in Hertfordshire had no pre-Conquest church of its own and its first vicarage, under St Albans, was ordained about 1200. Its lord, Nigel, can only therefore have looked to Fingest for its ecclesiastical needs as we have already deduced.

It is at this point in our dogged attempts to weave together the early, too scanty, threads of local colour that we begin to perceive a shadowy pattern emerging in the fabric at the Conquest.

Fingest: the Aftermath of the Conquest

Abbot Leofstan died in 1064. It used to be thought that St Albans's next abbot was Frederic, but the cathedral historians now seem to think Harold appointed one Egfrid to the vacancy, and that Frederic, another Saxon nobleman, did not succeed until 1070. Frederic was a patriotic leader of the Saxon party who had done his best to impede William's progress after Hastings, and at the Berkhamsted surrender had obliged him to swear to observe the ancient laws of Edward – an oath very soon disregarded.

His attitude to the Normans in the end led to harsh treatment of his abbey and confiscation of part of its patrimony. How much was lost is disputed, but his losses were William's gains. They are likely to have included Fingest Manor and parish with its Saxon wooden church, lying in what had been part of Harold's earldom.

Now, conventionally at least, under William's personal lordship, Fingest would have merited exclusion from the Domesday survey which was finally completed the year before the Conqueror died. That Fingest's titular lord at this stage was indeed the Conqueror gains plausibility from Thomas Delafield who, the reader will remember (Chapter VI), unearthed documentary evidence that Fingest was once 'Antient Royal Domaine'.

After Hastings, the Norman force made a lengthy, circuitous and destructive march towards London, skirting the Chiltern hundreds to cross the Thames at Wallingford, and thence moving to Berkhamsted to receive the formal submission of the English. This route left much of the south-west Chilterns relatively unscathed including, I suggest, the township of Fingest with its wooden church which was then still nominally at least under St Albans's obedience. A small township at first hardly aware, no doubt, of the momentous surrounding changes.

The Post-Conquest Parish

These changes however soon had a harsh intrusive effect locally, starting with the Hambleden estate. The Domesday record of the post-Conquest hidation of Buckinghamshire shows that after Queen Matilda replaced Earl Algar as tenant-in-chief of Hambleden, the reckoned extent of her new possession swelled to twenty hides, much the largest estate in the Desborough hundred (K. Bailey, 1992; Rec. Bucks, vol. xxxii, p.1). Hambleden Manor, like the Roman Yewden estate centuries earlier, expanded up the valley to reach Fingest's graveyard, which lying indisputably in Fingest Manor territory proscribed further encroachment. This left Fingest church in a manor and parish which despite owing as much temporal allegiance to the Conqueror as spiritual obedience to St Albans Abbey, had become punishingly diminished in an age when it was only rights of access to adequately productive arable land that kept tenant families from starvation.

At William's death in 1085, William Albini would have known that the survey established the long-standing claims of another abbot, Faritius of Abingdon, to seventeen hides of Lewknor and to the territory of Abefeld lying over the Oxfordshire border to the north and also to Ackhamstead, an enclave of Lewknor in Buckinghamshire. If the manor of Fingest was to resist threats of encroachment from this direction also, and to maintain its prescriptive self-sufficiency, Albini needed (with the connivance of its next royal overlord, Rufus) to take advantage of the local upheaval of land tenancy that followed the Conquest, and commandeer as much as he could of the productive arable land lying at the county border to its north-east. The best of this was the five or so hides between Ibstone (now held by William's legate, Hervey) on the west, and on the east the Marlow estates which were, like Hambleden, now Queen Matilda's. To the north, across the ill-defined county boundary, were the lands Abbot Faritius laid claim to.

In the event, Fingest Manor succeeded in appropriating the hamlets of Boulter End, Wheeler End and Cadmore End. This accretion had the effect of shifting its population balance so that henceforth – and indeed until the nineteenth century – these three hamlets, though furthest from the church, nevertheless housed a majority of

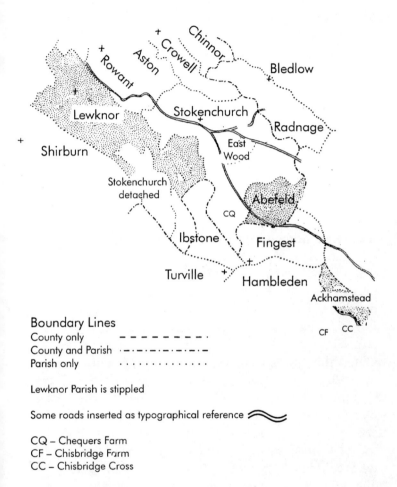

Boundary Lines
County only   – – – – – – – –
County and Parish   ·–·–·–·–·–·–
Parish only   · · · · · · · · · · · · ·

Lewknor Parish is stippled

Some roads inserted as typographical reference ≈≈

CQ – Chequers Farm
CF – Chisbridge Farm
CC – Chisbridge Cross

Fig. 15: Map from A. Morley Davies's *Abefeld and Ackhamstead: Two Lost Places* (Rec. Bucks, *vol. xv(3). pp.*166–171, 1949). The Oxon–Bucks county boundary ran through Ibstone parish until 1896.

Fingest's parishioners. What's more, it left Fingest church eccentrically sited, as it still is, in the extreme south-west corner of its parish.

Skirmett, as we have seen, was subsumed into the Hambleden Manor estate, and eventually into Hambleden parish.

Abefeld? Ackhamstead?

These two obsolete place names appear on no recent maps and on few surviving older ones. They are a pair of what Morley Davies called 'lost places' (Rec. Bucks, 1949, vol. xv, pp.166–171); but they once existed, and they have something to tell us about how Fingest parish settled its final relationship with the Oxon-Bucks county boundary.

First, Abefeld. Morley Davies's paper, as his accompanying map shows (Fig. 15), identifies Abefeld as a detached part of Lewknor parish, one of the dozen or so parishes of the hundred of Lewknor in Oxfordshire. Fig. 16, from the *Victoria County History of Oxfordshire* (vol. viii, p.1), shows the parishes making up the old Oxfordshire hundred of Lewknor as their boundaries were in 1840. Lewknor parish extended to include Studdridge, Cadmore End separated from Studdridge by the part of Aston Rowant parish where Chequers Manor lies (Fig. 16), and the detached hamlet of Ackhamstead, in Bucks. This trio of hamlets in the hills above Lewknor village, which were collectively known as 'Lewknor Uphill' were relinquished to Buckinghamshire in 1844.

Another hamlet, Plumbridge, also in the hills and no less a part of Lewknor parish and of Oxfordshire, was not part of Lewknor Uphill but rather of Ibstone, which as the Domesday survey found, straddled the Oxon-Bucks border. The upshot then is that what Morley Davies labelled as 'Abefeld' roughly corresponds in the 1840–based

The Hundred of Lewknor

A Studdridge ⎫
B Cadmore End ⎬ Lewknor Uphill
C Ackhamstead ⎭
D Plumbridge in Ibstone
E Padnells in Rotherfield Greys
F Wormsley
G Unnamed detached part (now in Cuxham with Easington)

A,B,C,D,E and F are now in Bucks

Fig. 16: The 1840 boundaries of Lewknor parish, showing the separated Ackhamstead portion (from V.C.H. Oxfordshire, viii, 1).

parish map (Fig. 16) with the Lewknor Uphill hamlet of Cadmore End.

In his paper on the Chiltern feld (discussed in Chapter VII) Dr Baines builds on Morley Davies's idea of early mediaeval Abefeld, throwing more light on its true origins and extent, its fate and its relationship to Cadmore End. He argues that Abbefeld (with an added 'b') was 'Aebbanfeld' ('Aebba's open country'), the large heathland tract of the Chiltern plateau north-east of the Fingest valley, extending into Stokenchurch and Aston Rowant.

According to the *Abingdon Chronicle*, Abbefeld had been held by that Abbey before it was lost in the Danish invasions. Some of it – 'Lewknor and its members' – was restored to Abingdon before the Conquest by the Danish thegn Tovi, who then (as we saw in Chapter VI) also held the Bucks part of Ibstone. Baines identifies (Fig. 6) what is called 'Old Abbefeld' in the *Calendar of Inquisitions Post Mortem* (vol. ii, pp.318, 384) of 1284, as the portion of Lewknor Uphill that Davies labels 'Abefeld'.

Abefeld, Cadmore End and the de Scaccarios

The rest of the moorland around Cadmore End that had been lost to the Danes was not finally restored to Abingdon until after the Conquest when Abbot Faritius recovered it for his abbey in 1106 by charter of Henry I.

What was regained included 'the land which Algar holds in Abbefeld, which Nigel de Oilly returned to the same church to hold in demesne' (*Hist. Mon. Abingdon*, vol. ii, p.110). This implies that the appellation 'Abbefeld' initially applied to more than just the land around Cadmore End, and this is confirmed if we move on nearly two hundred years to look at the land holdings of another Norman family, the de Scaccarios. To quote Morley Davies again: 'All through the thirteenth century the history of Abefeld is bound up with the family de Scaccario'. And indeed a number of escheat reversions of lands held by different members of this family, and enumerated in detail in the *Calendar of Inquisitions Post Mortem* for Edward I's reign (for example Nos. 528, 586, 820, 821) clearly indicate that some of the land in question lay between Ibstone, Fingest and Cadmore End – the area labelled 'Little Abbefeld in Stokenchurch' on Baines's map (Fig. 6).

The de Scaccarios at the time were grand ushers of the King's exchequer (*scaccarium* = a chequer-board, used for money calculations). Chequers Manor farm on the same land keeps their name alive today, not to mention The Chequers public house in Fingest.

Some of the *Inquisitions* of 1284 deal with agreements over disputed pasture rights on the Cadmore End moorlands. It seems that intermixture of holdings long persisted around Cadmore End and across the county boundary; at a post mortem inquisition on the death of Simon de Scaccario a writ of 'the Monday before the Purification 20 Edw. I' (Simon died on the Friday before) mentions the following valuation:

Tingehurste: 38s yearly rent from 2 virgates of land, and 12d pleas etc held of the earl of Lincoln by service of 10s and suit of court twice yearly.

So it looks as if even by the thirteenth century a tenancy in Little Abbefeld could still include Fingest land, with little regard to the ancient county border (Cadmore End = Cada's 'maere' or boundary).

The earlier history of the Cadmore End land is revealingly attested in a paper by G.R. Elvey in her paper *Buckinghamshire in 1086* (Rec. Bucks, vol. xvi, p.342) dealing with the use of the Saxon term 'hide'. Mrs Elvey says that by 1086, when the Domesday Book appeared, the word 'hide' was only used in Bucks to denote the fiscal unit on which the 'geld' of Saxon times had been levied, and never as a measure of area which by 1086 was always in carucates, i.e. as much land as a team of oxen could plough in a year. Thus description of land in later documents in terms of hides shows that there existed before the Conquest a settlement with a developed agricultural economy based on arable farming. As an example she quotes (from the Bucks Record Society publication *Feet of Fines for Buckinghamshire* (ed. N.W. Hughes) an agreement of the year 1235 ('68/25; 20 Hen III, Westminster, morrow of St Martin') as follows:

> Rog. de Scaccario pet. [plaintiff] and Hen. de Scaccario ten. [defendant], ½ hide land in CADMERE; H. ackn. right of R.; R. gave H. a moiety of the whole wood of Cademere lengthways in open as well as in covered places [.]

This makes it certain that arable land was already being worked at Cadmore End when Edward the Confessor levied his last geld in 1051, and this in turn may well explain why, when Fingest Manor had to give up territory to Hambleden after the Conquest, it lost no time in claiming some of what was traditionally good land in Cadmore End. That the land in question had once been under the Danes perhaps increased the interest it had for Fingest which had its own Danish antecedents.

We must remind ourselves that the redrawing of the county boundaries in 1896 completely changed the map, bringing the whole area surrounding Stokenchurch into modern Buckinghamshire (Fig. 15). The hamlet of Cadmore End with Cadmore End common, for many centuries part of Fingest parish, by 1852 had become detached as part of a new consolidated chapelry with its own newly built church. In the Oxford diocesan plan of

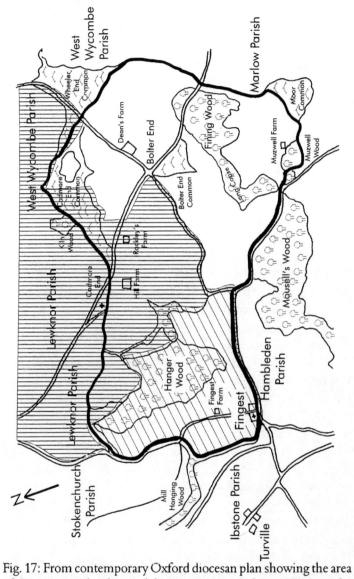

Fig. 17: From contemporary Oxford diocesan plan showing the area of Fingest parish (diagonal lines) incorporated in 1852 into the newly formed consolidated chapelry of Cadmore End.

this new chapelry published at the time (Fig. 17), the area north of the Lane End-Stokenchurch road, that Morley Davies's plan identifies as 'Abefeld' is marked 'Lewknor Uphill', lying alongside Cadmore End common. Likewise, the 1883 Ordnance Survey map (16 in/mile) marks as 'Lewknor Uphill' in Oxfordshire the area that includes Baines's Little Abbefeld in Stokenchurch and Old Abbefeld (Fig. 6), both alongside Cadmore End common on the Bucks side of the then county boundary.

Next, Ackhamstead. Morley Davies thought that this 'lost hamlet' was probably included in the seventeen hides of Lewknor recorded in the Domesday Book as held by Abingdon Abbey; as Fig. 16 shows, it was detached from the rest of the parish, lying well within Bucks. He quotes *The History of Abingdon Abbey* as describing the gift of Lewknor to the abbey in 1052 by Edward the Confessor's queen Eadgitha because of her sorrow at its young monks' undernourishment; and further notes that Henry I's queen Matilda (Maud the Good) at Council in about 1112 decided that the abbey owed service only to Lewknor hundred, not Pyrton. The Hundred Rolls of 1278 confirm that Matilda indeed gave the manor of Lewknor to the abbey in alms, and that one Thomas de Lega held tenancy from the abbot of two carucates of land called 'Achamstede' and 'Chissebech'; Chissebech is the modern Chisbridge (Fig. 15).

Morley Davies goes on to say that *The History of Abingdon* further records Ansgerus, a clerk of Lewknor 'making a good bargain' with Abingdon's Abbot Ingulf between 1154 and 1158 to obtain a member of Lewknor called Hacamsteda. Baines thinks that Ansgerus probably built Lewknor's parish church and may also have founded the Moor Chapel in Ackhamstead. In the thirteenth and fourteenth centuries the chapel seems to have served the needs of what were then quite numerous parishioners,

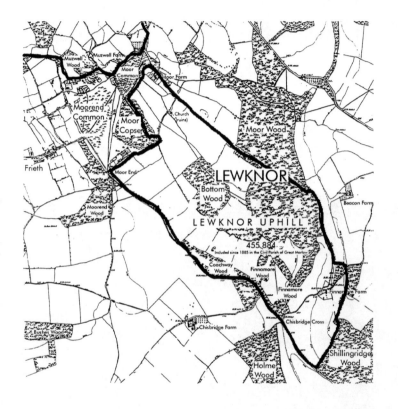

Fig. 18: 1883 Ordnance Survey map; the relationship to Fingest parish of the Ackhamstead portion of Lewknor is outlined.

though when it was built is doubtful. It was perhaps rebuilt about 1415. By the end of the sixteenth century the chapel had become decayed, with services held irregularly and poorly attended by a scanty population of Lewknor Uphill folk. When Delafield came to Fingest, Ackhamstead had popularly surrendered its old name for that of 'Moor Chapel'; he writes (Bodleian Library, *MS Top*, vol. D88,58):

> More Chappel, though entirely surrounded with the Parishes of Fingest, West Wycombe, Great Marlow and Hambleden all in the county of Bucks and quite detached from Oxfordshire, is notwithstanding a Branch of the Parish and Hundred of Lewknor, part of the cure of the Vicar there, who receives the Profits and supplies the church service, and is subject to the Bp of Oxford as Ordinary; and in temporal matters follows the Courts of the County of Oxford.

This suggests that the chapel was until then at any rate not in a ruinous state.

In an unpublished paper compiled for the Frieth Village Society in 1969, Dr G.H. Wyatt quotes from *The Oxford University, City and County Herald* of 1849 a hearing at the Consistorial Court of the Diocese of Oxford of an application for a faculty, later granted, for the demolition of Ackhamstead chapel and its rebuilding at Cadmore End. For the building of the church at Cadmore End, which was consecrated in 1851, much material from the old Moor Chapel was in fact used. Today virtually nothing of the latter remains bar its site, overgrown with cherry, holly, brambles and ivy, near where a footpath crosses a track in Moor Farm, south of Lane End. The parish boundary between Hambleden and Marlow now cuts right across the lost living of Ackhamstead. Fig. 18 shows how it lay in relation to Fingest parish, with Moor Common in between.

Finally on the subject of Ackhamstead, to return for a moment to the 1883 Ordnance map which, as we have noted above marks as 'Lewknor Uphill' on the Oxon side of the county boundary the areas Baines identifies as Little Abbefeld and Old Abbefeld (Fig. 6). Likewise, the OS map marks as 'Lewknor Uphill' (Fig. 18) the area labelled 'Ackhamstead' in Fig. 15. Between these two portions of 'Lewknor Uphill' lies that part of the Buckinghamshire parish of Fingest which we have concluded was commandeered at the Conquest when Skirmett was lost to Hambleden. Thus what Fingest parish acquired after the Conquest upheaval was Oxfordshire land hitherto part of Lewknor Uphill's land extending to and including Ackhamstead. It is more than likely that the resulting isolation of Ackhamstead within Bucks provoked the founding there of a chapel-of-ease of its own – the only one in the Lewknor hamlets – thus keeping the administrative link with Lewknor.

The Post-Conquest Church

Abbot Frederic died in Ely in 1077, still at loggerheads with William. The post-Conquest uprisings in which he with other English leaders had had a hand led very soon to the replacement of Englishmen by Norman magnates in much of the government of both church and state. The next abbot of St Albans was a Norman, Paul of Caen, a nephew of Langfranc, Archbishop of Canterbury. Abbot Paul, a strong disciplinarian, had little respect for the provincial ways of his Saxon predecessors, and less for their buildings. He started the immense task of physically rebuilding the Abbey and, determined to promote the standing of the monastery in the Christian world, drastically reformed its rules and those of its dependent churches.

This major refurbishment took place at a time when, under the direction of the papal envoy, a code of penance had been imposed upon the Conqueror's army for the unknown numbers killed at Hastings. The Normans, acknowledging papal support for their invasion, and strict in observance of such Church ordinances, saw to it that many village churches were built or rebuilt as acts of penance. What is more likely (and fits well with the architectural dating we have been at pains to deduce) than that Fingest's pre-Conquest wooden church, in a manor coming under William's lordship, was rebuilt in stone with Saxon labour during the abbacy (1077–1093) of a Norman prelate in papal favour? The building that resulted, with its two-storey tower and relatively spacious chancel-with-apse, was suited to celebration of Divine Office and high Mass on occasions when the abbot himself or members of his retinue were sojourning in Fingest during the peregrinations of abbey lands usual in mediaeval times.

The Tower's Third Storey

Abbot Paul died in 1093, six years into William Rufus's reign, but it was not until 1097 that the next abbot, Richard Daubeny, took office. Abbot Richard, says Delafield, was:

> A great favourite of the Two Royal Brothers William the 2nd and Henry the 1st by whose means be obtained many honours and Possessions and bravely maintained them when he had gotten them.

Matthew Paris, making the first surviving written reference to Fingest, says in his thirteenth century history of St Albans monastery that 'the manor of Tingehurste, with church and tithes', was one of several, royal grants procured for the monastery by Abbot Richard after Henry I had succeeded to the throne in 1100. From what we have argued above, it looks as if these were grants restoring to the abbey some of the lands it had lost under the Conqueror.

In 1115, during Richard's abbacy, the great new abbey church at St Albans begun by Abbot Paul was completed. With a grand and solemn service of dedication imminent, Abbot Richard sought to underline the sum and substance of his great monastery by enriching its newly reacquired daughter churches. We may imagine, moreover, that to Richard especially, Fingest manifestly deserved attention with its dedication to St Bartholomew being a reminder of both the Canterbury relic of the apostle's arm and the withering of his own arm and its miraculous cure. Whatever was in his mind, he proceeded to top Fingest's recently built stone tower with a handsome bell-chamber of good Norman stonework with generous Romanesque openings to carry the pealing of its bells to Chiltern folk far and wide in witness of the spiritual authority of St Albans.

The Fingest Rectory

Rectors, to quote A. Hamilton Thompson in *Leics. Archaeol. Soc. Trans.* (vol. 22, pp.2–32; 1941–45):

> are parsons of their churches, the *personae* who give the church or benefice, in itself an abstract idea quite distinct from that of the church as a fabric, its concrete individuality and legal identity. When the rectory of the church, with its revenues arising from the great tithes […] has passed into other hands, the cure of souls cannot be alienated from the church, or served from a distance, but requires to be discharged by a resident. The new rectors, whether they be individuals or (as often) corporate bodies of persons,

are, properly speaking, *parsons* of the church, and
must be represented by a deputy, or *vicar* in priest's
orders, to administer the sacraments and preach to
and instruct his flock. The rector or rectors have to
arrange to ensure his stipend from certain fixed
sources, and guarantee him an adequate residence.
This arrangement, confirmed and sanctioned by the
diocesan, has the effect of establishing the vicarage as
a freehold benefice, which can be vacated only by
death or resignation.

A rectory may not have been so precisely defined in the
twelfth century, and anyway lack of contemporary documentation means that we cannot be sure whether in its St
Albans days the resident chaplain serving Fingest was
appointed as rector or vicar. What we do know is that when
in 1163 the patronage of the benefice passed with the
church and manor to the Bishops of Lincoln, they certainly
treated it then and thereafter as a rectory. Perhaps the
abbots of St Albans had treated it likewise to favour the
chosen priests they installed here; their names, sadly, we
shall never know. At any rate, the Fingest benefice
continued as a rectory until it was subsumed into that of
Hambleden in 1978.

The Flowering of Fingest in St Albans's Sunshine

The Church grew in wealth and zeal under the Norman
kings and with the growth of monasticism around the turn
of the eleventh to twelfth centuries, the influence of St
Albans's Norman abbots and their Benedictine monastery
grew likewise.

Paul of Caen, a nephew of Langfranc, who was consecrated fourteenth abbot in 1077, had well established the
place and power of his monastery by 1088 when by

William's command the old Anglo-Saxon see at Dorchester was translated to a new site at Lincoln, from which a Norman bishop, Remigius of Fécamp, ruled the vast new diocese. Paying little regard apparently to this upheaval, Paul continued to build his great abbey and his monastery's reputation, founding the scriptorium for which it was to become famous. He succeeded moreover in freeing St Albans from the jurisdiction of the Archbishop of Canterbury, and proceeded to subsume under its patronage a number of neighbouring benefices, mostly in Hertfordshire but several in Buckinghamshire. Over half a century later this group of churches linked to St Albans was to achieve open recognition as a 'liberty' of the monastery, remaining independent of any bishopric but that of Rome until the Reformation.

Meanwhile, however, the next abbot, Richard Daubeny – he who regained Fingest from the King for St Albans – was in no hurry to change his monastery's obedience; and indeed when the new abbey church was completed in 1116, it was the Bishop of Lincoln who dedicated it.

Delafield's panegyric which I quoted earlier speaks eloquently of the grace and talent traditionally attributed to Abbot Richard. There can be little doubt that during his abbacy Fingest, as well as acquiring its church's handsome belfry, shared as a minor dependent in the flowering of the sum and substance of the monastery. With its advowson firmly in the hands of the Norman abbots of St Albans, the benefice of Fingest acquired a degree of ecclesiastical repute.

What the resulting effect was on the village we can only guess. Sadly, knowing nothing of the extent and nature of the manor house of the times and even less of any living quarters available for lesser clergy, we can scarcely take it for granted that when abbots Paul or Richard or their successors visited this church they housed themselves and their large retinues here – or indeed that this was ever practicable. Even in the comparative peace of Henry I's reign a numerous armed escort was needed, if not for protection then at least to make much of the power of an abbot of St Albans visiting his monastery's dependent Chiltern churches. Such numbers of clerics and servants would have imposed commissariat demands far beyond Fingest's scope. It is likely, rather, that it fell to a detachment of lesser souls, a prior and a few clerks perhaps, to provide the ceremonial processional body representing the patron abbot when high liturgical occasions were to be celebrated in the new stone church. Indeed until the third-storey belfry was added by Abbot Richard, the considerable room in the tower's second storey was very likely intended and probably used as secure quarters for such clerical visitors, or even resident priests. The later installation by Abbot Richard of the bells and their bellframe and the need for room for bellringers and their gear would have reduced this living space in the church itself. It may have been this – and the added circumstance of Richard Daubeny favouring the church with his own attendance on festivals such as St Bartholomew's day – that led to his building near the church a considerable manor house appropriate to an abbot's residence, however brief its occasions.

The Last Three Abbots to be Lords of Fingest Manor

Richard Daubeny, the fifteenth abbot, died in 1119. Another Norman, Geoffrey de Gorham, succeeded and held the abbey for a span of twenty-seven years that saw the death of the able and successful King Henry in 1135, and his replacement by Stephen, whose shaky hold on the throne was to plunge the country into misrule. Henry's plans for his daughter Matilda to succeed had come to nothing, and she precipitated instead a chaotic civil war that divided the country at the baronial level, revolving mainly around castles and their capture. Stephen, preoccupied with these troubles and his own position, failed to defend his throne's rooted interests in Normandy. After a series of conquests in northern France ending with the surrender of Rouen, the Plantagenet Geoffrey of Anjou, Matilda's husband, won from Stephen the dukedom of Normandy which had provided the Conqueror with his victory at Hastings. This loss of suzerainty over Normandy put an end, if only for the time being, to the cross-Channel structure of the Anglo-Norman aristocracy; and when the abbacy of St Albans fell vacant again on Robert de Gorham's death in 1146 its next abbot, the seventeenth, was Ralph Gubian, an Englishman. When Ralph died five years later (1151), another Robert de Gorham, nephew of the first, became the eighteenth abbot, still under obedience to Lincoln.

Stephen in his struggle for power made many promises to the Church. From 1139 onward the primacy was held by Theobald 'the last archbishop to wield unquestioned influence as the first advisor of the crown, in virtue of his ecclesiastical position' (F.M. Powick, *Stephen Langton*, 1928, p.109). As we shall see in the next chapter, the calibre of St Albans continued to grow despite twenty years of Stephen's unhappy rule. Thus we need not suppose that during this period the ecclesiastical standing Fingest church and parish had acquired under St Albans's wing was in any way diminished.

Chapter X
The Manor Episcopised: First Rectors Collated (1163–1234)

Pope Adrian IV was an Englishman, born Nicholas Breakspear in the town of St Albans. Although as a young man he had been refused admission to the order by the abbot, he retained a particular devotion to both the saint and his birthplace. Having studied in Paris, and later in Rome, he found favour with Pope Eugenius III and in due course was elected cardinal. Eventually in 1154 he succeeded to the papal chair when, it is thought, he took the name Adrian in deference to the eighth century pope Adrian I, who was held to have canonised Alban.

The discerning reader will here be wondering what possible hand Pope Adrian, Bishop of Rome, could have had, directly or indirectly, in Fingest's fate. The determining event was that Robert de Gorham, the eighteenth abbot, hearing of the new pope's accession, journeyed forthwith to Rome where, although initially less than popular on the papal scene, he lodged and persisted in lodging complaints of oppression of his monastery by the Bishops of Lincoln. At length he carried the day, and obtained from Adrian bulls securing for his abbey juridical independence of the bishop's see. The bull *Incomprehensibilis*, for example, laid down that *any* Catholic bishop could be invited to conduct the blessing of the abbot and perform ordinations and consecrations; other bulls ensured that the abbey's clergy were to be free from diocesan excommunications and could not be summoned to the diocesan synod.

What happened next Delafield describes in his *Account of Fingherst*. In fact he describes it twice over, first in his chapter on Fingest under the abbots (which he titles '*Dominium Religiosum*'), and again in the chapter '*Dominium Prelaticum*', which is about Fingest under bishops; both versions are in his best antiquarian manner, appropriate he thought to the disturbing effects these papal pronouncements were to have on the parish. Such is the persuasive immediacy of Delafield's descriptions that in what follows I unashamedly quote from them *in extenso*. In '*Dominium Religiosum*', speaking of Abbot Robert's arrival back in England, he says:

Upon his Return a Synod being assembled at London In Lent 1154/5 there the Abbat exhibited his Charters of Priviledges; the Proxies of Robert de Chesney, Bishop of Lincoln (who was in person absent) appealed to the Pope; but by the interposition of Friends, upon a meeting at St Neots a composition was made and signed by both parties. Soon after this, in the beginning of March, our Abbat sends two monks [...] very likely his kinsmen [...] to Rome with a Present of Two Candlesticks of Gold and Silver, most curiously wrought. Who returning home on the feast of the Passion of St Alban [...] brought many Relicks, Vestments, ornaments, a Gold Ring [...] received with great joy by the whole convent.

After this Dissension fell out again between the Bishop of Lincoln and the Abbat; for Ambition and a Thirst of power and pre-eminence cannot long rest unsatisfied. To compose which several Bishops and

Noblemen met several times; but a concord could not be brought about.

Delafield continues, the reader now being treated to the full, antiquarian style:

> Till at last Adrian dying In 1159, and Roland his secretary succeeding by the name of Alexander the 3rd (he that, after Adrian had humbled him by making him dismount and hold his stirrup while he alighted from his horse, had trod on the neck of Frederick the Emperor, as he kneeled down to receive absolution in St Mark's church in Venice, with this verse of the Psalmist uttered from his mouth: *Super Aspidem et Basilicam ambulabis, et conculcabis Leonam at Draconem*, i.e. Thou shalt walk over the Asp and the Basilisk and tread on the Lyon and Dragon); the Abbat applying to him got the former Priviledges granted to his Monastery to be confirmed by the Dint of many presents given and more promised.

Delafield takes up the tale again in his '*Dominium Prelaticum*' chapter:

> However this Agreement did not long subsist, but a dissension arose between the Bishop and the Abbat which by the Interposition of Friends was often set to rights but never continued long. Till at last, the Bishop of Lincoln being favoured by the King, then in France, attended by a number of Prelates came to the Abbey with visitational Authority, commanding the convent to attend him in Procession, and to supply him with Provisions and Entertainment in his Visitation: which the Abbat denied; and the Bishop

made a second complaint to the King; who issued his mandate to Robert de Bellomont, surnamed Bossu, Earl of Leicester, Chief justice of England, to cite before him the Bishop and Abbat, and to summon Hilary, Bishop of Chichester, Richard, Bishop of Chester […] William Turbus, Bishop of Norwich, and Laurence, Abbat of Westminster, to be his Assessors to hear the Allegations on both sides and to make report to the King.

This hearing was on the Fryday before Candlemas day in the castle of Winchester […] when Gilbert Bishop of Hereford pleaded for the Bp. of Lincoln, and one Master John de Tillebire was advocate for the Abbat.

The Issue was that the Commissioners put off the further hearing to mid-Lent: but before that came the King, by letters sent from beyond the sea, had taken the Affair into his own hand. Here it rested for about a year, and then was finally accorded in a Council at Westminster in this form. That the Bishop should renounce all claim of Power or Authority over the Abbey: and that the Abbey should give to the see of Lincoln for ever our church and manor of Thinghurst, then valued at Ten Pounds.

This Agreement was made, upon the suggestion of the King, Richard de Humetz Constable and Richard Archdeacon of Poitou in the month of March A.D.1163, in the presence of the King himself, of the two Archbishops (viz. Thomas Becket of Canterbury and Roger of York), of eleven Bishops, five Abbots, Two Archdeacons, Three Earls, Two Constables, the King's Chamberlain and many others.

So that in the year 1163, the 9th of Hen.2 (though the Print of M.Paris hath it by mistake the 12th) and the 16th of the Pontificate of Bishop Chesney, our parish underwent a new change, passing into the Personal Possession of the Bishops of Lincoln; who from that time made it one of their places of usual residence.

To finish the matter, Delafield, again in *'Dominium Religiosum'* concludes with:

All that I shall add more is that the expence of this Dispute (beside giving up our church and manor of Fingherst) cost the Abbey 140 marks, not reckoning the expences of more than one journey to Rome, presents made there, and one Hundred Pounds given at one time to King Henry the 2nd and many other presents. That the Abbat the following Easter, wearing his Mitre, with his Ring, gloves, Sandals and other proper Ornaments celebrated Mass at the Great Altar, not being molested. That twice in a year he held a Synod with his clergy. And leaving the conferring of Holy Orders, the consecration of churches and Altars, of Oyl and chrism, and the blessing of the Abbat and the Bells, to any Bishop he should request: performed all the offices of his charge and jurisdiction without any interruption, and left them undisputed to his successors.

At length, having ruled 15 years, 4 months and some days, he dyed of a Pleurisy on cal. Nov. 1166.

Delafield's account of Fingest being lost to St Albans and gained by Lincoln follows what Matthew Paris wrote in his thirteenth century *Chronica Majora*, and Dugdale in his *Monasticon Anglicanum* of 1655, doubtless taken from Paris.

(To interpolate here what can be no more than a guess, I wonder whether Master John de Tillebire (Tilleberie?

Turville?), anxious to substantiate St Albans's ancient claim, used the opportunity to severe the monastery's mandate over Fingest to free it for bestowal on a new vicarage and church in Turville to be instituted only a couple of decades later?)

The Manor House – Bishops' Palace?

Local Fingest legend still speaks of the old manor house as having once been 'the bishops' palace'. Although Delafield claims it as a 'usual residence', whether in fact Fingest Manor's first episcopal lord, Bishop Chesney, ever resided there we do not know. By the next century, though, it had indeed become usual for his successors to spend a few days there yearly on their diocesan travels. It seems likeliest that it was in reality more of a bishop's lodging – though no doubt a comfortable one – since the bishops already had a fine palace less than ten miles away at Wooburn Green. We noted in a previous chapter that the manor of Wooburn had been bestowed on the See of Lincoln in the Conqueror's foundation charter; and Wooburn Palace became traditionally a bishop's residence, continually enriched until alienated to the King after the Reformation. Fingest folk-memory perhaps envisaged its own ancient manor house as another Wooburn, but in a Parliamentary survey of the prebendal manor of Fingest in 1650 (we shall see more of this survey later) which gives a detailed description of the building as it was then, there is no hint that it could ever have been more than a manor house suited to lodging a bishop.

Ten Pounds?

At first sight it seems the abbot had by far the best of the bargain. The valuation of 'ten pounds' amounted to the annual dues and rents customarily owed to the lord (the abbot), excluding the temporalities due to the rector, viz. tithes, church-scot (first fruits on St Martin's Day), plough alms (a penny for each plough, paid fifteen days after Easter), light dues and soul-scot (mortuary fees); both would have been no more than average for a parish of Fingest's size (one thousand three hundred acres). What appealed to the bishop more than its monetary value may have been that adding this church (with its fine bells and new manor house) to Lincoln's polity, which already embraced Wooburn, in effect limited further extension of St Albans's jurisdiction in this part of the Chiltern plateau – although John de Tillebire planned matters otherwise.

There may well be nothing more than this to explain why the abbot and the bishop (though only after prolonged dissension) agreed the terms of the king's ruling and singled out Fingest – of all parishes – for exchange.

All the same, perhaps we might get closer to the heart of the matter by stepping back from the parochial to note the change the relative powers of Church and King were undergoing in England at the time. In 1164, a year after he had put his archiepiscopal signature to the St Albans–Fingest Agreement, Thomas Becket finally and fatally refused to accept the limitation of papal legal authority embodied in Henry II's *Constitutions of Clarendon*; he appealed to the Papal See, and in consequence had to flee to France. The sensational outcome of his intransigence on returning to Canterbury in 1170 does not concern us here. What is relevant, though, is that an open clash between the English crown and the Church had been increasing in likelihood from the beginning of this twelfth century. King Henry's resolve to assume all legal jurisdiction – including that over 'criminous clerks' – under his own hand was given public utterance, as it were, with his order to remove a Chiltern parish from an abbacy now unalterably under direct Roman authority, and award it to an English bishop who unequivocally acknowledged his kingly prerogative in ecclesiastical matters.

The Benefice Under Bishops' Patronage

On assuming the abbacy in 1097 Richard Daubeny had formally professed obedience to the Bishop of Lincoln and until the Agreement of 1163 his successors had followed suit. In practice this had meant that the abbots, though as patrons possessing the advowson of Fingest, had had to present candidates for the benefice to the bishop for 'institution' and 'induction'. The Agreement once concluded, the advowson with the lordship passed to the bishop. The bishop himself thus becoming patron, presentation and institution were thereafter combined into a single procedure known as 'collation', which avoided the absurdity of the bishop presenting a candidate to himself. Accordingly, in the bishops' registers for the next three hundred years or so, appointments of incumbents to Fingest are always 'collations'. As we have already noted, though, the bishops never thought to appropriate the benefice as a vicarage; it remained, as before, a rectory. As to whether any arrangement emerged about dividing the proceeds of the rectorial tithes, records are silent.

For the first three or four decades after the change to episcopal ownership the church building seems to have suffered little alteration. In this it differed from many parish churches with advowsons in the hands of wealthy lay patrons, often lords of local manors. During the twelfth century it was becoming common for a lay patron to endow a chantry chapel in his parish church, with the express purpose that he and his should be remembered daily at its altar and that the salvation of their souls and their deliverance from the cleansing fires of purgatory should be constant topics of prayer with the chantry priest(s). In

Fingest's case, however, although both lord of the manor and patron of the benefice, the bishop would make provision for endowing his chantry, often on a grand scale, in the cathedral of his enthronement. For the whole period from the Conquest to the Reformation Fingest's lords were such mighty prelates; the parish never boasted lay families of comparable wealth.

Early Episcopal Collations at Fingest

The earliest recorded names of Fingest rectors I can find (or, I believe, anybody else has found) are in the oldest surviving rolls of HUGH OF WELLS, the second Bishop Hugh of Lincoln (1209–1235) (*Lincoln Record Society*, vol. iii, pp.43, 70). Between the years 1209 and 1219 (the first decade of his bishopric) entries for the archdeaconry of Bucks name two collations to 'the church of Tinghurst', the first being 'Magister Willelmo de Denningwortha', and the next 'Petra de Cumba clericus'. Before this, neither Bishop Robert de Chesney (he who, the reader needs no reminding, in 1163 acquired both the advowson and lordship of Fingest) nor the first four of his successors kept any regular written records of diocesan benefices and their incumbents. Among these was the first Bishop HUGH (appointed, *pace* Becket, by Henry II), a Carthusian who had the reputation of being the most learned monk in the country. He travelled the diocese ceaselessly to consecrate churches, confirm children and bury the dead. He vigorously opposed anything tending to isolate the cathedral body from the rest of the diocese, and constantly encouraged the parochial clergy to bring their people to the annual Pentecostal procession at Lincoln. After fourteen years spent at this level of pastoral activity he died in 1200 and was canonised in 1220.

No written record of incumbents being kept during St Hugh's office, we have no names. His reputation for energetic administration, though, points to his choosing priests for his diocesan parishes with care. He set high standards his successors did not close their eyes to, and when Hugh of Wells took office he added substance to the care of parochial matters by initiating orderly written records of institutions and collations in his diocese, in part no doubt to discourage disputes over livings and rights of patronage. As to Fingest, it is noteworthy that of the thirty-six parishes in the archdeaconry of Bucks for which institutions before 1219 are entered in the rolls of Bishop Hugh II, there are only three in the S.W. Chilterns other than Fingest, namely Marlow, Aston Rowant and Bradenham. This paucity of episcopal institutions locally tallies with our conclusion that in the early thirteenth century Fingest's was still the sole parish church in the Chiltern valley region of the bishop's diocese.

Only a quarter of the rectors instituted in Bucks in Bishop Hugh II's time were priests; the rest were deacons, subdeacons or other clerks in minor orders. The title 'Magister' tells us that the first named rector of Fingest was a university graduate, a schoolman – another sign of the bishop's favour. In addition, Bishop Hugh's surviving charters show that there were other priests described as being 'of Tingehurst' (*Registrum Antiquissimum: Lincoln Record Society*, vol. xxxiv, p.169; vol. lxii, p.107; vol. lxvii, pp.173, 175, 181). There is mention of William de Tinghurst (and de Thynghyrste) and Ricardo de Tinghurst, both clerks, as witnesses of collations, charters and grants in different parishes around the diocese.

Furthermore, it was while 'apud Tingehurst' – staying at the manor house, in fact – that Bishop Hugh II instituted clergy to other benefices, for example one Geoffrey de Lafford as chaplain for Great Missenden. In the twenty-fourth year of his rule he collated the next rector to the church of Fingest, one 'Walterus filius Terici de Colon, civis Londoniensis'. In the same year (1233, two years before he died) the Bishop made his will, which included a bequest of six marks to one 'Henrico Cauchais de Tingehurst'. It appears that the manor accommodated household clergy whose duties included documenting and witnessing the bishop's edicts promulgated both here and elsewhere in the diocese. These clerics would have had their own quarters in the manor; and it is more than likely that the rectors of Fingest, with their duty of residence in the parish, used it as parsonage for the next three, if not four centuries.

The Chancel

Earlier, I promised the reader I would be matching, where possible, changes in the benefice's use and ranking with changes in the church building – relating the ecclesiastical to the ecclesiological. A good case in point is that the addition of the chancel resulted from the continual peripatetic use of Fingest by Bishop Hugh II, his entourage and his successors as an administratively convenient and comfortable halt.

Visiting prelates, celebrating Mass with their attendant clergy or participating in liturgical processions and saints' festivals in this favoured parish, began to feel the need for more ceremonial space (and more daylight) in the small dark Norman church. To match this need the apsidal east end (with its small deeply splayed windows) was pulled down and in its place a relatively roomy chancel was built with the tall lancet windows of the time, a surviving pair of which still grace its north wall.

The semicircular apse had spanned the full width of the church, so there was no requirement when the chancel replaced it to shape a stone arch. The new chancel, given walls less high than those of the adjoining nave, needed a pitched roof of its own. This meant doing away with the original apsidal roofing arrangement; and at the same time the nave itself was re-roofed, perhaps to match the tower more grandly, with the sturdy and steeper pitched oaken framing that to this day commands admiration.

The Victorian south chancel door was installed by Street. It was stepped up to match Street's stepping-up of the chancel floor. The thirteenth century door it replaced had opened at ground level for priestly access and for processional rites.

A 'Low-Side' Window

We have already noted outside the remains of the jamb of another lancet window at the junction of the south walls of the newly built chancel and the nave.

Forsyth's drawing of the south elevation (Fig. 8.2) shows the low sill of this window, still recognisable when he surveyed the building. The sill was only a foot or so above ground level, and we have seen that the section of the surviving stones of this window's east jamb is identical with that of the jambs of the lancet windows in the chancel's north wall. It seems unarguable then that the 'low-side' window was integral with the building of the new chancel. It would have had openable shutters rather than glazing, since probably its purpose was to give parishioners and anybody else outside the church when the sanctus bell rang during the celebration of the Mass an unobstructed sight of the elevation of the Host and to let them hear the priest repeat the words of consecration.

By the thirteenth century – the heyday of mediaeval Church power – the ceremony of elevation had acquired in the popular mind a mechanical, almost magical efficacy in bringing benefit to those witnessing it. The belief stemmed from the eucharistic theology laid down in 1215 by Pope Innocent III at the Fourth Lateran Council, developing the idea of the Mass as a distinct sacrifice in itself, not deriving sacrificial character from its relation to the sacrifice of the Cross; each Mass was therefore said to be a re-immolation of Christ.

As a consequence, theological emphasis was less on the communion of the faithful than on the formal consecration of the elements by the priest. As Keith Thomas puts it in his *Religion and the Decline of Magic* (1971):

> [...] the operative factor was not the participation of the congregation, who had become virtual spectators, but the special power of the priest [...] In the actual miracle of transubstantiation the 'instrumental cause' was the formula of consecration.

It was this dogma that the Lollards and Protestant Reformers later ridiculed, holding that it was nothing but a magical notion that the mere pronunciation of words in a ritual manner could effect a change in the character of material objects; even less that mere attendance at Mass was enough to secure material benefits. John Myrc, an Austin canon, was still in the fourteenth century quoting St Augustine to claim, in his *Instructions for Parish Priests*, that anyone who saw a priest bearing the Host would not lack meat or drink for the rest of that day, nor be in any danger of sudden death or blindness. The institution in 1264 of the Feast of Corpus Christi, with its adoration of the Host, gave rise to the popular idea that to see the Host was itself a safeguard against evil – hence the regular use of such low-side windows for the purpose.

The 'Popular Mind'

To achieve empathy with the religious zeal of thirteenth century Fingest parishioners is a difficult wresting of the mind. These were times when the 'continual tintinnabulation' of the church's bells called men to the daily celebration of Mass, to the Sunday services of mattins, Mass and evensong, and heralded many holy days, baptisms and weddings. There was tolling of a bell at the elevation of the Host, for the passing of souls, for the curfew and for alarms for fire or tumult.

Most of the laity did not attend weekday celebrations because of the demands of labour and service; but when they were at Sunday Mass, what did the village worshippers have in mind as they watched the priest vesting before the altar? They took little part in the service, gossiping and chattering during the most sacred parts of a liturgy that was mumbled in Latin by priests, and there was little sense of corporate worship. People thought of the Mass as something offered *for* them, not something shared; the culmination of the service was the communion of the priest. The people communicated outside the service, very often only at Easter, and then in one kind only.

The Mass was not intended to advance the cause of religion by appealing to the unconverted or stimulating professing Christians. The laity enjoyed no mental or spiritual independence. If not always obeying the Holy Church's teaching, they would never doubt its authority, and accepted without question what they were told. Among the seven sacraments of Grace was Penance, which rested on an intimate relationship between priest and people. In confession the penitent's parish priest probed the most secret places of his life at least once a year in searching cross-examination.

154

The possibility of being condemned to Hell's fire and torture was constantly in men's thoughts. The only things that could avail were the mercy of God, the prayers of the saints and the worship of the Church. That the mercy of God was revealed in the Passion of Christ men were thankfully aware; in the Cross lay the only hope of salvation. But to claim its virtue, they knew, they must have recourse to the saints and especially to the Virgin Mary. Laymen were everywhere taught to direct their prayers to the Virgin in the form of the 'Ave Maria'. At the same time the devout, however illiterate, were convinced of the reality of the Lord's Presence, and they showed this by their worship of the Blessed Sacrament. The greater part of the ordinary man's share in public worship was made up of devotion to the Blessed Virgin Mary, desire to see the Host, concentration on the Passion of Christ and devotion to the Cross.

Today, even the few remaining fragments of its church's 'low-side' window are a powerful reminder that in matters of religion the villagers of mediaeval Fingest in truth shared a 'popular mind' – a sharing that has long since faded and fragmented, as it has in many communities.

Bishop Hugh II

The episcopate of Hugh of Wells was by no means un-eventful. Chosen for the see by King John in 1209, he lost no time in going to France under a pretence, Delafield tells us, of being consecrated by the Archbishop of Rouen but in fact professing canonical obedience to the English cardinal Stephen Langton. When Pope Innocent III, pushing his claim of papal supremacy gave the vacant archiepiscopal see of Canterbury to Langton in direct opposition to the King's plans, John's response was wholesale persecution of the English clergy, which included seizure of Hugh's bishopric.

The next four years saw first the whole country put under a papal interdict, with John excommunicated; then his total resubmission as a papal fief in what proved to be a vain hope of gaining allies to recover the lands in France. This was a move that in 1213 had the effect of restoring Hugh to his bishopric, although for siding with the barons against the King he later incurred a papal debt of a thousand marks. Delafield in his *Dominium Prelaticum* quotes Matthew Paris as saying that Bishop Hugh of Wells was:

> of a fine Inquisitive Temper, and not implicitly to run into belief of the Miracles then so rife in the Church. For It being found of a Recluse Virgin Votaress at Leicester that for seven years she never tasted any food, unless on Sundays she received the communion of the Body and Blood of our Saviour, our Bishop ordered the fact to be strictly enquired into, and shut her up for fifteen days, being watched by Priests and clergymen, and at last found that for all that term she received no nutriment at all; yet had she a face as fair as a lily and as fresh as a rose.

As we have seen, the bishop's staying at Fingest did not disallow official duties. Their performance made him no stranger to the rector, and when there were episcopal deeds to be signed, the rector was often included in the necessary host of witnesses. Thus, for example, a confirmation of a grant saving the rights of the mother church at Laxton, dated at Fingest the Kalends of June (year indecipherable), bears among the signs of other witnesses the signature of William de Benningworth. Likewise, a year or so later, the next rector, Peter de Camb, had to put into effect the bishop's granting of a perpetual render of five marks from the church at Fingest to the choir at Lincoln.

Delafield underlines the bishop's autocracy:

I find him Personally residing at Fingest (where the Bishops all along had without question a Palace) and that he here exercised some part of his Episcopal Function. For in 1226 11 Hen 3 Martin de Ramsay Abbot of Peterborough being newly elected received the blessing of Hugh Wallys Bishop of Lincoln on the feast of St John the Evangelist at his Palace of Finghurst.

Peter de Camb was evidently careful to maintain the glebe rights accruing to the rectory. *The Calendar of the Roll of the Justices on Eyre* for the year 1227 specifies an instance where:

Robert son of Wm. who had brought an assise of mort d'Ancestor against Peter parson of Tinghurst for ½ v. of land in Tinghurst came and withdrew. Robert and his pledges Laurence de Tyrefeld and Rans de Tyrefeld are amerced [fined].

This case was considered as *Jus Utrum*. The jury:

came to make recognition whether ½ v. of land in Tinghurst was in frankalmoin belonging to the church of Peter parson of Tinghurst or a lay fee of Robert son of Wm. They [the justices on eyre] say the land is frankalmoin of Peter and of his church of Tinghurst and he may remit it for himself, his heirs and successors and the said church in perpetuity. Therefore may Peter have the seisin [possession].[1]

---

1 Transcript: Bucks Archaeolog. Soc. Rec., 1942, vi, 9, 10.

Two last questions arise regarding the office and benefice as rectors of William de Benningworth and Peter de Camb. First, the bishop's register gives no dates for their collations. Browne Willis and such authorities take them to be 1217 and 1218 respectively, but give no hint as to why Peter replaced William after only a year.

Secondly, why was it that while both were unequivocally collated at Fingest as rectors, the living at Wooburn Palace both then and later was always a vicarage? The reason perhaps is that at Wooburn Palace, while the cure of souls unquestionably accrued to the bishop by his office, it could be passed as required to a stipendiary vicar. At Fingest the situation was different. By past royal edict the bishop's official position there was 'lord of the manor', and exercising as such his advowson to provide a cure of souls in the parish he had no choice but to collate in this office a priest with full rectorial rights.

Chapter XI
Bishops Foster the Benefice: *Quo Warranto* (1234–1279)

During his prelacy Bishop Hugh II as lord of Fingest Manor had begun to use it as an episcopal residence from time to time each year during his peregrinations around his diocese. You will deduce, reader (and you will be right), that this would have had no inconsiderable effect on the calibre of the rectors. It was relatively rare for a parish to have as lord of its manor a bishop; when this was the case, as patron of the church the bishop himself exercised the advowson to nominate incumbents to the living; he then donned his mitre to collate them. This double dose of episcopal blessing confirmed the living as a rectory, not a vicarage, and as I've suggested very likely encouraged successive rectors to seek room and board in the bishop's manor house, making a separate manse unnecessary, at any rate for the time being.

The rector, like other village parsons of the times, would not have lived alone. In his quarters in the manor house he would have had some parochial staff – *capellani curati*, that is unbeneficed priests – and a boy to make his bed and tend the horse he kept for visiting his parish. Further, he may, like many contemporary clergy, have escaped Pope Innocent III's efforts to enforce clerical celibacy, and have found room for a consort, whether wife or concubine. Domestic arrangements apart though, in practice he had no choice but to divide his parochial energies between his spiritual and his natural sheep, which meant providing housing on the glebe for his animals – oxen for ploughing, and pigs maybe as well as sheep – and a good barn and granary for storing rectorial tithes. Thereafter for Fingest rectors an unwritten right of lodging in the manor house very likely persisted until Reformation times. Only then, when the lordship of the manor had passed from episcopal into prebendal and finally into lay hands, the rector found himself *persona non grata* in the manor house. By the end of the sixteenth century or thereabouts he had perforce to build, or get built, a separate rectory house for himself and his household. The natural site for this was the glebe alongside his farm buildings, and the resulting parsonage with its sixteenth century origins was to become known in due course as The Old Rectory.

More Bishops and the Fingest Rectors they Collated

To return to the thirteenth century benefice. As had been Bishop Hugh II's custom, his next seven successors in the see all made some residential use of the manor house, thereby for the most part adding lustre to the parish and conferring on its rectors a degree of wider recognition as churchmen of the archdeaconry of Buckingham.

First of these seven was ROBERT GROSSETESTE, bishop from 1235 to 1253, about whom a few words indicating his local as well as general influence may not be amiss. Of outstanding intellect, Grosseteste was one of the very few mediaeval Oxford scholars (he became Chancellor), to know Greek; he translated the *Testimony of the Twelve Patriarchs*, for example, with great exactness from Greek into the Latin more comprehensible to theologians of the time. The broad scope of his many writings reflects the new scientific approach to philosophy that his friend Roger Bacon developed from the canon of Greek influence that the crusaders' taking of Constantinople in 1204 had released to Western culture. In the field of statecraft, Bishop Grosseteste wisely and adroitly used his influence as a member of the Great Council to restrain the misrule of Henry III, and in the process furnished Matthew Paris the St Albans historian (a favourite of Henry's) with a first-hand view of contemporary political as well as ecclesiastical affairs.

Although relatively old (sixty-five) when a compound of his own ability and royal favour brought him to the bishop's throne, Grosseteste proved the newest of new brooms. Among his many other reforms he launched a rigorous visitation system within the church, beginning with the deposition of eleven heads of religious houses in his diocese (including the monastic superior of St Frideswide's, Oxford). He strongly resisted the customary papal patronage in England in favour of Italian clerks and insisted on careful choice of diocesan clergy and parish incumbents. His rejection of a good number of the latter on grounds of ignorance can have done nothing but good for village rectories like Fingest.

A detailed itinerary of his travels around the diocese has survived and shows that he customarily reached Fingest twice a year and stayed for varying periods of days, unless his political or ecclesiastical duties took him overseas – '*in partibus transmarinis*' – on behalf of the Great Council or to visit the Pope with whom in fact he seldom saw eye to eye. 'Of an inflexible resolution in the cause of the Church and religion', as Delafield writes, he had many disputes with the Roman court, of whose corruption 'he would say: *O pecunia, pecunia, quantum potes praecipere in curia Romana*; and scrupled not to brand the Pope with the name of Heretick and Anti-Christ'.

At length he died at another of his manors, Buckden, maintaining episcopal principles to the end. Delafield tells the tale thereafter of 'his Apparition in the Night to Pope Innocent the fourth in Bed at Naples, striking him on the side with the Crook of his Pastoral Staff, so as to leave a bloody mark and Impression'.

As to parish parsons, Grosseteste's rolls for his eight diocesan archdeaconries show the many institutions he made each year to benefices *cum onere et pena vicariorum* or sometimes *cum onere ministrandi personaliter in eadem*. The latter would have been expected of Fingest rectors, including parson Walter who had in fact been collated by Hugh of Wells two years before Grosseteste's enthronement.

In a list of institutions in the archdeaconry of Buckingham that Browne Willis compiled from the archives of Lincoln Cathedral, entries for 1237, 1243, 1247 and 1249 are missing (Bodleian Library, *Willis MS*, vol. i, pp.21–25). This may explain why they do not record Rector Walter's death, nor the collation of his successor, Peter de Powyck (who, Willis puzzlingly records, had formerly been ordained vicar).

Peter de Powyck (seemingly the only Fingest rector collated by Grosseteste) continued in the living after Grosseteste died in 1253, and indeed outlived the next bishop, HENRY LEXINGTON (1254–1258), and was still at Fingest until 1269, when he resigned (we do not know why) in the eleventh year of Lexington's successor, RICHARD DE GRAVESEND.

Lexington held office for only five years, during which Willis found no record of him making parish institutions. However we know that he carried out some of his episcopal business while staying at Fingest, since Peter de Powyck witnessed some of it.

The next rector was Nicholas de Malmsbury, collated to the living by Bishop Gravesend in 1269, but he died within twelve months and Gravesend instituted the next rector, Roger de Stachenden, in April 1270.

Gravesend's itinerary as bishop during his first five years is conjectural, but at Fingest Peter de Powyck probably saw little of him at first; he seems to have been mostly in France with Henry III and Queen Eleanor of Provence. But the King squandered royal treasure and tax receipts in a series of failed attempts to win back in France what John had lost to the crown. This, together with the gross misgovernment of the kingdom under the Queen's Provençal uncles and foreigners in high places, and the king's subjection to demands from Rome for money, led to the barons with Simon de Montfort at their head forcing through the Provisions of Oxford of 1258 that conferred regulation of taxation directly on the Great Council.

Bishop Gravesend by now had sided with Simon de Montfort's national party, but Simon's victory over the King at Lewes in 1264 was only the next year followed by defeat at Evesham, and this put an end to Gravesend's political career. He found himself among the bishops that the papal legate was denouncing as traitors, and was sentenced to seek the Pope's absolution; but he took his time before visiting Rome and did not get to Italy until 1st January, 1272. He was back in England by the end of March that year.

So Roger de Stachenden seems to have had the run of Fingest Manor on this and a few other occasions when the Bishop was away, such as attendance at the coronation of Edward I (19th August, 1274). Otherwise, however, the customary episcopal travel around the manors of the diocese was resumed and Fingest was a good centre for the local deaneries of the archdeaconries of Oxfordshire and Buckinghamshire. Thus, as Delafield tells us, an abbot of Oseney priory, near Oxford, was in 1267 'on the day of St Vincent the Martyr consecrated by our bishop, then being at his Palace at Fingest'.

Bishop Gravesend visited the manor twice in most years between 1263 and 1276. His episcopal rolls date these visits precisely and show that towards the end of an almost unbroken decade of regular diocesan travel – his health at last beginning to fail – he began to spend longer and longer periods each year before and after Christmas in the peaceful Chiltern manor of Fingest. Delafield says that he gave his name to the part of the manor land still known as 'Gravesend'. His last sojourn at Fingest was in January 1276 and he died at Stow Park in 1279.

'Quo Warranto'

It was during these last years of Gravesend's life that the 'Hundred Rolls' came under royal scrutiny. When Edward was proclaimed king on his father's death in 1272 he was campaigning with his brother Edmund in the Holy Land on the Seventh Crusade; it was two years before he arrived home to be crowned at Westminster with his queen, Eleanor of Castile. Thereupon one of his first acts as feudal lord paramount was to challenge the powers of the over-weening nobility and gentry that more and more during the long reign of Henry III had usurped and defrauded the Crown of its rights of holding lands and courts, and other *jura regalia*. In 1274 Edward's writ of '*Quo Warranto*' ordered a commission to enquire forthwith into the state of his demesnes and of royal rights and revenues alienated without licence. Three years later the commission returned their 'Rolls of Inquisitions' in which landowners' titles to the estates they claimed were set out hundred by hundred for minute examination. (The membranes on which these 'Hundred Rolls' were written were kept for centuries afterwards in the Tower or in the Westminster Palace exchequer – both decidedly less than perfect conditions of storage. Despite this, the Rolls remained for the most part remarkably decipherable and in 1812, by order of George III and Parliament, they were finally recovered, transcribed, printed and published.

In the appropriate resulting volume the enquiring reader will find entries for the hundred of Desborough in the county of Bucks. These include confirmation of the manor 'Tinhhurst', 'kept in the hands of a bailiff', as a legal holding of the Lord Bishop of Lincoln. Thus we have evidence that during the years of their respective lordships the bishops provided bailiffs for the day-to-day management of their Fingest manor. Dwelling at the manor as he did, Roger de Stachenden, the second of two rectors Gravesend collated to Fingest, no doubt knew the bailiff well since he held the benefice for thirty-five years (1270–1305), outliving both Gravesend and the next bishop OLIVER SUTTON.

The pleas of '*quo warranto*' also established the background of episcopal claims to the manors of both 'Woubourne' and 'Tyngehurst'. The plea for the latter traces its warrant to an agreement between Abbot Robert of St Albans and Bishop Robert Bluet (though, you will remember, the agreement was in fact with Bishop Chesney). But we are reminded in the *Calendar of Inquisitions Post Mortem* for 1291 that on Simon de Scaccario's death, a writ of assignment of dower to Petronella his wife arose from his right to part of a tenancy in Little Abbefeld which, as we have already seen, lay in Fingest Manor territory.

Chapter XII
A Bad Apple Among the Good (1280–1347)

BISHOP OLIVER SUTTON was enthroned in 1280, the year after Gravesend died. He proved a thorough disciplinarian, determined to uphold the authority of canon law and the rights of his see. By canon law he was entitled, when travelling as bishop, to claim hospitality for himself and a train of thirty horsemen, apart from an escort of knights to further ensure his safety; in 1290 these were led by the marshal Sir John of Bayton. Bishop Oliver's baggage was carried on packhorses. His registrar, John de Scalleby, carried also the official records of the see, including the rolls of past institutions of Hugh of Wells, Grosseteste and Gravesend – records which (we may be thankful) mostly survived this rough peripatetic treatment.

Oliver Sutton gave particular attention to maintaining the standing and good order of the parish clergy, conscientiously invoking for example the 'assise of darrien presentment' to declare, if there were dispute, who had presented the last parson to a church, and strictly requiring parish clergy to take priest's orders within a year of their institution.

Browne Willis notes that Roger de Stachenden had already been ordained chaplain when he was instituted rector by Grosseteste. Sutton doubtless approved this rector's priestly footing, meeting him as he often must have at the manor. The Bishop found town life uncongenial. He liked to escape to Theydon Mount in Essex, his family's house, or to his manors at Fingest and Buckden, and these seem to have been his three favourite retreats in the country; he spent Christmas at Fingest or Buckden whenever he could. Whether on each such visit Fingest Manor had to accommodate as large a bishop's train as that described above we do not know; perhaps the visits were sometimes less formal in nature. Whatever the occasion, John de Scalleby's entries in the episcopal rolls and registers carefully date the bishop's stays in Fingest each year and record the institutions he made on each occasion.

One or two of Scalleby's notes give us vignettes of episcopal domestic life in Fingest Manor as the Bishop knew it towards the end of the thirteenth century. In 1291 Scalleby writes:

> *V Idus Januarius anno primo apud Tinghirst summo mane in camera sua sedens sub fenestre ex parte australi Dominus Episcopus contulit Thome de Skendleby capellano cantuariam in ecclesia de Riston.*
>
> [From Fingest where the Bishop was sitting in his room under the south window early in the morning of January the ninth he collated Thomas of Skendleby chaplain to the chantry at Rushton.]

And again in 1292 he notes that Sutton sealed his will 'in the bishop's chamber at Fingest after vespers' on 28th January, 1292.

Bishop Sutton did not escape the obligation of supervising Rome's customary taxing ('*plenitudo potestatis*') of ecclesiastical benefices. In 1253 during Lexington's rule the first fruits and tenths that had long been paid to the see of Rome were given to Henry III for three years – the *Norwich Taxation* or *Pope Innocent's Valor*.

In 1288 Pope Nicholas IV:

> granted the Tenths to King Edward the First for Six years towards defraying the Expence of an Expedition to the Holy Land and that they might be collected to their full Value a Taxation by the King's Precept was begun in that year and finished as to the Province of Canterbury in 1291 [...] the whole being under the Direction of John Bishop of Winton [Winchester] and Oliver Bishop of Lincoln.

More than half the money did not get to the Pope but went as commission to the collectors. The bishops' listings of this *'taxatio ecclesiastica'* for dioceses and archdeaconries show separately the taxings of churches with benefices of ten marks and less; in Wycombe deanery these included Fingest, Radnage and Turville.

To the end of his life Oliver Sutton continued his customary travels around his diocese. At Biggleswade, a few months before he died, he appointed 'Richard of Fingest' bishop's proctor – further evidence that as well as the rector it was usual for there to be other priests (*'capellani curati'*) residing at Fingest Manor.

John de Scalleby tells that the bishop worked *'in magna senectute et bene constituto'* until a fortnight before he died (on 13th November, 1299). He goes on:

> he was a man constant by nature, prudent in directing things both spiritual and temporal, and a good ruler over his household neither greedy nor extortionate.

Fingest, with its parson and other clergy, must surely have benefited from this episcopal rectitude.

More Lords Episcopal and the Rectors they Collated

Accustomed as we have become to consulting the collection of institutions Browne Willis so assiduously assembled by manuscript copy from the original Lincoln rolls, we now look to him again for the next incumbents and episcopal patrons of Fingest benefice (*Willis MS, vols. ix, x, xciv*).

Roger de Stachenden died early in 1304, in the fifth year of the rule of JOHN DALDERBY, Oliver Sutton's successor. During the next fifteen years of Dalderby's bishopric the Fingest living changed hands no less than five times. In April 1304 Dalderby instituted as rector Simon de Blatherwick, described in the rolls as a presbyter (that is, a priest). By the end of the next year (1305) Simon had resigned the benefice in favour of Robert de Bolton, an ordained chaplain. Four years later, in June 1309, this Robert also resigned the living to take up a vicarage at Cadenaye, and in December of that year Dalderby instituted as rector another presbyter, William de Burwell.

How long this William managed to stay as Fingest's rector is not shown in the bishop's rolls, at least as copied by Browne Willis's scribe Mr Sympson (*Willis MS,* vol. i). They merely say that next came Robert de Mayhen de Chippingnorton, who in turn resigned in February 1314 (no reason given). His successor was Richard de Chippingnorton, against whose name Willis's scribe writes 'acol', meaning perhaps that he was an acolyte. An acolyte, as a minor cleric, could not celebrate Mass or have cure of souls, but this would not necessarily have excluded him from the benefice; he had only to arrange for an unbeneficed but ordained priest – perhaps one of the clerics domiciled at the manor – to undertake these solemnities.

The next entry for Fingest in the Willis copy of the bishop's rolls for the archdeaconry of Buckingham rather puzzlingly gives the name of this last incumbent as 'John de Norton'; but in another MS (vol. xciv, pp.77, 78) Willis writes in his own hand 'Richd. de Chipping Norton'. Whatever his soubriquet, this Richard was also not long in the living, exchanging it after five years in 1319 with another presbyter, William Mayhen de Deddington, for the prebend of Trethyn in the collegiate church of St Berian in Cornwall. (Being appointed a prebendary implies that in the meantime he had achieved full ordination.)

Delafield describes Bishop Dalderby as remarkable for his piety and devotion, so much so that after his death 'he was esteemed by the common people as a Saint'. Despite having instituted five rectors there, we do not know how often, if ever, Dalderby came to Fingest. As lord of the manor the right of patronage – the advowson – was his, so he would at least have presented the Fingest rectors collated during his bishopric; and he might have used local visits to induct them himself.

At all events, with his death the invigorating effect on Fingest church and parish of bishops constantly visiting as lords of its manor began to fade. Inevitably there was an accompanying decline in the ecclesiastical rank the benefice had achieved after more than two centuries with notable prelates as its patrons – centuries that had witnessed a flowering of Fingest amongst small parishes within the *ecclesia Anglicana* till then so firmly established as a model of the mediaeval Universal Church.

Perusal of the Lincoln episcopal rolls shows Dalderby collating William Mayhen de Deddington rector in December 1319. In the unbroken year-by-year series of bishops' institutions in the archdeaconry of Buckinghamshire we find no further mention of Fingest until September 1349, thirty years later, when we note BISHOP GYNWELL conferring care of souls at Fingest by the hitherto usual process of collation upon one William Bolbeyn de

Federynghay. The entry gives no hint whether William Bolbeyn succeeded William de Deddington or someone else as rector.

The dates in question (1319–1349) cover the twenty year bishopric of HENRY BURGHERSH (1320–1340) and the five years of THOMAS BEK (1342–1347) who after a two year vacancy succeeded him. To get a very different picture of an episcopal lordship at Fingest, we have only to consider a description of Bishop Burghersh – *'cupidus et avarus'* – in Thomas Walsingham's *Historia Anglicana* (vol. i, p.255) and the tale that Thomas Delafield tells with relish of his nature and the fate it brought upon him.

Henry Burghersh was of a noble Sussex family. Delafield tells us he:

> ascended to the chair of Lincoln in 1320. He was an active, not, to say a turbulent man, and a great opposer of his prince, King Edward 2nd. He was scarce warm in his seat before he incurred the displeasure of the King, and had his Temporalities seized and detained for two years [...] His disaffection was deeply rooted [...] not long after be took part with Queen Isabel against her Husband [...] whom he assisted her to depose [...] He was among the commissioners sent to take the resignation of King Edward at Kenilworth Castle, persuading him to resign his crown to his son.

Edward III rewarded him with the highest offices of state, and in 1326 made him Chancellor of England. As such he played a big part as ambassador abroad in Bavaria, Flanders and France, promoting Edward's claim by right of his mother Isabella to the crown of France; and it was in these foreign employments that he died in Ghent in Flanders in

1340. Delafield again:

> [...] as riches and years increased upon him, he grew excessive covetous and encroaching. As an instance of which be is said to have enclosed a great part of the Common of this Manour of Thinghurst, or Tynghurst, now Fingest, in prejudice of the rights of his Neighbours, to make a Park, and kept it from them to the day of his Death.
>
> Though he perished in this injustice to the last Date of Life; yet (if report says true) it so affected him that be could not lye at quiet in his grave. For he is said to have appeared to one of his Gentlemen in the dress and accoutrements of a Keeper or Ranger; with a green jerkin on his Back, a Bugle horn hanging at his side, and a Bow and Arrows in his hands. And to declare that he was doomed to this Penance till his Encroachment should be disparked by being again thrown into the Common, and desired the good offices of the Canons of Lincoln to see it effected. This message from their late dead Bishop the Gentlemen delivered (as it is said) and the Canons were so wise as to give credit to the report [...] and deputed one of their number (William Bachelor by name) to see it effected. Which being done, the Bishop (as I think) was at rest and never more appeared.

Delafield also quotes the very similar tale Dr Fuller tells in his *Church History* that Burghersh:

> took in the land of many Poor people, therewith to complete his Park at Tinghurst. These wronged Persons, though seeing their own bread, Beef and Mutton turned into the Bishop's venison, durst not

contest with him who was Chancellor of England
[...] only they loaded him with curses and execra-
tions.

Both Delafield and Fuller clearly base their stories on
Dugdale's 1676 *Baronage* (vol. ii, p.35), which in turn
derives from Walsingham's Latin version in the *Historia
Anglicana* (vol. i, p.255).

These vivid accounts of Burghersh's harsh treatment of
Fingest's peasants and his posthumous repentance agree
that thereafter the canons of Lincoln ordered the cutting
down of hedges, the filling up of ditches and the restoration
to the poor of their inheritance.

Thomas Delafield's opinion was:

There is probably a great deal of truth mixed with
falsehood in this Romantick Story [...] traces of the
Mounds, in high Banks and deep and wide Ditches,
being after more than 400 years (as I observed in a
late Parochial Procession or perambulation) even at
this Day frequently to be seen, and called even now
the Park ditch [...] Bachelor [...] there being a gentleman of that name, one of the Prebenderies from
1327–1341.

Sceptical Anglican cleric as he was, Delafield comments:

But the apparition of the Bishop, the Bow and
Arrows, the green Jacket and the Horn (it is wonder
that Quarterstaff was left out) have all the Air of a
Fiction; and seem to be an improvement of the
Monks on the circumstances of Fact. Such Fictions
keep up the Best Part of Popery (viz. Purgatory)

Fig. 19: Area of Fingest parish imparked by Bishop Burghersh outlined on current Hambleden footpath map (deduced by Daphne Phillips).

whereby their fairest Game, and greatest gain is preserved.

Daphne Phillips of Booker gives us an idea of how much of Fingest common land Burghersh appropriated for his park. Carefully matching local topography with what detail is described in surviving manuscript and printed sources, she has put together (*Bucks Free Press*, May 24th, 1985) a likely picture of how things were in the parish between 1330 and 1340 or so, when the bishop had put into effect a royal grant of 'free warren' in his manor and a royal licence to impark three hundred acres of land enjoining his woods (Fig. 19).

Both the manor house, serving as a convenient hunting lodge, and the church itself lay within Burghersh's park from which villagers were summarily excluded, whether as farmers or churchgoers. The care of souls in the parish, dependent as it was upon celebration of Mass before a congregation in church, ceased; and the Bishop, with his passion for the chase in his park, would have had little compunction in foregoing his patronal right of advowson. So it is hardly surprising that his episcopal roll records no hint of collating a new rector at Fingest during his bishopric.

This is not to say that Burghersh did not use the church as his episcopal chapel for ceremonial occasions of worship. He may well have furnished it suitably to house his doubtless large clerical retinue; indeed it is likely that it was during his rule that the decorated two-light window in the eastern end of the nave's south wall – then still part of the chancel – was installed to replace the old small Norman one and provide better light for the celebration of Mass.

That Burghersh when not hunting used time he spent at the manor for episcopal purposes is vouched for by Browne Willis (*Willis MS,* vol. xii, p.12) who notes the bishop signing grants and deeds from 'the bishop's palace at Thingherste'. Willis remarks that 'Bp. Burgwash's Register is the most voluminous of all, the latter part of which contains 388 folios'. None of them mention Fingest; it seems then that William Mayhen de Deddington, who had been collated to Fingest in the year before Burghersh became bishop, sooner rather than later found himself lacking the pastoral duties to justify his residing at the manor (now a hunting lodge) and took himself elsewhere.

The next rector was not collated until nine years after Burghersh's death – perhaps when the disparking procedure had been completed and a congregation restored to the church?

Before we leave the saga of Bishop Burghersh's moral turpitude and its outcome, the reader may be wondering how creating his private park within parish land impaired so grievously the villagers' supply of 'bread, Beef and Mutton'? Daphne Phillips's map (Fig. 19) seems to show that the area emparked, three hundred acres, would not have left villagers – most of them by now having lived for long in the Cadmore End–Bolter End region of the parish – too badly off for land capable of food production. We have to remember, however, that in wooded parishes in the Chilterns such as Fingest there was then an almost total absence of open fields. The mediaeval villagers were able to maintain themselves only by exploiting their rights to the wooded commons (M.W. Beresford, Rec. Bucks, vol. xvi, p.5) that the Bishop appropriated into his park. What arable land escaped could have played only a subordinate role in the village economy, since cleared land was but a small proportion of the whole parish, providing no more than a patchwork of individual fields, quite unlike the extensive open fields usual elsewhere.

The 'subsidy of the ninth'

In 1338, two years before Burghersh died, Edward III's warlike intent regarding the French crown took him to Flanders and to the start of the Hundred Years War. Parliament voted him the necessary money in the form of a two year 'subsidy of the ninth', that is the ninth lamb, the ninth fleece and the ninth sheaf – or in lieu an equivalent tax, the liability falling on 'the Prelates, Earls, Barons and the Commons of the Realm'. According to the 1341 transcript of the *Nonarum Inquisitiones in Curia Scaccarii*, in the case of 'Tynghurst' the amount due was eight marks, as presented by 'Hugh at the Stompe, William of Mosewell, Roger of Cademer, Henry Jurdan and Richard of Bolters', presumably freemen of the bishop's manorial court jury. (These are places still known in the parish – Muzewell, Cadmore End, Bolters End). The same transcript notes that in estimating the 'ninth', land was taken into account that had been *includit in quondam parco de novo constructo* – Burghersh's park.

A two year vacancy of the Lincoln seat followed Burghersh's death before the consecration of its next occupant, THOMAS BEK in 1342. Not surprisingly, perhaps, there's no record of the new bishop renewing visitations to Fingest Manor during the five years of his rule. A note by Willis (*Willis MS*, vol. i, p.142) says interestingly that when on Bek's death in March 1347 the bishop's throne was again vacant, it was the same William Bachelor, the canon who saw to the disparking of Burghersh's land encroachments, to whom fell the undertaking of episcopal spiritualities until the next bishop, JOHN GYNWELL was consecrated in October of the same year.

As we have seen, after the naming in the bishops' register of William Mayhen de Deddington as collated to the office and benefice of Fingest in 1319, there is a thirty year gap before mention by either Willis or Delafield of the next named rector, William Bolbeyn de Federinghay. In the year 1349 we are in the thick of the most horrifying country-wide disaster of mediaeval times.

Chapter XIII
The Black Death and After
(1347–1419)

John Gynwell ruled for fifteen years (1347–62). He set about his episcopal duty with a will, beginning with a series of energetic visitations of the numerous deaneries of his extensive diocese. His registers for 1347–50 provide an exemplary record of his day-to-day movements which has been analysed in detail by Professor A. Hamilton Thompson (*Arch. Journal*, 1911, vol. lxviii, pp.301–360).

By the winter of 1348 his travels had brought him into the southern archdeaconry of Buckingham and in due course to the deanery of Wycombe, where from the 30th November onwards he visited the benefices of Penn, Great Marlow, Wooburn, the Chalfonts, Great Missenden and Hughenden. He left Hughenden on 18th December for Fingest Manor where he stayed until the middle of February 1349 before setting off again.

On arriving at Fingest it is unlikely he was welcomed by an incumbent rector; for as you will remember, heedful reader, we have already argued in some detail that during Burghersh's and Bek's years of offices there was no rector – let alone local care of parish souls – at Fingest.

As to filling the vacancy, Gynwell's register for 1349, the third year of his episcopy, dates precisely the collation of the next rector, William Bolbeyn de Federinghay. The date itself compels particular attention, for it was 9th September, a month when the first outbreak in England of bubonic plague, the pestilence so fitly called the Black Death, had reached and was just passing its height in Wycombe deanery no less than everywhere else.

The countrywide spread of deaths from plague was so swift that there was little chance of it being documented exactly where it struck and where escaped, in times well before the keeping of parish registers. How people fared in particular villages – Fingest for example and its neighbouring parishes – even with all we have since learnt about the epidemiology of the Black Death, can rarely be figured. We get some idea, however, from Hamilton Thompson's paper in which he assesses the local impact everywhere of the infection as it swept across the diocese. His ingenious method of quantifying plague mortality from region to region was to work out from Gynwell's register the rate at which the bishop was instituting new clergy in benefices falling vacant. He meticulously analysed the register's entries in this way for each of the diocese's eight archdeaconries.

From April 1349 to March 1350, Hamilton Thompson noted for each month the occurrence of benefice vacancies due to incumbents' deaths. From fifteen in April these rose to forty-three in May, then to one hundred and twenty in June, peaking at two hundred and thirty-five (over a fifteen-fold increase) in July. In August there were two hundred and one new vacancies due to death; by September they were down to ninety-one, and the number went on falling slowly through October (fifty-three), November (forty-four), and December (twenty-four). In January 1350 there were still twenty-six death vacancies and in February eighteen; by March they were down again to nine, near to normal. This is the classic pattern of preva-lence and mortality in a plague outbreak – erupting at the end of spring, rapidly peaking in late summer and declining with autumn frosts.

Mortality in Buckinghamshire

Narrowing matters down, among the one hundred and ninety benefices of Buckinghamshire archdeaconry we find there were seventy-seven vacancies due to death (forty per cent) over this same period – a more than six-fold rise compared with the two previous years. Wycombe deanery was as badly hit, ten out of its fifteen benefices falling vacant over the same period. Month by month these were: in May, Great Marlow and Medmenham; in June, Saunderton; in July, Bradenham; in August, Hughenden; in September, Radnage and Fingest; in October, Little Marlow; in November, Turville; and in the following March, Saunderton again. The register shows all these as death vacancies except Bradenham and Fingest, for neither of which is a reason given. The Bradenham one may have been due to a resignation; but, as we have already satisfied ourselves, the Fingest vacancy was attributable rather to Bishop Burghersh's patronal neglect.

When the plague struck, Bishop Gynwell, who had only the year before stayed for two months at his Fingest Manor, doubtless felt that as the plague was rife in the Wycombe deanery as in the rest of the diocese, he was diligently doing his Catholic duty in remedying the persistent vacancy there as readily as he was replacing death vacancies elsewhere. Whatever the precise reason for the new rector, William Bolbeyn de Federinghay, being collated to the living at this particular time, he was fortunate indeed to escape the infection that was then peremptorily launching sixty per cent of Wycombe deanery priests into eternity.

Rattus Rattus and Xenopsylla Cheopis

The indulgent reader will perhaps allow a digression attempting to account for William Bolbeyn's deliverance. The epidemiology of plague concerns us here only so far as it identifies as a necessary precursor of a human plague epidemic the local occurrence of an epizootic of rat plague. Rat plague takes an invariable form: a fatal septicaemic infection of the black rat *Rattus rattus* with the plague bacillus *Yersinia pestis*. An epizootic of rat plague can develop when rat fleas (*Xenopsylla cheopis*) take blood from rats already infected with *Yersinia pestis*. In such a flea which has ingested infected rat blood, the rat plague bacilli rapidly multiply to an enormous degree, forming sticky masses within what amounts to the flea's oesophagus, which block further passage of blood into the insect's stomach. Still hungry, therefore, the flea continues to suck highly infected blood, the excess of which can only pass back again to the flea's mouth parts. The infection is thus readily injected into the next animal the flea bites in its ravenous attempt to satisfy its hunger, having deserted the now unattractive and cooling corpse of its erstwhile host; flea activity is much dependent on local warmth. It is when living conditions are such that black rats are commensal with man – that is, are house rats – that the urgent jumps of such a 'blocked up' flea in search of another meal are as likely as not to land it on a human subject as on another rat.

This brings us to how, possibly, William Bolbeyn escaped infection in Fingest. Mediaeval bubonic plague was chiefly, it seems from contemporary accounts, a disease of the poor, the better-off often fleeing away from epidemic areas. In the early fourteenth century the country poor, for the most part still bound to their lord's land and service, were living on the manor in dwellings that were no more than hovels. Straw being in short supply through the relative scarcity of arable land in these villages of the Chiltern plateau, the cheapest and most readily available roofing material was turf. Roof turf provided ideal quarters for the house rats of the times, and they lived, nested, bred and died therein. With a rat plague epizootic supervening, it is not difficult to imagine infected fleas, starving on rats dying in people's roofs, jumping (or just falling) in liberal numbers on to the humans below.

Manor houses though, even then, were different. With stone or wooden walls and stone, lead or shingle roofs, they gave little shelter to house rats. Resuming his predecessors' custom of residing in the manor, as we believe he must have, master William Bolbeyn very likely had this to thank for escaping the Black Death. In contrast, the housing of most other parish priests then was little better than that of the villeins.

The Toll in Lives

Hamilton Thompson's study shows that during the year 1349 benefice clergy were dying from the plague in every deanery throughout the whole of Gynwell's diocese of Lincoln. Though there was variation in clerical death rates between deaneries and even between archdeaconries, his findings indicate that overall something like forty-five per cent of all parish priests succumbed to the plague; and studies of other dioceses over the same period have given figures between thirty-nine per cent and forty-nine per cent. The sixty per cent finding for Wycombe deanery makes it certain that the plague was just as prevalent here, if not more so.

So much for the deaths of beneficed clergy. To what extent these reflected the general death rate in the population is a question that has elicited a range of answers, and the truth of the matter is still argued. However, on evidence from all sources so far available, a not too misleading estimate is that at least a third of the population of England died of the Black Death in the year of its first outbreak. In particular areas deaths may have been as high as forty per cent or as low as twenty-three per cent (Philip Ziegler, *The Black Death*, Penguin, 1969, p.232). Therefore, we can hardly avoid concluding that in 1349–1350 a proportion of Fingest village folk somewhere within these limits died of the Black Death unsung save for the continual tolling of the passing bell, and soon unremembered.

For Bishop Gynwell and his diocese however, as for most of the rest of the country, this was by no means the end of it. In 1361, towards the end of his episcopate, there was another epidemic – 'the second pestilence' – the herald of a series of further, if somewhat less virulent, outbreaks that recurred throughout the rest of the Middle Ages. The entries in the bishop's register for 1361/62 repeat the pattern of mortality: numerous appointments of parish priests to livings vacated by death. Of the seventy-nine livings falling vacant in the archdeaconry of Buckinghamshire between April 1361 and April 1362, sixty-five were due to deaths, the peak incidence in October falling to more customary levels in December. This time however Wycombe deanery fared better; death vacancies in 1361 occurred in only four livings. These were Haveringdon (West Wycombe), Hambleden, and Saunderton – and Fingest, where William Bolbeyn, having escaped the first outbreak, had survived in office for twelve years. What caused his eventual death we do not know; though it is possible that priests tending the sick and dying – if any did – even if escaping flea infestation may have directly acquired pneumonic plague by respiratory contagion.

The Aftermath

During the second half of the fourteenth century, against a darkening background of plague, war, taxes, bad government, insurrection, schism in the Church and heresy, what had seemed to be the fixed order of things in England began to undergo changes. It is far from easy to distinguish separately scars that the plague, even on such a scale, left on English life and society. Much less perceptible are the imprints that the pestilence left on the slender ribbon of Fingest's unfolding annals.

This being so, the critical reader must surely be thinking that with so forbidding a gap in local records, we have little choice but to suffer a period of silence. Not so, I suggest; instead we will take it that matters here took much the same shape as elsewhere in the country.

A revolution in land tenure in England was then unarguably well under way, whether engendered by the plague's depletion of the population, or already afoot. It is clear that for at least twenty-five years before the Black Death, England's main exports (wool, for example), its agricultural production and the area of its cultivated land had all been shrinking. Among serfs and villeins unemployment was becoming rife; landlords were finding themselves unable to work the whole peasant tenantry of their demesnes to good effect, and instead many of them began to commute their feudal rights, substituting wages and rents in monetary terms for labour service – a change altering the occupation of land.

The Black Death can only have increased this tendency, though for opposite reasons. With the inroads made on the size of the workforce whether hitherto employed or unemployed, labour became so scarce, dear and difficult to procure that survivors who had already worked for wages were for the first time empowered to demand more money, while even those who had not were now reaping the general benefit of free socage.

The famous Statute of Labourers of 1351, enacted with the object of reversing these trends by pinning wages and prices to pre-plague levels, aimed to force peasants back into feudal tenure and servility. It reimposed restriction on the right of freemen and villeins to leave their place of work, compelled labourers to accept work offered, forbade the employer to offer increased wages and fixed the price of bread, meat and fish.

It has been held that the Statute was from the outset a dead letter, but recent opinion is rather that for a time it did achieve reasonably well what it set out to do. Prosecutions with fines were brought against employees and against some employers too. A few years after the immediate shock of the Black Death wages and prices fell back to near pre-plague levels; and on top of this, landlords began to reimpose old burdens such as heriot, denial of the peasant's right to dispose of his chattels, and many other unloved customs of the old feudal manorial system.

To these manifold peasant grievances the renewal of the French wars was soon to add another – the imposition of poll taxes.

The Peasants' Revolt

The first poll tax of 1377 (the year Edward III died and Richard II acceded) was graduated by wealth; all labourers over fourteen years, men and women, 'except true mendicants', paid a groat (four pence). Returns for the three Chiltern hundreds show that in Wycombe four hundred and eighty-two people paid 4d, in Hambleden one hundred and sixty-nine, in Turville and Ibstone ninety-seven and in 'Tynghurst, forty-two (L.J. Ashford, *History of High Wycombe*, 1960). This probably accounts for about two-thirds of the total working population, life expectancy being short. The tax of 1381, at three groats a head for all, cost Wycombe deanery £130.6s.8d, Fingest contributing £5.6s.8d (*Willis MS,* vol. i, p.542). Such repeated taxation fell with ever more grinding severity upon the poor and ultimately provoked widespread violence towards tax collectors and investigating justices. It was in Essex and Kent that the deepest resentment accumulated for decades and erupted in rebellion directed against London and its seats of power. Peasant leaders fuelled insurrection to the point of mob-killing of bailiffs and lawyers – not least the Chief Justice of England – sacking of manors, burning of records, opening of prisons, the seizure of the Tower of London, the murder of the Chancellor of England Archbishop Sudbury, and the burning of the Savoy Palace.

The rest is common knowledge: the rebels parleying at Smithfield with the young King Richard; Mayor Walworth's sword striking down Wat Tyler as he drew a dagger; and Richard riding forward alone 'with the regality of his crown' to promise pardons and grants of freedom. Within a month the revolt died, the leaderless peasants dispersing to their homes only to suffer brutalities when – at Parliament's rather than the King's wish – men-at-arms rode throughout Kent and Essex in punishing retribution.

Meanwhile at Fingest Manor…

In the face of these days of wrath and anguish, you may well wonder whether perturbing calamities and miseries enacted in London, Essex and Kent echoed widely enough to resound in manorial Fingest and affect day-to-day living in this remote Chiltern valley?

We can take it, at any rate, that the bailiff, acting for his landlord the bishop, had by feudal custom been using villein labour to tend the lord's animals and work the home farm and demesne land to provide for the manor on the scale the bishop expected for himself and his retinue.

After the Black Death, with wages rising, labour scarce, demand reduced and hence prices for saleable produce falling, the bailiff found himself in a weak position to put the feudal clock back, the Statute of Labourers notwithstanding. As the bishop's agent, he had little choice in serving his master but to make the best of things by dividing off parcels of the manor demesne. Some would have been put to pasture for sheep – paying one shepherd instead of a score of labourers – and some let off for cash rents, or even sold off to freemen of the manor who, long accustomed to working its patchwork of individual fields, found themselves tenant-farmers. How much of the manor farm estate was lost to the demesne in this way we cannot tell; it is likely that the bailiff's parcellings mapped out farms that eventually established themselves as holdings around the manor's periphery – for example Hill Farm, Rackley's and Mozwell's.

It is likely, then, that from rents and cash payments the bailiff was able to make up for the loss of manorial rights to feudal villeinage and serfdom that were now inevitably on the wane. Whether the manor continued to produce income enough in cash and kind to satisfy the expectations of future bishops regarding use of the manor house as a residence we cannot be sure; but there can be little doubt that successive rectors continued to make what use they could of it for parsonage purposes, though their readiness thereafter to give up the living when the opportunity offered (as we shall be seeing) implies that a degree of retrenchment was inexorably in hand.

And the Church?

Another factor contributing to the decline of feudalism was discontent with the established Church, which emerged from the Black Death with diminished credit. Perhaps this was especially so in Chiltern towns and villages, where endemic anticlericalism had long fostered contempt for the priesthood. Although clergy both high and low persistently preached the plague as a sign of God's gross displeasure at worldwide human sinfulness, they had signally failed in their sermons to transmit any warning of divine anger before disaster struck.

When it did strike, it became clear that the clergy, whether by repeated penitential procession or by self-flagellant extremes of religiosity, were totally unable to stay its progress. All could see that the parish priest, lacking divine preservation and just as likely to succumb to the plague as his parishioners, was likely also to deprive dying laymen of the absolution that spelt deliverance from the fires of Hell. It was all too plain a challenge to the credulous awe with which custom had hitherto invested the cloth.

To disillusionment was added growing resentment at the wealth and luxury that numerous purchases of indulgences and deathbed chantry bequests were heaping on an already affluent Church, and a new acquisitiveness was likewise evident even among lower clergy seeking vacancies as parish priests. The register of Bishop JOHN BUCKINGHAM, Gynewell's successor, exemplifies this trend; it is full of records of exchange of livings between incumbent priests, sometimes to churches in another diocese. Hamilton Thompson (*Leics. Arch. Soc. Trans.* 1941–45, vol. 22, p.2) describes the exchange system as fostered by brokers who arranged exchanges in large numbers, often of one church for another, and then a day or two later exchanging the latter for a third, the transactions bringing the clerics concerned some emolument, and benefit to the broker. By 1392 exchanges like these had become so common that Archbishop Courtenay of York saw fit to issue a mandate denouncing such 'choppechurches as accursed consorts in guilt of Gehazi and Simon Magus'.

In the benefice of Fingest, clerical 'chop-church' was at first, characteristically perhaps, slow to catch on. Of the two rectors that Bishop Gynewell had collated, the second, instituted in 1361, continued to hold the living until 1390, untempted by the possibility of exchange. Browne Willis names him as Roger Belleclerc in *Willis MS*, *xciv*, though he writes it 'Roger Bellerbun' in *Willis MS, x*.

Nine Successive Rectors in Eighteen Years

When Belleclerc (or Bellerbun) died, a string of exchanging priests took up their successive brief offices at Fingest; between 1390 and 1408 the living saw a nine-fold exchange of incumbents, Willis (*Willis MS,* vols. i, xciv) names them:

John Crisp of Oxford, deacon, collated 14th January, 1390 on the death of the last rector.

He exchanged it for Toft Newton with Master Thomas Ryder on 13th July, 1392.

He exchanged it for Cattemer, Bucks, with Master Laurence Breton on 30th September, 1393.

He exchanged it with Master Thomas Colyn, perpetual vicar of Dorney on 28th October, 1395.

He exchanged it for Basilden vicarage, Co. Berks with Master Stephen Balingham collated in 1400 by Bishop Beaufort.

He exchanged it for Stapleford with Chaplain John Martin on 27th July, 1401.

> He exchanged it for North Scarle, Co. Lincoln with George Colne, collated by Bishop Repingdon on 21st April, 1406 (1408 in *Willis MS*, vol. x).

> What George Colne's fate was is not recorded, but the register goes on to record a further exchange with

> Master William Skinner who in turn exchanged office for Polesgrave, Bedfordshire with Master William Etyngdon on 3rd November, 1408.

That most of these exchanging clerics are 'Master' (in the Latin *'dominus'*) suggests that they were ordained priests, qualified to celebrate Mass – if they were ever to do so at Fingest. The reader will note too that from the collation of Roger Belleclerc onwards, the French 'de' is dropped in specifying provenance; henceforth the latter is used directly as surname. These were Chaucerian times when Norman French, until then the preferred language of king and court, nobility and educated clergy, was being replaced at all levels by native English – a change officially recognised in fact by a 1362 order for the use henceforth of English in courts of law.

… and Three Bishops

JOHN BUCKINGHAM was Keeper of the Privy Seal when by papal provision, though at King Richard's peremptory instigation, he was made Bishop of Lincoln. It was he who began the prosecution of priests for holding the opinions of Wyclif, but in 1398 Pope Boniface IX, on the grounds that he lacked due compliance with the Roman See, ordered his translation to Lichfield, a see half the value of Lincoln. Recognising this as the demotion it was, Buckingham refused it and retired to Canterbury where he died the same year.

Boniface moved him in fact to make room for HENRY BEAUFORT, the natural son of Katherine Swynford by John of Gaunt, though subsequently legitimised by his parents' marriage being made good in 1397 by an Act of Parliament and a bull from Rome. Beaufort was Chancellor of Oxford when he was preferred to Lincoln in 1398; he held office as bishop there until 1404 when, with Henry IV now settled on the throne, he became Chancellor of England. The next year the Pope translated him again, this time to Winchester – the first Bishop of Lincoln to consent to removal to another see.

From Fingest's viewpoint we have little reason to follow further his glittering career in State and Church as 'the rich cardinal' who was nominated (unsuccessfully) for the papacy; he died in 1447, having served as bishop in one see or another for forty-seven years.

In 1405, a year after Beaufort's papal translation to Winchester, PHILIP REPINGDON was advanced to the see of Lincoln, again by papal provision, this time of Innocent VII. In his youth at Oxford as a pupil of Wyclif, Repingdon had at first strongly supported the latter's views on such matters as man's responsibility to God alone, the invalidity of sacraments celebrated by priests in mortal sin and the justifiable confiscation of property from a negligent Church. But by 1382 he had recanted the whole Wycliffian doctrine in twenty-four articles at St Paul's Cross, and in 1394 he became abbot of the canons regular of St Augustine at Leicester. In 1397 and again in 1400 he was Chancellor of Oxford University. For the fourteen years of his bishopric, Delafield tells us:

he was a severe persecutor of the Wycliffites or
Lollards: and was termed 'Rampingdon' by the poor
People he so much molested.

Then in 1419, unprecedentedly, he left office to return to
private life.

The registers of these three bishops give no indication
that they visited their manor or church at Fingest.
Repingdon's register mentions his visiting eight of his other
manors in the diocese, but not Fingest.

This is not to say that he was unaware of his position as
lord of this manor and, so far as the church was concerned,
its patron. We may here remind the observant reader of our
resolve to match changes in the church building with
changes in its patronage and in the manor's lordship. As we
know, architectural judges agree that the chancel's east
window with its stone tracery dates from about the time of
Repingdon's office; so we may conclude that it was he who
sanctioned its installation, replacing an earlier lancet
window or windows which had matched those on the
chancel's north side. In the style of the times he caused the
new window to be glazed with historiated stained glass, one
of its three lights presenting a representation of the Virgin
Mary that Willis described three hundred years later. For
Repingdon, we may surmise, this finer (and quite elegant)
east window focused attention more surely on priestly
celebration of Mass in the sanctuary as the kernel of the
Church's catholic faith.

Wyclif and Lollardy

Senior churchmen, apprehending the decline in the
prestige and authority of the Church, blamed it on the
incoming host of mendicant friars who, they claimed, were
undermining both with their popular outdoor sermonising.

They petitioned Pope Clement VI to forbid friars from usurping the functions of parish priests; but instead Clement turned his wrath on priests themselves for their arrogance, covetousness and neglect of the ways of God. In England Cardinal Thoresby, Archbishop of York, determined to correct the neglect of teaching and ordered parish priests to rededicate themselves to expounding to the people the Creed, the Ten Commandments, the Gospel Precepts, the Seven Works of Mercy, the Seven Deadly Sins, the Seven Virtues and the Seven Sacraments of Grace.

But friars or no friars, the liturgical boot was already being fitted to the other foot. By the 1380s Wyclif's Oxford had become a centre from which his influence was spreading everywhere. It certainly reached Chiltern parishes – Amersham, Wycombe, Great Marlow, Henley – where already Lollardy with its rooted hatred of the priesthood was cultivated in fertile soil. We need not concern ourselves here with the theological differences, fundamental as they undoubtedly were, that had emerged between John Wyclif and schoolmen like William of Ockham and, Duns Scotus about the nature of the Eucharist and of human knowledge of God, but they were differences that his 'poor preachers' were enthusiastically expounding in churchyards and on village greens. More practically relevant were Wyclif's commission of an English translation of the Bible 'as its own interpreter, open to the understanding of simple men'; his denial of the mediatory function of the priesthood; and his support for the Lollards' rejection of the sacerdotal system which after his death became expressed in their 'Twelve conclusions for the reformation of Holy Church in England'.

Perhaps a trace of the paganism inherent in their Scandinavian forbears re-emerged in its villagers; it is hard to believe that Fingest in its Chiltern enclave spawned no Lollard sympathisers of its own. One can hear Wyclif's words ringing out to vilify its changing rectors as 'idolatrous, leprous and simoniacal heretics' – descriptions they may well have deserved. But Bishop Repingdon would have none of it, whether surrender of church property or denial of the validity of the priesthood. During his term of office the Church doctors of Oxford pronounced Wyclif's theses heretical; and by 1401, within three years of Henry IV taking the throne, the statute *De Haeretico Comburendo* was law, passed by the clergy in Estate. Wyclif had died in 1384; it was now Lollards who were being pronounced heretical and their heresy punishable by burning.

As to the doctrinal orthodoxy of the rectors after William Etyngton who held the Fingest living during the rest of Repingdon's lordship of the manor we have nothing to go on. How long Etyngton remained rector and whether he died or resigned, there is no record. The register for the fifteenth year of Repingdon's rule (1419, his last before leaving office) simply states that on 28th April that year the bishop collated as chaplain Walter Hammond in the living vacated by the death of one Simon Acres.

The Tower's Twin Gables

Fingest villagers apparently took the hint that such a theologically hot potato might do more than burn their fingers. Shrewdly confirming tradition, they left maintenance of the chancel's fabric to the responsibility of the rector (as we concluded earlier, the church's chancel or presbytery initially included most of the nave). The parishioners' lay wardens now turned their hand to maintaining only the part of the church they saw as their own – the church tower and bells. It is more than likely that to be kept weatherproof the tower by now needed a new roof. Lead was costly and the wardens' practical solution was to build two ordinary village roofs side by side – the saddle-back gables which have done the job ever since.

With such work in hand much attention was given to brewing for the highly popular 'church ales' held to meet the expenses of fabric repair. We do not know for certain of course (as with so much in Fingest's history) but it seems at least likely that with the parishioners' space within the church being restricted to the floor of the tower, the wardens and the people now set their minds to obtaining a 'church house' which would provide for parish clerk and sexton, and not least for merry-making on feast days and at church ales. Other 'ales' – bride-ales, scot-ales lamb-ales, scythales and especially funeral wakes were all popularly held after (or often in place of) services marking the seasons of the church year.

The Church House

When and where a 'church house' first appeared is a teaser. In 1740, while looking through the papers of 'Thomas Ferrers, late lord of the manor', Thomas Delafield found two relevant entries which he noted down at the back of the parish burials register he had charge of. One concerned a grant to Fingest churchwardens on '4 Apr. 23 Eliz. Regina' (1581) of a waste plot opposite the church house next to the king's highway; the other, of '18 Dec. 32 Hen 8' (1541), detailed the renting from the lord of the manor by church-wardens John Robinson and Henry Coker of a piece of ground 'and a building thereon' lying between the land of the rector on the south and the king's highway on the west. Both of these cuttings strongly suggest that the mediaeval 'church house' of Fingest survives, give or take the inevi-table repairs of centuries, in the Church Cottage on the same site today.

The jovial life of mediaeval England portrayed in the *Canterbury Tales* has a darker side, that of the poor peasantry presented by Langland in his monument of Lollardism *The Vision of William concerning Piers the Plowman*. At any rate after church ales, and mediaeval hunger and poverty, a church house still stands opposite the church, looking perhaps, save for brick infilling, much as it did when the village people first built it. It proved, as things turned out, a last blossoming of the mediaeval Church in Fingest – a flowering on ever stonier ground.

Chapter XIV
The End of the Middle Ages
(1420–1485)

Any attempt to sketch Fingest with its rectory and manor as it was during the last few decades of the Middle Ages, is hard put to identify local features that speak of the disturbances which shook and in the end destroyed feudal power in England and changed the nature of English kingship. But survey these we must in the hope of descrying, however imperfectly, changes that colour our picture.

A Chronicler's Survey: Crown and Church

These were times that saw the ending of the Hundred Years War and the loss to the crown of the French Plantagenet inheritance and to the great families of England of the wealth that had flowed from these southern provinces. At length the umbrage that greeted these troubles at home broke out in the Wars of the Roses with their desperate battles for the right of succession to the throne. The topographically nearest battles at St Albans (1455 and 1461) and Barnet (the last, in 1471) – for all we can tell left people in Fingest untouched. The long lists of casualties suffered on the battlefields were mostly among the royal or noble commanders, their families and their private retainers.

Otherwise, as civil war sparked, died and sparked again, the daily business of the moneyed classes and burgesses in the towns, and of squires and merchants in the country was little affected. For a time after Henry V's death, such persons of the emerging 'middle class' continued to share the rights of freedom from arbitrary taxation, legislation and imprisonment that the feudal baronage, the Church, and the knights of the shires in Parliament had over the years won from the crown. During Henry VI's long reign commerce continued to increase, but at the same time the great regional noble families in the Common Council under a weak king were increasingly restricting these rights; franchise and freedom customarily claimed since the reign of Edward I were continually diminished.

In 1461, with the Yorkist King Edward IV taking the throne and the unhappy Henry VI deposed, the last hopes of the House of Lancaster were crushed. Secure as king, Edward began to change the character of English sovereignty, putting in place of the old, 'the new monarchy', as J.R. Green calls it in his *Short History of the English People* (London, J.M. Dent & Son, 1915, chapter vi).

He vastly increased the crown's resources by trading overseas on an unheard of scale in tin, wool and cloth, swelling the royal exchequer on the pretext of resuming an invasion of France that never in fact took place. His powers were the stronger because his victory over the Lancastrian nobles at Towton had put the wealth of enormous estates into the royal treasury, wealth which increased the more when Warwick was killed at Barnet and Queen Margaret defeated at Tewkesbury. As to government, with the feudal strength of the regional aristocracy in tatters, Edward had no further cause to honour the now dwindling constitutional rights of Parliament and people.

The storm of the Wars of the Roses not only left the baronage in ruins, but – and more relevant to our interest, reader – weakened the independence of the Church. Fearful that its vast estates might also fall to the King, the churchmen became supinely devoted to the service of the Royal Council, surrendering their Church's tradition of independent spiritual life and repudiating the centralising tendency of Christendom. As Green puts it, 'the old English kingship faded suddenly away, and in its place we see, unrestrained, the despotism of the New Monarchy'.

An Historiographer's View of Contemporary Fingest

The bishops now became no more than a part of a landed aristocracy shorn of former power. As early as Bishop Repingdon's time we may infer the declining self-assurance of the Lincoln bishops from a small local clue – an unprecedented collation of a Fingest rector. This is to be found in listings in Browne Willis's hand of bishops' institutions in the parishes of the deaneries of Buckinghamshire, (*Willis MS*, vols. x, xciv).

Therein are Browne Willis's descriptions of many Bucks churches and parishes he visited; from perusal of the relevant Lincoln episcopal registers he is able to give for each a comprehensive list of its parsons past and (for Willis) present. Accordingly, in the list of rectors accompanying his description of 'Fingherst' there appears one 'Walter Hammond' (we have mentioned him earlier) who was collated to Fingest rectory in 1419, Bishop Repingdon's last year of office. What is of interest here – our clue – is that elsewhere in *Willis MS* (vol. xciv) the vicars listed for 'Tyrefeld' include the same 'Walter Hammond', presented to the vicarage there on 13th November, 1413. We have here then incontrovertible evidence of a vicar instituted at Turville in 1413 being translated in 1419 to Fingest rectory.

Considering this, the reader will call to mind the inveterate dissension that simmered two and a half centuries earlier between the Abbot of St Albans and the

Bishop of Lincoln regarding the latter's claim to authority over the pastoral mandate of the former. As we learn from Delafield, the argument was finally settled in 1163 in the presence of the King himself (Henry II) and the two archbishops Becket of Canterbury and Roger of York. It was agreed by all parties that the Bishop renounced his claimed authority, and that in return the abbey surrendered to the Bishop the church and manor of Fingest.

We can scarcely believe that so arbitrary a settlement of a delicate pastoral matter did not engender estrangement between the two proud prelates – a difference well inherited by their equally proud abbatial and episcopal successors. One cannot imagine Grosseteste, Sutton or even Gynwell agreeing to collate to a rectory in their own diocese a Turville vicar obedient to St Albans.

Thus it speaks somewhat ill of Bishop Repingdon's husbanding of the episcopal office to which he had in due course succeeded that he ignored, or overlooked, the incongruity of such a collation. Lord of Fingest Manor he might be, but he evidently gave little thought to using his power of advowson to its benefice to protect the prestige which its church had over many years been acquiring within the diocese. We may note, too, that at this time the Abbot of St Albans, John of Wheathampstead, preoccupied though he was with restoring his abbey's rule of monkish discipline, calculatedly offered no objection.

The upshot, so, far as it affects our picture of Fingest in the twilight of the mediaeval age, is that we glimpse here in microcosm the ebbing away of the tide of proud episcopal independence that had hitherto lapped the Fingest benefice.

Fingest's Rectors Left to Their Own Devices

In late mediaeval times a distinctive development of parochial life in many villages was the endowment of chantries, with priests to say daily Masses for the souls of benefactors and their families, usually lords of the manor or of estates within it. In Fingest's case, as we have more than once pronounced, its manorial lords were Lincoln bishops, and they predictably chose to found their chantries in their own cathedral church; their Fingest Manor otherwise boasted no parishioners wealthy enough for such a venture. (Bishop Burghersh eschewed custom by endowing a chantry for himself and his family in the priory church of St Frideswide, Oxford which later became Oxford cathedral.)

Thus unlike most other village churches, Fingest was fated to acquire no stipendiary chantry priests and acolytes. Left to himself, this stringently tested the rector's integrity as a parson, for it meant he had no more clerical support in the parish than a deacon perhaps and a clerk, and virtually none from a shadowy bishop. Nevertheless, he was responsible for the care of souls of villagers who still felt themselves unquestionably belonging to the Church, and looked on their parson as wielding the power to deprive them of spiritual comfort in this world, and give them tickets to either endless bliss or unspeakable torment in the next. Without superior guidance, with parishioners mostly illiterate, credulous and uncritical, the rector found himself ministering a Christian faith overlaid with the myriad superstitious beliefs of the times, and defending the authority of his cloth as best he could.

So what of Walter Hammond? That he was collated to the rectory as 'chaplain' following a string of 'magister' rectors perhaps suggests a demotion of his office. We know nothing of him, not even whether he was ordained. If he was, the masses he celebrated as rector were never graced by the supporting presence of his bishop and seldom by senior churchmen. His assumption of living quarters in the manor house was no doubt still honoured by the bishop's bailiff as a matter of convenience. But his yeoman parishioners, finding little authoritative support now from the Church for their fiscal and common rights, became disinclined to fund church expense as they had before, or to enhance, let alone repair, the building. The church's wardens however did not so easily give up; within a decade or two, perhaps more, they felt it right to install a locally carved stone font, probably placed near the south door. Dogma then being rife regarding the almost magical properties of holy water, they also took care to fit a stout wooden lid with an iron hasp, no doubt at the behest of a superstitious rector.

We do not know how long Hammond held the benefice. The episcopal registers record no further collations to Fingest rectory during the offices of the next four Lincoln bishops. The first of these was bishop RICHARD FLEMING appointed to the see in 1420 by Martin V, the pope elected after the Great Schism. In 1424 Fleming was advanced to the archbishopric of York, again by papal provision; but the dean and chapter of York objected and the Pope was forced in 1425 to issue a contrary bull translating him back to Lincoln. Discomposed, no doubt, and seeking papal re-approval, Fleming at once gave effect to the sentence of the Council of Constance by exhuming the bones of Wyclif (buried forty years before in Lutterworth churchyard), burning them and casting them into the River Swift.

After Fleming's death the next bishop instituted to Lincoln in 1431 was WILLIAM GRAY, formerly Bishop of London. A note in Fuller's *Worthies of England* (1662) suggests that he may have spent more time locally in Buckinghamshire than some of his predecessors. Particularising the 'Names of the Gentry of Buckinghamshire returned by the Commissioners of the twelfth year of King Henry the Sixth, 1433' Fuller mentions 'William, Bishop of Lincoln'; so Gray evidently qualified as at least a resident in the county. This may, of course, have been in Wooburn Palace rather than Fingest Manor house. Interestingly, among one hundred and fifty gentry of Bucks that Fuller names is one 'Robert Dalafield'.

Gray died in 1435 to be succeeded by WILLIAM ALNWICK. Delafield tells us that Alnwick was 'Father confessor to that virtuous, Devout and Religious Prince, King Henry 6th'. He held the see for twelve years (1437–1449), to be followed by MARMADUKE LUMLEY, bishop for only a year (1450).

In the registers of successive bishops, there is a long gap after Hammond before Fingest rectors are named again. The next is Thomas Roger, presented to the living in 1461, according to the register of Bishop JOHN CHEDWORTH (1452–1471). The register does not specify the cause of the vacancy filled by Thomas Roger. That it occurs forty-two years and a span of four bishops later than the Walter Hammond entry must raise doubts about the completeness in this regard of the intervening records. In another volume (vol. xxv) in which he outlines how he assembled his collections of Lincoln institutions in Buckinghamshire livings, Browne Willis notes that Bishop Fleming's register lacks entries for clergy instituted during the years after he was retranslated back to Lincoln from York (1425–1430); and that in Bishop Alnwick's register there are no entries for 1436, 1437, 1449 and 1450. It is clearly possible that even if the registers are otherwise complete, in these absent years the collation of one or more Fingest rectors went unrecorded.

An Errant Rector

This possibility apart though, a paragraph in one of the folios of Bishop Chedworth's register dealing with provincial acts in his diocese (*Linc. Epis. Reg. Bp. Chedworth*, m. 10) makes intriguing mention of a Fingest rector whose name otherwise does not appear among incumbents instituted in the diocese either before or during Chedworth's rule. The paragraph in question, written by the bishop's registrar or scribe, describes in some detail how in 1454 one Master Richard Dyvett, rector of the church in the parish of Tyngehurst, assaulted the rector of Newnham in the act of distributing holy bread to the poor after Mass; and notes that for this action Master Richard Dyvett incurred *commissio corrigenda*, that is, official bishop's censure. The parish of Newnham in the north of Hertfordshire was one of the sixteen parishes of the 'Liberty of St Albans' before the Dissolution. What Richard Dyvett was doing there, quite a way from Fingest, we are not told; he was clearly a pugnacious cleric. He may have been trying to register again the long-standing hostility between Lincoln and St Albans we inferred above; or perhaps he was a Lollard sympathiser protesting against the superstition of the 'holy' bread?

Further Ill-Documented Collations

Oddly enough, Browne Willis describes Bishop Chedworth's registers as 'the Best Registered of any of the Books I have seen in the Archdeaconry of Buckinghamshire'. Despite this compliment, it is apparent that like some of their precursors they lack necessary detail, at least in respect of Fingest rectors. For example in Browne Willis's list of 'Fingherst rectores' (*Willis MS*, vol. xciv, pp.77–78) compiled from Chedworth's register, the next entries after Thomas Roger's collation on 28th June, 1461, say simply 'Tho. Smith resigned 1465 and was succd. by Richd. Smith collated 23 Jan. 1465 subdiacon.' They continue: 'Robt. Wymbush last Rr. died 1471 & was succd by Richd. or Robt. Scot collated July 20 1471.'

Such patchy entries of collations of Fingest rectors in the registers create doubts whether Master Richard Dyvett was altogether atypical as an incumbent at Chedworth's time, and indeed whether Chedworth himself was ever more than in name lord of the manor and patron of the church, or ever set foot in either. Perhaps a long illness, which we hear from Delafield preceded his death in 1471, in part explains his lack of supervision of parish affairs. Delafield also writes that 'he is said to have been negligent about his Manour Houses; and that his Executors paid to his successor 2,000 pounds (a vast sum in those Days) for Dilapidations'. It's likely, the reader will agree, that if Fingest Manor house was equally neglected, it made it difficult at this stage for the rectors to enjoy there the living room hitherto taken for granted.

Bishop Chedworth died in 1471. After him came THOMAS ROTHERAM, consecrated to the bishopric in 1472. Chancellor of Cambridge University in 1469 and Chancellor of England in 1475, he had little time, if inclination, to consider let alone visit his patronage of Fingest. In 1480 he was again translated by papal provision, this time to the archbishopric of York. Delafield names him as 'Thomas Scot alias Rotheram' and suggests that the 'Robert Scot' collated rector of Fingest 1491 might have been a relation. Delafield goes on to say that in 1500, aged seventy-six, the bishop died at his palace at Cawood 'of plague'. (There had been further plague outbreaks in 1464, 1471 and 1479.)

Next in the see was JOHN RUSSELL (1480–1494). He had been Bishop of Rochester, and was 'in great favour with Edward 4th, was Keeper of the Privy seal, and tutor to the King's eldest son, Edward Prince of Wales' Delafield says. (This was the ill-fated 'Edward V'.) He was also Chancellor of Oxford University and Chancellor of

England, so it is unlikely he had time to devote to his manor and church at Fingest.

Rector Robert Scot was, it seemed still in the living when Russell died in 1494 at his manor in Lincolnshire. Even at Scot's time Fingest was still paying 'Peter's Pence' or 'Rome-scot'. This was an ecclesiastical tax due to the Pope, payable each midsummer, anciently first paid by King Offa. Browne Willis (*Willis MS*, vol. i, p.553) has a note about it, as usual unpunctuated:

In the Archdeacon of Buckingham's office kept at Aylesbury is an ancient Book of Peter's Pence collected by his officers and remitted to Rome in it is a list of all the churches and chapells that paid them and over against the vicarages is wrote the names of the convents they were appropriated to it is wrote in a sheet of paper in double columns as here transcribed but being ill kept is somewhat obliterated and torn I have attempt to copy on its being lent to me October 11 1757 by Mr Registrar Bell's deputy.

The title is

'Quaturnus Redditum Archdiaconatus Bucks extractus ex veteri rotulo Mr R, est ft Ao primo Edwardi Quartus' [1460]

There follow the Peter's Pence amounts levied on the deaneries of Buckingham and Wycombe, together totalling £1.15s.2d: Hambleden and Fawley contributed 3s/4d, Turville 20½ pence and Fingest 13½ pence.

In 1483 Edward IV died. Richard III took the throne and the crown rightly that of Edward's young son, the uncrowned and mysteriously missing Edward V. He was to lose both in 1485 at the Battle of Bosworth Field to Henry Tudor, Earl of Richmond. Henry, though the last remaining scion of the House of Lancaster claimed the throne less through right of birth than right of conquest. His marriage in 1486 to Edward's daughter, Elizabeth Woodville, united the warring houses and ended any possibility of further civil war. As Henry VII he continued the 'new monarchy', the personal rule Edward IV had so inflexibly imposed.

Returning to Lincoln and its bishop we come upon WILLIAM SMITH. He had held several high offices, including the bishopric of Lichfield and Coventry, before Pope Alexander VI translated him to Lincoln in 1495. In 1501, when he was in Wales as President of the Council of the Marches, Henry sent him his elder son Arthur. This makes it unlikely that he saw much of his little Fingest Manor, but at least on reaching the year 1503 in his register we begin – this time after a thirty-five year gap – to find again named Fingest rectors being collated.

Chapter XV
The Tudor Crown:
Mediaeval Cobwebs Blow Away
(1486–1547)

As powerless to vindicate liberty under Henry Tudor as under Edward IV, the Church trembled the more at the progress of heresy. John Foxe in his sixteenth century *Book of Martyrs* luridly describes Bishop William Smith's rule by the statute *De Haeretico Comburendo* in persecuting Lollard sympathisers in Buckinghamshire, where they especially persisted in denying the doctrines of the Romish church. One such was a confessed heretic, William Tylesworth of Amersham, sentenced by the Bishop to be burnt at the stake. His only daughter Joan Clerk, a married woman, 'was compelled', Foxe tells us, 'with her own hands to set fire to her dear father'; and Delafield, quoting Foxe, goes on to say that her husband John was made to serve penance by bearing a faggot at the burning, as did twenty-three other persons: all afterwards were compelled to wear penitential badges abroad in Buckingham, Aylesbury and other towns.

Foxe deplores the punishment of Bucks people of heretical thinking who received no quarter from Bishop Smith. Of Thomas Chase, also of Amersham, Foxe says, 'he could not abide idolatry and superstition, but many times would speak against it'. The poor fellow was confined in the Bishop's prison at Wooburn – a cell called 'little ease', too small to allow either standing or lying. Refusing to abjure he was eventually strangled. The Bishop's men gave out he had hanged himself, and buried the body in unconsecrated ground in Norland Wood on the highway between Wooburn and Little Marlow.

At Fingest, with the fate of heretics brought so vividly before their eyes – and what is more, Bishop Smith residing as he often did in nearby Wooburn Palace (he died there in 1514) – both rector and parishioners became strongly inclined to tread in church the way of catholic orthodoxy.

Some More Fingest Rectors

The next rector of Fingest named in the bishops' registers is Roger Cowper, collated by Bishop Smith in 1503 'on the resignation of the last rector'. If 'the last rector' was indeed Robert Scot, collated in 1471, he held the living for thirty-two years before taking the opportunity to resign; we may think this unlikely and wonder whether an intervening incumbency has been lost.

Whatever the case, in the Archdeacon of Buckingham's court rolls of the time we find hearings of Fingest cases that would have fallen within a rector's remit, whether Robert Scot's or another's (*The Courts of the Archdeaconry of Buckingham 1483–1523*, ed. E.M. Elvey, *Bucks Record Soc.*, No. 19, 1975). There are four of these, to wit:

[…] *in ecclesia parochiali de Magna Merlow* [16th July, 1493]: *Willelmus Clerk ad instanciam rectoris de Tyngest: rea comparuit actrix non ideo dimittitur ab officio una cum refusione expensarum.*

A will of Reginaldus Davy de Hamelden [30th November, 1493]: *Item lego ecclesie de Tyngehurst quattuor modios brasii* [four measures of malt].

Magna Wycombe [27th February, 1496]: *Thyngehurst; Thomas at Felde ad instanciam Ricardi Stacy. Pax et dimissus.* [Stacy is a recurring name in Fingest parish registers later].

Magna Wycombe [8th October, 1496]: *Thinghurst; Injunctum est ijconomis ibidem quod provideant aquabaijulum citra festum Omnium Sanctorum iam proximo futurum sub pena xls. Pax est et dimissi sunt.*

This command to the wardens to provide a holy water clerk before the next feast of All Saints under pain of a forty-shilling fine suggests that the font was already there; and suggests as well that the rector conscientiously conducted the customary processions around the church on saints' and other holy days.

As to parsons whose names we know, the register says nothing of Roger Cowper's fate; it simply mentions that his successor Humphry Hassall resigned in 1505 and was in turn succeeded by Will Barrot, who was collated by Bishop Smith on 20th February, 1505. It goes on that on Barrot's death the living went to Henry Penkyth, collated on 18th May, 1509. Penkyth lasted at Fingest only a month or so, leaving *per dimmissionem* (being with the bishop's authority ordained in another diocese) in favour of John Gerard, collated on 24th June, 1509.

The Future Cardinal Briefly Patron

In 1514, the fourth year of Henry VIII's reign, the appointment by papal provision of the young king's favourite THOMAS WOLSEY as Bishop of Lincoln was but one of many links in the chain of preferments in Church and State which led eventually to his acquisition of a cardinal's hat and with it virtually sole secular and papal authority within the realm, though always as servant of his royal master.

Wolsey held the Lincoln see for only a few months before proceeding to the archbishopric of York and thence to further heights; it seems beyond the bounds of likelihood that he knew much of his Fingest Manor.

As to the Fingest rectory, the rolls say that on 14th September, 1513, John Gerard in his turn gained bishop's authority to proceed to ordination outside the diocese and one Roger Travesse took the living.

Willis and his followers Lipscomb and Delafield appear to have thought that Travesse was collated by Wolsey. Nevertheless, the authoritative *Guide to Bishops' Registers of England and Wales* (Smith, David N., London, 1981) unequivocally dates Wolsey's brief translation to Lincoln as in 1514, the year his predecessor there died. So, if the rolls are right, the likelihood is that Travesse was collated by William Smith, not Wolsey. Adding to confusion, Willis (*Willis MS*, vol. xciv) names him as 'Travesse or Graves'; but all soon becomes clear as we see below.

Bishop Atwater

In the year 1514, then, three bishops of Lincoln found themselves in the episcopal chair. The third, WILLIAM ATWATER, was advanced to the see again by papal provision; like Wolsey he was a fellow of Magdalen but *sanctae theologiae professor* as well.

The year after his consecration Atwater found himself in the role of gospeller in the solemn ceremonial Mass celebrated when Wolsey received his cardinal's hat at the high altar in Westminster Abbey. After this occasion of high pomp and circumstance, however, we hear little more of Bishop Atwater, save that, like most bishops of his time, he made regular diocesan visitations which were duly re-corded. His yearly itinerary included frequent visits to Wooburn, where he settled many diocesan matters '*in capella manerii*'. In his episcopal court book are his 1519 'visitations' in the archdeaconry of Buckingham, where especially he found churches forlorn and ill-kept, repairs to towers and walls neglected by parishioners and to chancels by rectors, and everywhere churchyards desecrated by cattle, sometimes the rector's own. Of one hundred and fifty churches visited, rectors were non-resident in thirty. Of the twenty-two churches that passed muster, Fingest, under his own patronage, was one. Atwood's visitation book has the entry under Wycombe deanery: '*Tingest: Parochiani dicunt omnia bene. Dominus Robertus Traves Rector*'.

Thus Willis's 'Graves' was a misreading of 'Traves', which clearly fits better with 'Travesse'. (In the English court handwriting of the time the capital 'G' and capital 'T' were not unlike.)

Immorality was much sought out. Atwater's roll of '*detectiones*' (things discovered or made known to him as visitor) names a Fingest couple – John Plumrige (another recurring name in later parish registers) and Agnes Tyles – brought before him in January 1519 having confessed that her pregnancy had preceded their marriage – a circumstance apparently, if surprisingly, causing more remark then than it might have done now. The Bishop's injunction in John Plumridge's case was that on the next Sunday he was to lead the customary procession around Fingest church, bare-headed and bare-footed, bearing in his hand a lighted candle. In Agnes's case (heard a week later) she was (appropriately) on the feast of the purification of the Virgin Mary to walk about the village publicly bearing a lighted four-penny candle (*Linc. Rec. Soc.* vol. 61, pp.133, 139).

An old man when consecrated, Atwater very likely chose
to spend a good deal of time at his palace at Bishop's
Wooburn; at any rate he died there at the age of eighty-one
(it is said) in 1521.

The 1522 Musters for Buckinghamshire

Henry's Spanish marriage to Catherine of Aragon had by
1513 led to war with France. Peace was restored when his
sister Mary married Louis XII, though within three months
she was widowed. In 1520 Henry crossed to France with
his court and met the new King, Francis I, both sides
putting on a lavish display of tournaments, feasts and balls
at the 'Field of the Cloth of Gold'. A couple of years later
Henry joined Charles V, now Emperor of Germany, in
making war again on France. Charles, already ruler of
Spain, Austria, Naples and the Netherlands, was not short
of funding or men for his armies, but Henry's warlike
intent was not matched in England by either his troops or
the money to pay them.

In Tudor times the method of raising troops was to hold
musters in the various counties. Every free able-bodied
man over eighteen was expected to keep ready for use the
arms suitable for his wealth and rank. The provision of
armour (known as 'furnishing of harness') was the responsibility of towns, villages or hamlets.

Wolsey, ostensibly to assess potential strength in the
field, appointed muster commissioners countrywide to
inspect harness and assess every man's quota of the cost to
his locality. In their *Certificate of Muster for Buckinghamshire in
1522* (ed. A.C. Chibnall, HM Stationery Office, 1973) the
commissioners, parish by parish, named men answerable to
muster, giving for each man the annual value of any land,
tenancy and/or goods he held. The 1522 muster roll for
Fingest is of some interest for it is an early (perhaps the first

ever) listing of the names of its inhabitants. It reads as follows:

THINGESTE

	Valor terr' et tent'			Valor bonorum		
	£	s	d	£	s	d
Sir Rog Traver for his benefice	5	6	8			
Sir Thos Lovell stewarde ther Bishop of Lincoln	10	0	0			
Thos Umpton gent	4	0	0			
John Stompe		10	0			
Wm Callowe		n		5	0	0
John Miller		n		1	0	0
John Mere[1]		n		2	0	0
John Goodinge		n		4	0	0
Wm Ernolde[2]		n			n	
John Bowyer		n		1	0	0
Phil Wittington	4	0		2	0	0
Ric A Dene		n		3	0	0
Hen Paslade[2]		n			n	
Hen A Deane		n		1	0	0
John Sadler		n		10	6	8
Rob Anstye		n		2	0	0
Thos Tyler junior		n			n	
Thos Tyler senior		n		2	0	0

[1]One good bill   Four bills   [2]Two bows
(n = nihil]

Sir Thomas Lovell is named as bishop's steward. The office of steward of the lordships of Thame, Dorchester, Wobourne and 'Tynghurst' (all manors in the bishop's hands) had in 1480 first been granted by the dean and canons of Lincoln, under Russell's bishopric, to William Stonor, knight, with a fee of £6.20d from the issues of these manors and leave to appoint deputies (*Catalogue of Ancient Deeds, P.R.O.,* vol. vi, p.245). To appear on the Fingest muster of 1522, Lovell, a later deputy, may have resided at either Fingest or Cadmore End Manor. Another conclusion to be gleaned from the muster is that since a 'Sir Edward Unton' is known to have possessed Cadmore End Manor in the sixteenth century (J.G. Nichols, *The Unton Inventories,* London 1841, p.xxxvii) the naming of 'Thos Umpton gent' means that Cadmore End (and presumably its manor) was taken to be part of Fingest. We note, too, Rector Traves's name appearing again, but now with Bishop John Longland as patron.

The muster commissioners evidently found few Fingest men harnessed to carry arms; it looks as though they thought only John Mere had a bill he knew how to use as a weapon. Neither of the two bowmen, it seems, admitted to having land or property.

The Lay Subsidy of 1522/23

The underlying reason for Wolsey's muster was made clear the next year – it predicted with some certainty how much a lay subsidy would produce. Continual heavy war expenditure in France was putting the Crown in ever more urgent need of loans. Wolsey had already compiled a schedule of loans to be expected of those worth more than forty pounds a year; in Desborough hundred he identified as such nineteen persons, including one apiece in Hambleden and Turfield but none in Fingest. Soon after Bishop Longland's consecration, Wolsey obtained as well a Crown grant from Parliament of a general lay subsidy to carry on the wars with Scotland and France.

Again, in 1526, still under Wolsey's administration, further subsidy was collected, this time from clergy in the diocese of Lincoln. For each subsidy, and for the later *Valor Ecclesiasticus*, Fingest was appropriately assessed.

The lay subsidy was in effect a tax on land and/or goods; a shilling in the pound on annual income from land, and/or on goods, worth more than twenty pounds; sixpence in the pound on goods valued between two pounds and twenty pounds; 4d on goods worth less than two pounds, and for wage-earners, 4d per one pound wage.

The lay subsidy roll for the county of Bucks gives the names of its taxable inhabitants. Eighteen Fingest inhabitants proved liable; in the subsidy roll they are listed as follows:

Towne of Thynkhurst

William Calowe	£7
John Myller	£1-6-8
John Mere	£2
Richard Stacy	£2
Adam Grey	£1
John Helyar	£1
Thos. Shrempton	£3
Richard Deane	4m
John Deant	£1-6-8
Thos. Matthews	£1
William Collis	£1
Thos.Taylour	£2
Thos. Tylar	£3
John Sadyller	4m
Robert Austin	£3
Thos. Tylar the younger	£1

John Alen	w£1
John Robyns	w£1
[w = wage]	

At the rates agreed between Wolsey and Parliament, the sum collectable was 17s 8d (*Subsidy Roll for the county of Bucks: Anno 1524*, ed. A.C. Chibnall, and A. Vere Woodman, *Bucks Rec. Soc.*, 1950).

Although the muster roll and the lay subsidy roll for Fingest were both recorded within the space of two years, the two sets of names agree rather poorly, with only half appearing in both. This possibly suggests that the commissioners' agents did not name persons they knew as individuals, but used second-hand information; nearly all the names appear in parish registers later assembled.

The 1526 Subsidy from the Clergy

The subsidy from clergy in the diocese of Lincoln in 1526 was based on new valuations of clerical incomes within its hundreds of parishes; not the livings but the individual clergy were taxed, curates as well as incumbents, with no exemptions for even the poorest. Those with annual incomes of eight pounds or more paid a tenth (*quota mediatatis*) those with less paid a fifteenth (*quota tercie*). Certain deductions were allowed in estimating incomes e.g. the cost of repairing a rectory (including chancel) and stipends of curates.

The Subsidy Collected in the Diocese of Lincoln in 1526 (ed. Revd H. Salter, *Oxford Historical Soc., 1909,* vol. lxiii) details fifteen clergy subsidy entries under '*Wicombe decanatus*'. They include:

Tingehirst

Dom Rogerus Traves rec	vil
Inde proc. et sin.	xs vijd ob. q.
Pro visitationi episcopijs	iiijd
Dom Roberto Colins	xls
Repar.	xvis
Dom Robertus Colyns pensionarius	xls q.t.iis viijd
The total subsidy due:	q.m. iijs iiijd ob. q.

Again, Rector Traves was still going strong. Also named is another priest of the parish, Robert Colins or Colyns, in receipt of a pension; perhaps he was a retired curate.

Rector Traves carries on under Bishop John Longland

At Fingest Roger Travesse or Traves outlived Atwater. Listing names of parsons in 'Wicomb Deanery' in 1524, *MS Willis (i)* mentions him again: 'Tinghurst: Rog. Graves R'. The rectory's patron and manorial lord was now JOHN LONGLAND, consecrated Bishop of Lincoln in 1521, at a time when Henry VIII's plans to despoil the Church were already threatening.

Longland, who was born in Henley-on-Thames in 1473, entered Magdalen, Oxford, as a demy, became principal of Magdalen Hall and by 1511 was a doctor of divinity with a reputation as a theologian of hard study and devotion. 'In good favour with Henry VIII for his excellent way of preaching at Windsor', in 1519 he was made the King's confessor; his appointment to Lincoln two years later owed something to Wolsey, a close friend with whom he had been a near contemporary at Magdalen.

As Bishop he strongly asserted the rights and privileges of the Church and the duties of the clerical body, and in 1527 gave a monition from Cromwell requiring the parish clergy of the diocese to preach in person at least four times a year. He used his political influence strongly against the increasing tendency to enclose land for pasture 'to the hurt of the commonwealth of the King's realm'. In a letter to Wolsey he said, 'your heart would mourn to see the towns, villages, hamlets and manor places in ruin and decay, the people gone, the ploughs laid down...'

At Henley he built the fine bell tower of the parish church, and endowed a row of almshouses for the poor which still stand on the north side of the churchyard. On a more secular count, he agreed a lucrative composition with Wolsey to share probate fees for wills of over ten pounds.

The English Reformation Taking Shape

The twenty-six years of Longland's bishopric (he died in the same year as Henry VIII, 1547) was a time of unprecedented change in both country and the *ecclesia Anglicana*. It saw Wolsey's fall and his death in 1529, his place taken in the King's confidence by Thomas Cromwell. Rapidly assuming eminence, Cromwell made it his business to ensure that Henry VIII steadily acquired dominance over both Parliament and clergy. The King appointed Thomas Cranmer to the see of Canterbury and the stage was set for Cromwell and Archbishop Cranmer to preside over the beginnings of the Church of England.

Henry was utterly frustrated by Wolsey's procrastination and had become intent on somehow breaking with the Pope to achieve his marriage annulment. Cromwell suggested the simple but masterly answer – that the King make his supremacy plain by evicting the Pope from England. In just three years, 1532–1535, Cromwell induced

Henry to put through Parliament seven Acts that extended his sovereignty into all spheres of society. These were Acts cutting off diocesan and parish payments to Rome, forbidding appeals to Rome on any count, and abolishing not only papal consecration of English bishops but papal authority generally in England; Acts that made him, the King, supreme head of the Church in England with power to define doctrine and punish heresy. Finally, the Act of Succession gave parliamentary sanction to the divorce, and made it high treason to refuse to take an oath in favour of the new regime. On 23rd May, 1533, the year that he was made archbishop, Cranmer opened court to declare the marriage with Catherine void, and on 1st June Anne Boleyn was crowned Queen.

Longland shared the King's lack of sympathy with Luther's attack on the Sacraments for which the Pope (later to excommunicate him) had earlier titled Henry 'Defender of the Faith'; and there is no doubt that he had royal approval in being as severe a persecutor of heretics as William Smith had been. As Delafield puts it, 'he was a cruel vexer of the faithful so that there were more confessors molested in this small county of Bucks than in all England elsewhere for 20 years together'.

Foxe tells of Longland in the year of his consecration visiting the southern part of his diocese, leaving the Great North road at Hatfield to pass along 'the Bishops' Road' to Amersham, Wycombe and Henley. At Amersham he examined many who had been abjured on trial by Smith in 1506, and compelled them to denounce those who had shared their belief, forcing husbands, wives, parents, children, brothers and sisters to betray one another. In proceedings over several months local people suspected of heresy numbered over two hundred. Of the convicted, Delafield writes that 'by the cruelty peculiar to that sanguinary religion children were compelled to put fire to the Piles that consumed their Fathers'.

Longland was a member of the Convocation that drew up, at the King's command, the 'Six Articles of Religion' that were directed for the most part against the 'new learning' espoused by Colet and Erasmus. At the same time he seems to have concentrated on restoring proper monkish regimens to numerous English monastic houses, all of them anciently built on allegiance to Rome – the very allegiance that in the King's eyes unquestionably condemned them to dissolution and plunder. Henry, in fact, persecuted in both directions. If a good Catholic disowned his supremacy he was burned or hanged; if a Protestant denied one of the Six Articles his fate was as certain and severe.

Longland seems to have regularly observed his visitational duties around the diocese. Among fifteen entries in his visitation record for 'Wicombe deanery' in 1530 is noted:

Tynghurst. *Johannes Ho...inson* [Hodgkinson?] *subtrahit ad ecclesia ibidem iijs pro redditu unius domus ecclesie pertinentis.*

Who, then, was John Hodgkinson? Was he Traves's successor as rector, or merely a clerk in holy orders assisting Traves in parish duties, as was common at the time; or was he indeed an ordained priest at all? We get no help here from the register which, not otherwise mentioning Hodgkinson, goes on to name the next rector as 'Joh. Dormer', presented to the living by the bishop on 20th September, 1532, but says nothing of his predecessor. So how Traves ended his incumbency remains a mystery. Of added interest here, though, is the mention of rent the parish supplied for a house belonging to the church, since it implies a parsonage house already there, separate from the manor. The present house known as The Old Rectory has many early features that date it to this time.

The *Valor Ecclesiasticus*

By 1535 the King, again desperate for money through extravagance at home and expensive wars abroad, was putting into effect the second Annates Act of 1534 whereby the first-fruits of every benefice, formerly paid to the Pope, together with a tenth of the annual income, were to be appropriated to the Crown. The official valuation of ecclesiastical revenues detailed for every benefice was recorded in the *Valor Ecclesiasticus* popularly known as the 'King's Books'.

In the Record Commission's transcript (1819–1840) of the *Valor Ecclesiasticus* the valuations of Wooburn and Fingest appear together (Fig. 20) under 'Value of manors in the county of Oxford in the possession of John Bishop of Lincoln'. It will be seen that there is an allowance for the duties of John Bowell, the bishop's bailiff, now acting for both Wooburn and Fingest.

Church Courts Held in Fingest Manor

Longland's rolls record him twice holding church courts at Fingest for view of frankpledge (that is, requiring parishioners publicly to speak to each others' conduct) viz.:

> Tinghurst, alias Fingest, *Visus francplege cum cu baron Johis* [Longland] *permissione Divina Lincoln. Epis. Ibidem* on 17 Dec. 1537 (28 Hen. VIII)

and again on 13th December, 1541, (32 Hen. VIII) (George Lipscomb, *History and Antiquities of the county of Buckingham*, 1847, iii, 565). Courts were customarily held in the patron's manor house, so it is likely that as president Bishop

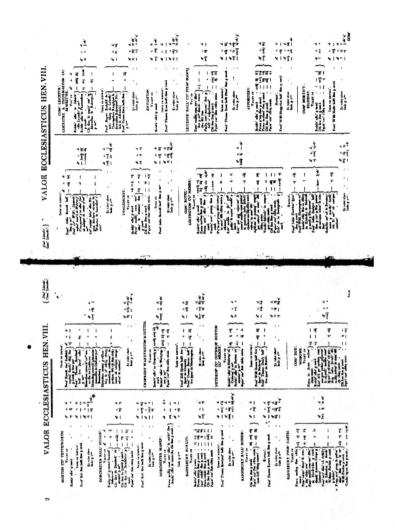

Fig. 20: Parts of pages 2 & 3 of *Valor Ecclesiasticus (1546)* vol. iv; 'Henricus VIII', 1821. Entries for Woborne and Tyngehurst. (Reproduced with the kind permission of Bodleian Library Service, Oxford. Shelfmark G.A.Eccl.Top.b.24 = R.4.70/4)

Longland was following his predecessors in maintaining living quarters at Fingest.

The Last Fingest Rectors Under Lincoln Bishops' Patronage

John Dormer very soon resigned his living and on 6th January, 1533, the Bishop collated John Garnett in his place. Rector Garnett would as the current incumbent have attended the 1537 court for view of frankpledge. On his death, William Gyllot, collated on 7th February, 1539, became the incumbent attending view of frankpledge held at the manor in 1541.

Gyllot was still rector of Fingest when, as the next chapter describes, in 1548 its manor and advowson were taken from the see of Lincoln.

Chapter XVI
The Reformation: Confusion and Conformity (1548–1606)

The undaunted reader will by now be asking himself how, in these Tudor times, actions and reactions in religion and government shadowed everyday life in Fingest. Firstly, was Henry VIII's strong opposition to the 'new learning' and the Protestant reformers at all reflected in local church custom? After all, he had let it be widely known that he did not wish to separate himself from Rome in doctrine, only in government, and his published views as head of the Church of England seemed to herald little change. Spelling them out, the Six Articles Act of 1539 confirmed the old central doctrine of transubstantiation, the adequacy of communion in one kind only, the necessity of clerical celibacy, the obligation upon the laity (for example ex-nuns and lay-brothers) to observe their vows of chastity, the importance of private masses, and the necessity of sacramental confession. The *King's Book* of 1543 further silenced doctrinal challenge against the ceremonies of the old religion. Despite this, in his attachment to Cranmer Henry saw fit to order copies of Coverdale's version of Tyndale's Bible in English to be placed in churches (in 1535 printing of the Bible was allowed); and he required people at Mass to repeat the Creed, Paternoster and Ten Commandments in English. These were injunctions likely to have met with Fingest's approval.

On his death in 1547 Henry left a will charging a body of sixteen executors and twelve privy councillors – his brother-in-law Edward Seymour among them – to protect the young King's interest and continue the management of state affairs and church policy as before. But under Seymour's powerful influence this regency council soon overruled Henry's supposed orthodoxy; and before long the boy Edward, whose education his father had perhaps astutely left largely in Protestant hands, was appointing his uncle Seymour Lord Protector of the realm, creating him Duke of Somerset into the bargain.

Somerset had the 'Reformed Religion' and the Protestant cause at heart, perhaps not least inspired by the enormous fortune from Church lands he was able to lay hands on as Protector. At his instigation Parliament, with young Edward's whole approval, formally set aside Henry's will. In the first year of the new king's accession, 1547, the Six Articles Act and the statutes against treason and heretics were repealed, and Cromwell's Injunctions of 1538 revived.

The changes in Henry's 'Church of England' that followed jolted the custom and authority of the Old Religion in every parish in the land. English was substituted for the old Latin ritual, images in churches and cathedrals were pulled down and pictures defaced, Mass was abolished, observation of fasts on eves of holy days (especially St Thomas Becket's) were forbidden, and in the face of hostility to the doctrine of purgatory and the commercialism of the teaching of the Dominican friar Johann Tetzel (1465–1519) that –

as the penny in the coffer rings,
the soul from purgatory's fire springs

– prayers and masses for the dead were done away with. Rood screens were pulled down (no trace remains of where

Fingest's stood), and bells were silenced, ending the people's custom of repeating *Aves* when church bells were tolling after service in the belief this induced papal pardons. Browne Willis (*Willis MS*, vol. x, p.19) speaks of 'the taking down from the tower and selling off of Fingest's fine peal of bells *tempore* Edward VI'. All in all, the old order of worship that had for so long given this Chiltern benefice its own special character was in Edward's brief reign irretrievably done away with.

Bishops' Patronage Melts Away

In this same year, 1547, Bishop Longland died and HENRY HOLBEACH (alias RANDS), formerly prior and dean of Worcester and then Bishop of Rochester, was elected to the see of Lincoln. Holbeach, a man entirely subservient to the court of Edward VI, was a chief leader of the Reformation and of the commissioners who condemned Bishop Gardiner of Winchester for opposing Reformation doctrines. Among his very first actions as bishop, Holbeach signed away to the Crown great numbers of manors and estates which for centuries had been diocesan properties of Lincoln; along with them in 1548 went the manor and rectory of Fingest.

In taking such a step some readers may find extraordinary (*Lincolnshire Archives Committee Report*, 1950–51), Holbeach very likely had his own survival in mind. Succeeding Longland, who had so sternly persecuted Lollard and Lutheran heretics, Holbeach at the beginning of the new reign realised the pendulum was swinging the other way. After the Reformation Parliament of 1529 religious reformation had been shedding its heretical label, but shedding it in a particularly Anglican way, for despite approving the dissolution of the monasteries and the deliberate spoliation of the property of the church, the

Church authorities showed no hesitation in repelling Lutheran and Lollard attacks on private property. This was especially the attitude in London and the large towns, where lands seized by the Crown had found ready purchasers among the new nobility seeking landlords' profits from the new dispensation.

In the countryside, on the other hand, the dissolution of the monasteries and now of chantries as well, with all the loss of their extensive lands and incomes, had an opposite effect, removing the mainstays of subsistence that monks of priories and convents and chantry priests had customarily provided for the country poor. Rural poverty became rife, and there were Catholic risings again for the Old Religion, especially in country regions like Norfolk and the West; but there was little evidence of resentment among the small-holders of anticlerical South Bucks, especially in Fingest, a parish where the church lacked even a single chantry chapel.

The removal of papal supremacy brought to an end the hitherto unlimited power of Convocations and Church courts to legislate for and discipline the laity. It no less impaired Holbeach's episcopal powers vis-à-vis the government of the Lord Protector and the new king. Lincoln was the see of a huge diocese, which by Longland's time had acquired twenty-four scattered episcopal palaces and residences, with their associated lands and manors; on top of this there were reserved rents to the see to the tune of seventeen thousand pounds. Lest such urban diocesan wealth were to occasion royal attainder – or alternatively rural diocesan poverty engender rebellion – Holbeach in his wisdom lost no time in relinquishing most of his see's estates to the possession of the Crown, a gift of which Somerset made himself a major beneficiary.

We see how Fingest's fate was thereby settled in the Patent Rolls of 1547 (*Pat. 2 Edw VI, pt. vi*) where the

Bishop obtained licence to alienate Wooburn manor and Fingest Manor to Edward, Duke of Somerset; and next, in 1551 (*Pat. 4 Edw VI pt.* viii), where the King 'at the humble Petition of our Dear Uncle Edward Duke of Somerset int. al. grants to him the m. of Tyngherst als ffingeste'.

Somerset improved matters further to suit himself. He obtained royal licence 'to grant the manor of Tingherst otherwise Fingherst, co. Bucks, to William Thynne, in exchange for the manor of Dultingcote. *Hanc licentiam predictam reperies semper in promptu in cancellaria domini nostri regis*' – a grant the bishop and chapter of Wells promptly confirmed (1551, 10th May, *Calendar of MSS of Dean and Chapter of Wells,* vol. 2, fol. 52, 1914).The revenue of the manor of Dultingcote had been the prebend supporting William Thynne's preferment to a canon's stall in the chapter of Wells cathedral; such prebends were usually good livings and Dultingcote clearly more so than Fingest. At any rate, William Thynne found himself prebendary of 'Dultincote alias Fingherst', the Dultincote revenue going into Somerset's pocket.

A Wells Prebendary as Patron

The sum of this ineffable mullarky was that Thynne and his prebendary successors, while retaining a canon's stall in Wells chapter, became patrons of Fingest and thus possessors of the advowson of a living in an entirely separate diocese. Though ordained priests, this gave them no cure of souls in their new prebendal parish. Patronage gave them only the right to nominate future Fingest rectors, and they had still to seek any such incumbent's institution in the spiritualities (though no longer 'collation') from the bishops of Lincoln. As before, the rector appointed retained the great tithes.

William Gyllot was in his tenth year as rector at Fingest when Holbeach became bishop in 1547. Like most parish parsons at the time, he found himself embroiled in the change from the Old to the Reformed; on top of this Somerset's contrivings meant that by 1551 the bishop who had collated him had lost the right of patronage to the Fingest incumbency. The advowson, appendant as it was to the manor, was now in hands outside the diocese, a change threatening the freehold of the benefice.

In that same year 1551 Bishop Holbeach died, and the see came to JOHN TAYLOR (1552–1554). It was during Taylor's brief occupation of the episcopal seat that Dudley, Earl of Warwick, conspired with the Council to get the young King's policy into his own hands; Somerset soon lost his head on Tower Hill on a charge of felony. As the new Lord Protector and now Duke of Northumberland, Dudley, although privately still a strong Roman Catholic, schemingly pushed forward the Reformation. He induced Edward, by then sick and dying, to alter the succession, shutting out his sisters Mary and Elizabeth, and in the Protestant cause settling the crown on Lady Jane Grey, granddaughter of Mary Tudor and wife to his own son Guildford.

Lacking sympathy with political machinations effected under the cloak of religious reformation (and, no doubt, detesting the further demeaning of the advowson of his own benefice) Gyllot, as a Catholic priest, was unwelcome as rector to the reformed prebendary at Wells; he was the last incumbent to celebrate Mass at Fingest in the old style. Two or three years before Edward died in 1553 he had given up or lost the living.

Mary's Papistry

Dudley's manoeuvrings ended by his joining Lady Jane and Guildford in the Tower for execution, while to wide acclaim Edward's sister Mary took the throne. So far as his microcosmic Fingest benefice concerned him, Bishop Taylor seems to have done little to oblige the Queen, nor did he recognise the prebendal effect on its advowson. In February 1554, filling the living *propter lapsum* after Gyllot's departure, he collated as by episcopal custom a new incumbent, William Adde. However, as Browne Willis (*Willis MS*, vol. x) explains, to do so he needed 'the consent of Will. Thynne, Gent, Prebendary of Dultincote in Wells cathedral'. Taylor was the last Bishop of Lincoln to exercise the Fingest advowson. Thereafter it was in the hands of the Wells prebendaries – another shortfalling in our church's diocesan standing.

To Queen Mary's great indignation her defiant attempts to restore England to papal obedience by reviving the heresy laws and the Six Articles initially suffered parliamentary defeat. But in 1554, with Cranmer arrested for treason and Cardinal Reginald Pole succeeding him at Canterbury, Parliament became obliged to re-enact the heresy laws and repeal all the anti-papal and anti-ecclesiastical laws passed since 1529. Further, steps began to be taken to repair some of the Protestant damage done in church buildings, for example broken roods, Easter sepulchres and fonts; although as we noted earlier it looks as if Fingest's fifteenth century font had to wait until Queen Anne's reign to find its way back into the church.

Though Mary found it impossible to recover for the Church the lands lost by the monasteries and chantries, she determinedly persecuted the reformers at whose door she laid the sacrilegious blame. By 1555 the burnings of Bishops Ridley and Latimer and Archbishop Cranmer at

Oxford, and the fires of heretics burning at Smithfield, did nothing but imbue the English with an undying hatred of the Pope and Roman Catholicism. Further, despite the Catholic Queen and her Roman Church, the people's long-standing anti-clericism, and the acceptance by the lower ranks of the clergy of the Protestant rule of preaching, made for increasing use of the English liturgy of Cranmer's 1552 Prayer Book in the ministration of religion. We may imagine William Adde at Fingest poring over Cranmer's *Book of Homilies* in preparing the lengthy sermons that especially in services ministered by village priests were taking the pride of place that the sacrifice of the Mass had for so long held.

In the third year of Mary's reign, 1556, when William Adde was in his second year in the Fingest living, Thynne at Wells resigned the prebend to George Carew DD. Carew was prebendary only briefly, for the Lincoln rolls show that in 1557 Richard Petre Esq., the next prebendary, was presenting Edward Bagshaw AM, to the church of Fingest to be duly instituted by THOMAS WATSON, the last of the Marian Lincoln bishops. His rolls do not say as much, but the living was vacant because Adde had died and Willis (*Willis MS*, vol. xciv) notes that his will was proved in 1557. There is a copy of it in the Bucks County Archives:

> I, William Adde, being sick in body but sound in mind bequeath my soul to Almighty God and Blessed Mary [...] and my body to be buried, in the chancel of Fingest Church. To mother church at Lincoln 4d to church at Fingest 6/8 to my brother my black gelding, my cow, 40/-, 6 of my best tegs, 6 lambs and my great kettle.

('Blessed Mary' perhaps recognises his institution by a bishop favouring the old order.)

Adde's will gives us a picture of the Fingest living as no better, indeed a good deal worse, under Mary than under Edward, and certainly than before the Reformation. Regrettably, his will tells us nothing of how he lived; it is only clear that he was a poor man farming a few animals, with little furniture in the parsonage house to will save his prized great kettle. Browne Willis (*Willis MS*, vol. xiv, p.52), however, found an '*extract ex Testamentis Tempore Regine Marie*' that speaks of Adde leaving a legacy – modestly saved, no doubt, from the rectorial tithes he could extract from his flock – to the Reverend Swanson, vicar of West Wycombe. If his expressed wish was observed, Adde was the first Fingest rector to be buried in the church.

In the next year, 1558, Mary died and Elizabeth succeeded. After only six months in the living Bagshaw resigned and the next rector, William Green, was presented by Sir William Petre, knight, of Ingatestone, Essex, on this occasion acting as attorney for Richard Petre. But within two years, Green too had given up the living.

Fingest and the Elizabethan Settlement

Looking at politico-religious rulings next to be enacted after Mary's disastrous reign, we may make a shrewd guess that the brevity of Bagshaw's and Green's incumbencies reflected their doubtful hold on tenure. Within months of Elizabeth's coronation in 1559 the government, more or less with Commons' approval, had introduced supremacy bills which the Lords, especially the spiritual lords, at first persisted in throwing out. But Protestant opinion eventually prevailed; indeed Bishop Watson of Lincoln, supporting Convocation's contrary views, found himself in the Tower for speaking against the supremacy. By April 1559 Parliament had passed the Act of Supremacy, sweeping away the whole of Mary's reactionary legislation, reviving the anti-papal statutes of Henry VIII, and vesting in the Crown power as 'supreme governor' (rather than 'supreme head') of the national church. An oath of supremacy was made compulsory for all clergy, judges, justices, mayors and persons taking orders, or degrees at university.

Next, in May 1559, an Act of Uniformity was passed by both houses, though with a majority of only three in the Lords and the spiritual peers still solidly against. This Act restored the second Edwardian prayer book as the directory of public worship, its provisions applying to the entire community, clerical and lay; clerical offenders were liable on repeated offence to imprisonment for life, and the laity to a fine of twelve pence for every absence from church. Whether or not it was the passage of these acts that decided Bagshaw's and Green's resignations, within the year Sir William Petre, again in his capacity as Richard Petre's attorney, was presenting Peter Rider to the Fingest living, this time to be instituted as rector by Bishop NICHOLAS BULLINGHAM, Thomas Watson having been removed for refusing the oath.

Peter Rider, a Long-Serving Rector (1560–1606)

The forty-six years that Peter Rider was rector spanned nearly the whole of Elizabeth's reign. A survey in the diocese of Lincoln taken within five years of Elizabeth's accession to determine numbers in every parish, has an entry under the deanery of Wycombe: 'Twyngest 24 families' (*Brit. Mus. Harleian MS 618*). About five members per family was then average (Julian Cornwall, Rec. Bucks, vol. xvi, p.258). For a parish so small to have a resident rector at this time was something of a rarity. During Edward's and Mary's reigns many priests had fled overseas for their opinions, while in 1559 as many as one thousand had been removed for refusing the Oath of Supremacy. As to the state of churches, a survey in 1585 found only two thousand ministers to supply ten thousand churches. Eight thousand parishes were without priests, and in many the church building was dilapidated:

> Numerous churches […] allowed to become utterly desolate […] in certain of them no service of any kind had been held for nearly 12 years […] no-one to look after the fabric, to keep up the fences of the churchyard […] swine often grubbed up graves […] doors' hinges rusted […] birds nesting through broken windows […] bells no longer needed, sold […] lead stripped […]

(Robt. Gibbs, Rec. Bucks, 1888, vol. vi, p.154.) With Peter Rider in the living throughout this period Fingest church seems to have escaped serious dilapidation. At any rate he kept the parish solidly Anglican, as bishops' visitation reports show (see below). Elsewhere, despite the Act of Uniformity, even in parishes that still had priests confusion often prevailed, some having the same clergyman as Anglican minister and Catholic priest in one.

The more extreme Protestants, meanwhile, were counter-attacking the settlement of 1559. Puritans seeking further 'purification' of the church from unscriptural and corrupt forms were urging replacement of the three orders of Church ministry by Presbyterian elders and deacons, and the Book of Common Prayer by a Book of Discipline. In 1563 a Puritan petition to Convocation (where they concentrated effort) sought to make a clean sweep of 'the dregs of popery' – the use of organs in churches, the ring in the marriage ceremony, the sign of the cross in baptism, kneeling at communion and the use of vestments other than the surplice. Their petition failed, but only just.

Undaunted, the Puritans held out for preaching in services, Sunday observance and the 'table-wise' position of the altar; and led by Cartwright of St John's College, Lady Margaret Professor of Divinity at Cambridge, published a long series of pamphlets, among them the 'Martin Marprelate' papers attacking the bishops and the state of the Church. A lengthy Puritan 'General Supplication' to Parliament in 1586 included 'A shorte view of the whole estate of the ministerie in the Comt. of Buck'. (*C.W. Foster, The State of the Church In the Reigns of Elizabeth and James I as Illustrated by Documents relating to the Diocese of Lincoln,* vol. i, *Lincoln Record Soc.,* vol. xiii).

The supplication document found the following state of affairs in Buckinghamshire in 1584:

Parsonages and vicarages furnyshed yet not all resident	150		
Curates serving	60		
		-	210
Whereof			
Diligent preachers	14		
Preachings now and then	16		
Non-residents learned	6		
Double beneficed learned	9		
		-	45
Unlearned and unprofitable non-residents	13		
Double beneficed unlearned	8		
Parsons vicars and curates unlearned and unprofitable	139		
		-	160
		-	205
Of this number infamous	26		

Note the number of fyve is wanting must be supplied
in the double beneficed men in the Shire to make up
210

The Puritan persuasion found such 'double benefices'
(pluralism) especially objectionable.

Subscribing to the Three Articles

Faced by this presbyterianism with its 'prophesyings' and
'classes' Elizabeth became bitterly opposed to Puritan
attempts to change the Church of England. John Whitgift,
master of Trinity College and Regius Professor of Divinity
at Cambridge, was appointed to Canterbury in 1583 and
aided her to the full with his Act of 1583 against 'seditious
sectaries'. Clergy were compelled to subscribe to Three
Articles, viz.:

1. That her Majesty hath sovereignty over all persons in the realm whether ecclesiastical or
   temporal.
2. That the book of common prayer contains
   nothing contrary to the word of God and that the
   subscriber will use it and none other.
3. And that he believes the Articles of religion set
   out at the 1552 Convention. [The Thirty-nine
   Articles]

Bishops and archdeacons were accordingly directed to
make parish visitations, listing the clergy and checking for
attendance and 'instruments exhibited' – that is, letters of
orders and institution, licences to preach, and dispensations
if the incumbent had any. Listings were entered in the
bishop's *Libri Cleri*, the 'Visitation Books'.

Churchwardens were under oath to present at the visitation any person or thing that needed 'correction'. Such presentments made known to the visitor were *detectiones*. Matters the visitor discovered were *comperta*. The *comperta* for 1585 reveal a few cases of nonconformity in the archdeaconry of Bucks; among these at Fingest the visitor found that 'their parson [Peter Rider] doth not read the lettanye on the sundaies and holidaies orderly'.

Peter Rider was otherwise a model of conformity. In 1584 he subscribed his name to the Three Articles: '*Ego Petrus Rider, rector de thy'ghest ex animo subscribo*'. In the *Liber Cleri* for the next year, 1585, he is entered under Wycombe, Archdeaconry of Bucks:

> Tingrift. Sir Peter Rider vicar
> ord pr. by the bp. of Chester
> 24 Sept 1558.
> i. 8d t. 8d.
> Bred in the schools.

That he was ordained in 1558 by the Bishop of Chester suggests that Lincoln's Bishop Watson was then already disapproved; Nicholas Bullingham did not take the see until 1560. The abbreviations 'i' and 't' refer to fees due from the parish to the episcopal visitor – in this case for letters of institution eight pence; and for letters testimonial (subscription to the articles of religion) also eight pence. 'Bred in the schools' means he was not a university graduate.

In 1597 Peter 'Ryder' and again in 1603 Peter 'Rider' are named as voting in Elections of Proctors to appear before William (Chaderton), Bishop of Lincoln at Stamford, in turn to be entered for election as proctors for the Convocations at St Pauls, London.

In the *Liber Cleri* for 1603 there is a further entry:

Finghurst. Q. P'ge prop. v.6 li 7s 11d
   P. Mr Barker prebend of Wells
   I. Peter Rider. D. Noe grad.
   R. est comm 84

(Here Q = quality, kind of benefice; P'ge = parsonage (i.e. rectory); prop = not appropriate or impropriate; v = value; P = patron; I = incumbent; D = degree; R = resident; comm = communicants.)

The Manor and Advowson Leased Out

The mention of patronage brings us back to Wells's prebendaries. Browne Willis (*Willis MS*, vol. x, p.22) says Richard Petre was outed of his preferment about 1570. In the 1979 edition by J.M. Horn of the part of Le Neve's *Fasti Ecclesiae Anglicanae* that deals with Bath and Wells diocese, there is a note that he was stated to be abroad in October 1571 and having 'confirmed to the Papist Religion' was consequently deprived of York benefices. The next prebendary of Dultingcote/Fingest, collated in 1572, was Walter Bayley MD, a layman and physician-in-ordinary to the Queen. Prebendary Bayley lost no time in arranging a leasing for twenty-one years to Thomas Collyns, register to the Archdeacon of Berkshire, 'the manor of Tyngerst, alias Fingest, Co. Bucks, and the advowson of the rectory of Tyngerst with power to cut woods and underwoods, rent £18'. (*Wells Chapter library, Ledger F, p.293*).

This marketing of the manor by a Wells canon to a tenant put an end to any right the Bishop of Lincoln or his bailiff might have claimed to living quarters there. The tenancy was soon recognised by law and as we have already seen (Chapter VI) Delafield, under the heading '*Dominium Regale*' in his *Account of Fingherst* quotes verbatim from documents to this effect that he came across in the manor house. These were presentments of homage to courts (presumably justices' courts) held there in 1576 and 1581. Delafield very reasonably thought their wording proved the manor to be originally 'ancient demesne'; but they provide also the first written mention of tenants being in the manor. They also carry the implication that Fingest's rectors had long ceased living in the manor house.

Thomas Collyns in fact lasted eighteen years at the manor. In 1590, as *Wells Chapter library Ledger F* (*fol. 119d*) tells us, there was a:

Lease by Wm. Whitlocke M.A., preb. of the prebend of Dultincott alias Dulcott otherwise called Tingherst or Fyngest, to Michael Farrar, alias Turner, of Great Marlow co. Bucks, yeoman, for 21 years of the manor of Tingeherst alias Fingest co. Bucks, except the advowson of the rectory, and all timber trees containing above 16 inches square; rent 20*l* and 26*s* 8*d* to the Master of the Fabric of the Cathedral. Confirmed by the bishop and the dean and chapter.

An entry of 1597–98 (*Ledger F, fol. 154d*) repeats this, except in describing Michael Farrar as 'gent'. Members of the Farrar family (appearing in the church registers later as 'Ferrers') were born in, died in, or married from the manor for the next one hundred years or more.

The Rector, meanwhile, was ensconced in the parsonage house opposite the church. The surviving Fingest registers dating from 1608, two years after he died, tell us something of his family thereafter. Elizabeth Rider, widow (most likely his wife), was buried on 28th June, 1625. 'Peter Rider sonne to Elizabeth Rider' married Cicely Davy on 8th October, 1620, and in 1621 and 1624 their daughters Anne and Jone were baptised. Two male Riders appear in the marriage register in 1643 and 1682; and as to further Rider births recorded in the seventeenth century register there are six between 1545 and 1686, two of which are entered, according to Commonwealth prejudice, as 'born' meaning not baptised.

Peter Rider predeceased his wife by all but twenty years. Bishop's transcripts of the church register record an entry under: 'Anno 1606: ffingest. The 19th day of August was buried Peter Ryder rector'.

He died the third year after James VI of Scotland with his royal cavalcade from Edinburgh reached London as King James I 'by divine right'.

Chapter XVII
Passive Obedience, Revolution, Restoration (1606–1660)

Leaving Fingest's conformity in Tudor affairs, we come next to the century of the Stuarts. Surveying as ever the unwinding scroll of our parish's history, we cast about now for perceptible patterns impressed thereon under this dynasty of royal despots, and especially the vicissitudes engendered during the years of civil war, regicide and revolution that interrupted its continuity.

The Stuart Motto: *Non desideriis hominum sed voluntate Dei*

James I (1603–1625), who held it as unquestionable on theological grounds that inheriting the throne of England meant inheriting the divine right of kings, found himself ruling a country much divided in ecclesiastical allegiance between a considerable number of inborn Puritan Bible-thumpers, a phalanx of High Churchmen of Anglican persuasion, and a sizeable group of Roman Catholic recusants rallying to the papal Counter-Reformation. He was at once presented with a 'Millenary Petition' voiced by a thousand Puritan clergy deploring the continued use of the Prayer Book, and what they saw as papist survivals in the Church of England, including the orders of bishops and deacons and not least the vestments they wore. At his

Hampton Court Conference, ostensibly to consider the petition, James mistook English Puritanism for the Scottish Presbyterianism he disliked, and would brook no argument dissenting from his own opinion. Except for royal approval of a new translation of the Bible that became the 'Authorised Version', the Puritans gained nothing for their cause.

James immovably upheld the link between the divine right of kings and the apostolic succession; but had hardly made it crystal clear that, for him monarchy and episcopy stood together – 'No Bishop, no King' – than the discovery of the Gun Powder Plot filled the serried ranks of English Protestants of all persuasions with more horror and dread of 'popery' than ever. Though personally inclined to leniency towards Catholics, James imposed an anti-papal oath of allegiance distinguishing those who were loyal to the state and those who were not. His Erastian policy discounted arguments against ecclesiastical dogmatism such as Richard Hooker had put forward in 1594 in his *Ecclesiastical Polity* with the aim of 'purifying' the church to make it truly 'catholic' and reformed. In his fixed belief in his divine right James, denying that tyranny could exist by the appointment of God, refused to ratify Convocation's reformist canons that made no attempt to contest this, simply because they advocated 'non-resistance to the King in possession'. The Court of High Commission, established in Elizabeth's time for inquisition of heretics, was brought into action again to provide for disciplinary action by bishops dealing with supposed transgressions against uniformity – both Puritan and Roman Catholic. These were ceremonial and ritual errors, clerical misdemeanour, recusancy, sectarianism, immorality and divorce. 'Passive obedience' to religious discipline as the King and bishops saw it became the order of the day, no less in Fingest than elsewhere.

Rector Edwards Succeeds Rector Rider

During Peter Rider's forty-six years of religious conformity under Elizabeth and then the Stuart James I, Fingest's advowson continued in the hands of the canons who successively occupied the prebendary stall at Wells. When Rider died in 1606 the latest of these, William Barker, appointed as rector Christopher Edwards, a graduate with an MA degree probably from Oxford, and in sympathy with James's High Church views. Edwards held the living nearly as long as Rider, his forty-one years spanning the reigns of both James and Charles. Evidently little affected when in 1642 Charles took on Parliament in the Civil War; he continued to lead the parish in its accustomed ways of 'passive obedience' and 'non-resistance' no matter what Parliament handed down until the year he died, 1647. By then even in Fingest national events could hardly have continued to escape notice and for the next thirteen years church life in the parish for priest and people alike turned upside-down, as we shall soon discover.

On James's death Charles succeeded (1625–1649), only to assert his divine right even more strongly than his father. Needing supplies for what proved to be wasted military forays against Spain and France, he had to call parliaments, however briefly, in order to fund the monetary demands of his army; not until 1628, in return for four hundred thousand pounds, did he find it necessary to give way and assent to Parliament's 'Petition of Right' which listed the major grievances it held against him. Notwithstanding, he continued to govern solely by royal prerogative, relying in secular affairs upon Thomas Wentworth, later Earl of Strafford, and in church matters on the Bishop of London, William Laud, whom he elevated to primate in 1633.

Religious Controversy Reawakens: Communion Table Versus Pulpit

Laud, a bitter opponent of Puritanism, more than over-stepped Hooker in striving to reform the Church of England as truly 'catholic and reformed'. Broadminded and conciliatory in doctrinal matters, he punished all opposition to his designs on ritual and liturgy. He held that it was not through the word of God alone, but as much through sacraments mediated by the priest standing raised above the laity at the altar, that the sinful could come to salvation. This passion for religious reform expressed itself in reviving ceremonial, and rigid enforcement of proper conduct of worship, with altar-wise communion tables re-sited to east ends and fonts used for baptism and in their right places. This insistence on putting the altar rather than the pulpit at the centre of the church was what aroused the most hostility in Puritan minds.

In 1629 Laud issued a further proclamation commanding archbishops and bishops to take special care that parish churches, many having long persisted in a state of neglect, be kept in decent repair; and to make use of the ecclesiastical courts to oblige parishioners to attend to this part of their duty. Rough drafts survive of the findings of a visitation of Buckinghamshire parish churches made in 1637 under the direction of JOHN WILLIAMS Bishop of Lincoln. The following are extracts from the report on Fingest, unmistakably Laudian in tone (Robert Gibbs, 1888, Rec. Bucks, vol. vi, p.247):

Fingestre: Church and chancel in decay in the foun-dation [...] the rails to be set a foot nigher to the Comm. Table [...] [to provide] a new Table; the seats on the S. side of the chancel to be made like them on the N: the chancel wants tiling and ceiling

246

> as the church is ceiled [...] the chancel wants sentencing [...] the boards upon the partition to be taken off, the uppermost lath on the S. side of the church 2 feet lower and also the seat on the N. side; the W. window in the belfry, and one window on the N. side partly dammed up [...] a new chalice and flaggon to be procured also; a cushion, pulpit-cloth and Altar carpet, all to be suitable, of green cloth and fringed, with tassels to the cushion; the partn. to be taken down, and the King's Arms to be set in a frame over the place where the partition is [...] 10 Commdts. to be set over the Com. Tab. The Service Book which is now in the church the year of the impression it seems was 1620 [...] no hood [...]

As rector in office, Christopher Edwards had both the will and, it seems, the means to respond to Laud's faultings of the nonconformist arrangements in Fingest church, and to see that his flock responded likewise. According to the epitaph Browne Willis saw on his tombstone in the church (turn back to Chapter VIII) – 'an Ordinary stone with a brass plate' – he proved 'a benefactor both to the parsonage House and chancel'. (Sadly, Lipscomb in 1847 in his *History and Antiquities of the County of Buckingham* writes that 'the stone has long been destroyed'.)

As well as correcting the church's dilapidations listed in Bishop William's report, putting right the chancel meant re-siting and re-railing the altar at its proper position under the east window, in the Laudian manner. 'Decay in the foundations of church and chancel' called for structural repair work, and the added courses of brick which, as the discerning reader will remember, we found built into the base of the south wall of the nave, show that the parishioners did their duty here. As to the chancel, the rector saw to it that the footings of its south wall were shored up to strengthen the fifteenth century rebuilding work when the old lancet windows were replaced with square-headed 'transitional' ones and the 'low-side' window was blocked out.

In the case of the parsonage house, Edwards's bene-faction was to enlarge it. It had been first built as a small, timber-framed, L-shaped hall-house with a kitchen and buttery having two pitch-roofed rooms over, and on its north side a hall with vents in its timbered roof for smoke to escape. The new rector built a second brick fireplace and flue in the hall, backing its fellow in the kitchen, and added a chamber with its own fireplace on the hall's north side. To both chamber and hall he put beamed ceilings, and from the latter built a dividing staircase leading up one way to a large room with a rebuilt pitched roof over the hall and chamber, and the other back to the older small rooms over the kitchen and buttery. These alterations expanded the hall end of the old parsonage into a two-storey four-bay wing; this done, it was faced with Flemish-bond part-glazed brickwork with wood-framed ground floor sashed win-dows. The parsonage house thus took on the appearance it has today as The Old Rectory.

Parson Edwards's family

Edwards certainly needed a larger house, for his wife Anne bore him ten children in the parsonage between 1610 and 1628, six girls and four boys. As for all infants born in the parish, he recorded the dates of his own children's baptisms in the church's register book he started; rather touchingly, for each of them he added notes as to the day and hour of their birth. For example, against the 1610 entry for his firstborn, John, he writes 'was baptized March 11, borne the Thursday before at 2 of the clock in the morning'; and for his tenth, Elizabeth, in 1628 'was baptized ffebruary

15th and borne the Saturday sennight before about 4 of the clock in the afternoon of the 7th day of the same month'. Perhaps unusually for the times, he noted in the burial register only one infant death among his children, that of Anne, baptised on 3rd February, 1621 and buried on 18th March, 1622. A second daughter Anne survived.

The Civil War

During these later years of his rectorship when Christopher Edwards was engaged in family, parish and church affairs at Fingest, in the country at large the King with Strafford's backing was persisting in his non-Parliamentary impositions, not least the infamous 'ship money', and Convocation was passing further canons tightening the bonds between King and church and furthering the schemes of Laud's party. By 1640 Charles had become intent on using military force to reverse Laud's failure to impose episcopalian reforms on the Presbyterian Kirk of Scotland; but in the resulting 'Bishops' War' it was English troops that suffered reverses, and Charles found himself facing an invading army of Scottish Covenanters in the north, which took Newcastle with ease. For their withdrawal the Covenanters demanded a harsh treaty, the humiliating terms of which Charles had to agree – including paying eight hundred and fifty pounds to the Scots each day they remained on English soil. Again debt forced him to recall a Parliament that by now was mostly Presbyterian nonconformist in religion and stubbornly opposed to him in government; it became 'The Long Parliament'.

Among this Parliament's first acts was the impeachment of Strafford and Laud, both later executed under bills of attainder, real evidence of treason being lacking. In May 1641, with all London approving, the 'Root and Branch'

Bill abolishing bishops in the English Church was brought before the Commons. By November it was presenting Charles with its 'Grand Remonstrance' reciting all his acts of tyranny and misgovernment.

His response was to enter the House forcibly and take the Speaker's chair, intending himself to impeach Pym, Hampden and their friends on a charge of treason – only to find 'my birds flown'. In January 1642 he left London, not to return until his trial and execution six years later.

Meanwhile, a breach was now irreparable between royalists loyal to civil government by the King and Church government by the bishops, and a militant Puritan Parliament dedicated to overthrowing the existing Church. In August, confident of support from well-equipped royalist troops, Charles appealed to arms, raising his standard at Nottingham.

Royalists Against Parliament Men

The royalists came off best in the initial skirmishes and battles. In the Thames valley, for example, royalist troops under Prince Rupert seized and looted Bulstrode Whitelocke's house and estate at Fawley; and at the Battle of Chalgrove Field, Parliament's forces could only mourn the loss of John Hampden, carried mortally wounded to Thame where he died in the hands of a surgeon named Delafield (of the same family as our Thomas).

The tide began to turn with Oliver Cromwell's victory at Marston Moor in 1644 where he demonstrated that his 'Ironsides', countrymen he had mustered and trained himself, were capable of halting and destroying royalist forces, however equipped. Then at Naseby in 1645 his New Model Army again broke the royalist charge and swept away the royalist foot; and in 1646 the fall of Charles's headquarters at Oxford spelt defeat and surrender. He chose to give himself up to the Scottish army, though when the Commons had paid off the treaty arrears, the Scots gave him into Parliament's hands.

The De-Laudification of Parish Religion

On the religious front, meanwhile, Parliament had passed an ordinance abolishing the Book of Common Prayer and ordering its replacement in churches everywhere by the Presbyterian Directory of Worship. In 1644 a 'Solemn League and Covenant' against 'popery', along Scottish Presbyterian lines, became law. Taking sole charge of government now, and assuming a supreme voice in Church affairs, Parliament in 1646 with The Lords' approval finally passed an ordinance positively imposing the Presbyterian religion throughout the country.

The gist of what all this meant for parishes generally is manifest when we examine the Fingest parish register for the times, which, luckily for our purpose has survived. Up to and partly into 1647, the year he died, Christopher Edwards, in his educated italic hand, meticulously entered every baptism, marriage and burial he conducted in his parish. His last entry was a baptism on 11th April, 1647 of 'Elizabeth, daughter of John Deane the younger and Mary'. His mode of keeping the register shows little influence of the Directory of Worship, for until the last he enters infants as 'baptized'. As we know from Browne Willis (*Willis MS*, vol. x, p.21), he died on 10th July and was buried in the church beneath an ordinary gravestone with a brass plate (provided by his wife?) under the south wall of the chancel within the altar rails.

During his last illness the proper upkeep of the register was abruptly abandoned; not even his burial was entered, and we only know when he died from Browne Willis's account of his epitaph. Thereafter the register mutely demonstrates the turmoil of Presbyterian parish government. From 1647 to 1653 there are no entries for baptisms, marriages or burials – save for two which speak for themselves:

Anno 1647

November 1st John Deane sonne of George Deane & Mary was borne

Anno 1650

November 20th Robert Deane sonne of George & Mary was borne

> Witness thereto. Mary wife of George Deane
> Thomazin wife of John Turner

These are again in educated italic script, but by another hand, which comparison with later post-Restoration entries identifies as that of John Richardson, the intended next rector. As had become usual, he was appointed by a prebendary at distant Wells (John Young BD), but was to find himself, an episcopalian Anglican, *persona non grata* at Fingest. That a 'sequestered' cleric such as he thereafter managed to enter any names, we may well wonder. At any rate, both infants being from one family (incidentally, that of Edward's last entry), the parents, solid Fingest folk, managed to get access to a register otherwise lacking contemporary entries, and Richardson obliged. However, conforming to a Parliamentary ruling that dates of birth rather than dates of baptism be registered, he wrote 'was borne' rather than 'was baptized', and in the 1650 entry even added names of witnesses.

Parson Richardson's Excursions During the Protectorate

The parish register has no further Richardson entries until 1659 when he was again the recognised incumbent. As to what he had to endure in the intervening years, there are clues to be found in *Walker Revised*. This is A.G. Matthews's 1948 Clarendon Press editing of John Walker's assembly of clerical histories, *The Suffering of the Clergy*, published in 1714. Walker called it *An attempt towards recovering an Account of the numbers and Sufferings of the Clergy of the Church of England, Heads of Colleges, Fellows, Scholars etc. who were sequestered, Harrass'd etc. in the late Times of the Grand Rebellion.* Of three Richardsons matching this designation, Walker identifies John Richardson 'rector of Fingest, Bucks 1657'. If true, this implies his sequestration elsewhere had by then ended. (In honesty though, acceptable as we may find the account of Richardson's movements that follows, a note of caution here. Walker's precise words in the foregoing are 'John Richardson or *namesake* R. of Fingest 1657' (author's italics). The reader must judge whether or not, for our purposes, the italicised word materially alters matters.)

Describing Richardson's 'sufferings' in the years before 1657, Walker says that he was inducted rector of Nether Heyford on 7th March, 1646, when he was violently assaulted, though he later (8th November, 1646) came into residence to take the place of Thomas Cole MA, rector there since 1600, who had been ejected by the Puritans. According to Walker, the next year Richardson himself was ejected, 'T. Butler' taking possession at Nether Heyford in September 1647.

This gives us a date that fits rather well with our John Richardson's becoming available in November 1647 in or near Fingest to register the first of the two births mentioned above.

He can scarcely have lived in the newly furbished parsonage house, however, for the government's Committee of Plundered Ministers seems to have sequestered him forthwith, whether as 'malignant', 'scandalous' or 'insufficient' we cannot tell; in any case they put in his place at Fingest William Reeves, a Presbyterian minister whom Anglican eyes would have seen as an 'intruder'.

William Reeves's Ministry at Fingest

Reeves supplanted Richardson in the living on 14th August, 1647, within a month of Edwards's death. We know this, and his subsequent history, from an entry under Reeves's name in *Calamy Revised*, A.G. Matthews's 1934 Clarendon Press editing of Chapter 9 of Edmund Calamy's *Abridgement of Baxter's History* which is subtitled *A Particular Account of the Ministers, Lecturers, Fellows of Colleges etc., who were silenced and ejected by the Act of Uniformity*. The Act in question was that of 1662. Richard Baxter was a seventeenth century Puritan divine and Edmund Calamy, writing in 1702, was a historian of Nonconformity.

Again, what Calamy tells us of Reeves fits with Walker's account of Richardson. He says that on 25th May, 1654, the Committee for Plundered Ministers appointed Reeves vicar of Wraysbury, Bucks (anciently Wyrardisbury), and that on 3rd October, 1656, he received in that parish the 'composition of first-fruits' which established him in full and lawful possession of the living. We may take it then that by 1657 Reeves had left Fingest; and it is likely that with the expiry of enforced puritanism imminent, Richardson at last (and thankfully, no doubt) felt able to take up the advowson Wells prebendary had bestowed on him ten years before. That he had benefited at all from an Act of 1657 which laid down that ejected ministers were entitled to an allowance of one-fifth of the profits of the living is unlikely.

It was not until 1660 that as rector Richardson resumed writing regular entries in the Fingest parish register. In the intervening decade, after a gap of four to five years, we find registrations in the irregular hands of lay scribes, the Parish Registers. The last of such entries were for 1660:

> Mar 7 Chrestofor Willcokes the sonne of ffrances buried
> Mar 14 Elizabeth Plomeredg wife of John Plomeredg buried

These overlapped John Richardson's first attempt at registration on his reinstatement as rector, again in his regular italic hand, but – to make his anti-Puritan point – in Latin:

> 1659
> *Aprill 11th Katharine Rockhall fil: Gulielmi Rockhall et Susannae uxoris ejus. bapt: fuit.*

The Parish Register's antepenultimate 1659 entries include two – one glad, one sad – for the Richardson family:

> William Brocker husbandman sonne of Edithe Goodspede in the parish of Stoak Talmage in the county of Oxon: and Alicia Richardson daughter of Mr John Richardson minester of ffingest in the county of Bucks maried the 31 October

and

> Martha Richenson daughter Mr Richenson minester buried ffebuary the 8 1659

At the Restoration in 1660 Reeves as a Puritan was ejected from the Wraysbury living, but he remained an inveterate preacher. *Calamy Revised* says that after his ejection: 'he preached nowhere statedly but here and there occasionally, and pretty much at Abingdon. He was once much troubled on occasion of a Charge of Treasonable Words, sworn upon him in a sermon he preached on Psalm 2, 1. But upon a Tryal be was Acquitted. He dyed Anno 1683.'

'Political Independents' and Oliver Cromwell

We shelve now consideration of what happened in minister Reeves's brief office at Fingest and, for the moment, our perusal of the confused state of the parish register that resulted. We turn instead to what had been going on meanwhile in the rest of the country.

The Civil War over, a split inherent in Puritan ranks became politically divisive. Parliament's victory had indeed limited the despotic power of the King, but at the cost to the country of much violence and radicalism. There began to be obvious among the nobility, gentry and settled persons a reaction against being brought under the political power of Presbyterian elders and ministers. In accord with a general nostalgic desire for pre-war stability and the conclusion of a treaty with the King, the Long Parliament aimed to resolve matters on its own terms though with no thought as yet of doing away with the monarchy. The army's pay being heavily in arrears, it was also planned to alleviate the tax burden that maintenance of so large an army was imposing by rapidly reducing it in size, putting Parliament's own generals in charge of the remaining force.

The Independent Puritans under Cromwell thought differently. In matters religious they opposed Presbyterianism, holding that each church congregation had the right to decide its own form of worship. Various sects proliferated – Particular Baptists, Muggletonians, Ranters, Quakers and a dozen others – each differing in theological standpoint but all cherishing a Puritan belief that God worked through the individual, not the priest.

It was the army's very successes under Oliver Cromwell that brought Independents to the fore. Disillusioned with Parliament's failure to establish a 'godly reformation', and in sympathy with the 'Levellers' of London, they looked for support to an army now of radical opinion and in mutinous mood at Parliament's neglect to satisfy its outstanding pay demands. In June 1647 the army's Cornet Joyce seized the King from his Parliamentary guards, and delivered him to Hampton Court as a prisoner, though well-lodged. The army's plan was, with the Independents, to force Charles to agree to the radical terms they both shared.

In August the army marched on and occupied London. In November Charles escaped (with Cromwell's connivance?). Hoping to play off Presbyterians against Independents he began intriguing with conservative factions in Scotland to promote a joint rising of Royalists and Presbyterians against northern England. In 1648 a second smaller Civil War was the result. With his New Model Army, Cromwell pushed back the Scots and proceeded to route them on their own soil; his commanders likewise suppressed pro-Royalist stirrings in Cornwall and South Wales.

Nevertheless, a critical divergence was now evident between Cromwell's army and the Parliamentarians, the army calling for a purge of Parliament and trial of the King as 'the capital and grand author of all our troubles', while Parliament still wanted to discuss possible treaties with him. Matters came to a head on 2nd December, 1648, when the army entered Whitehall for the second time. On the 6th, Colonel Pride and Lord Grey, standing at the door of the Commons, forcibly excluded one hundred and ten Presbyterian MPs, about two hundred and sixty others withdrawing 'voluntarily'. The purged remainder, the Rump – part Independent, part pro-army and part republican – held fierce debate which ended with Cromwell declaring further bargaining with the King useless. It was voted Charles be brought to trial 'for treason against Parliament'. On 20th January, 1649, sitting in Westminster Hall, a 'High Court of Justice' – not the Peers nor the Commons, but a revolutionary tribunal of sixty-nine members – tried Charles. A martyr to his belief in royal paramountcy, he conducted himself with calm courage and dignity throughout, as he did when he faced execution in Whitehall on 30th January.

The Rump, the Barebones Assembly and the Commonwealth Parliaments

In February 1649 the Parliamentary Rump abolished the House of Lords and appointed as Council of State a military junta headed by Cromwell. Making no appeal of any sort to popular consent – much like the king it had murdered – it passed an act declaring itself the sole source of power and the people of England to be a Commonwealth.

As to constitutional reform, apart from re-codifying the language of the law courts from mediaeval Latin into more intelligible English, for the next four years the Rump talked a lot but did little. It made a half-hearted order that everyone must attend a place of worship, and in churches replaced the Royal Arms with its own. Paying the arrears and regular wages of the army, it ensured for Cromwell the well-disciplined force he forthwith cruelly used in Ireland to suppress Catholic rebellion in favour of Stuart restoration. In Scotland, meanwhile, the King's son, Charles Stuart, had signed the Covenant in order to get the

Scottish crown, but in 1650 a Scottish force backing him was routed at Dunbar by Cromwell. At Worcester the next year an invading Scottish army led by the young Charles, newly crowned at Scone, was again utterly defeated. Charles escaped, via the Boscobel Oak Tree and Brighton, to Normandy.

Republicanism Under the Protectorate

In April 1653, having pledged precisely the opposite, the Rump voted to prolong itself – its last act, for an infuriated Cromwell forthwith dissolved it, emphasising the point by physically removing the Mace. Three months later he announced his new republican constitution to an unelected assembly of his own nominees – the 'Barebones Parliament' – sitting in St Stephen's Chapel of all places[1].

In the remaining years of his constitutional experiment Cromwell unquestionably proved an able ruler of England and Scotland. His navy under Blake took supremacy of the sea from the Dutch and launched England as a world trading power. But in trying to achieve the 'godly-reformation' he had always desired he perforce mixed a degree of religious toleration – excepting papists and 'delinquents' – with autocratic government under his regional major-generals. In 1654, by general acclaim now titled 'Lord Protector', he opened the first elected republican parliament. By 1657 the next Protectorate parliament was presenting him with a second constitutional instrument, the 'Humble Petition and Advice', superseding the first. As well as restoring the House of Lords, it authorised the Speaker to offer the Protector the title of

---

1 Properly, 'Barebone's' for its most frequent speaker was a merchant whose Puritanic parents had named him 'Praise-God Barbon'.

'King'. Hesitating, Cromwell at length refused – haunted, no doubt, by a spectre of the headless Charles. The next year he died, to be buried in Westminster Abbey after a grand lying in state with crown, orb and sceptre on his breast. But his republican revolution had failed, and his son Richard lasted only eight months in his father's shoes. In 1660 a Convention Parliament, nominated by the Rump and surviving members of the Long Parliament, invited Charles II to return to his inheritance.

Meanwhile, in the Parish…

The earliest surviving Fingest register runs from 1607 to 1671, the entries written on parchment sheets and paper pages, mostly on both sides and often in two columns per page to save space. The various loose leaves were probably kept as such, and it was not until 1773 that they were bound together in vellum to make a slim book tied with tapes. In its fourteen pages sequence and continuity were much confused, part reading from front to back, part reversed and part reading back to front. Disorder is especially marked in the Commonwealth years, where the reader finds half-pages seemingly cut out, and whole pages apparently missing. Whether this is due to haphazard assembly in binding, or to deliberate expunging at the time, it is hard to be certain, but most of the 1647–53 gaps appear to speak more of omission than commission. It is a puzzle, though, to account for the following on a quarter-page (the rest evidently cut out or cut off) bound in immediately after Edwards's last (1647) entry, and registering unsigned in a different, secretary hand, a marriage in a different county:

Marriages Anno Dom 1649
William Gregory of Wattleton in the county of Oxon
and Christian Yewstace of Pirton in the same county,
were maryed the one and twentieth day of June

This marriage registration antedates the Barebones Assembly enactment of 24th August, 1553, that took away from ministers not only custody of the registers but also their authority to solemnise marriage, which was entrusted to the justices. Accordingly, we find in the Fingest register a new page headed 'Marriages 1653' but containing only a single registration above the signature of the magistrate who wrote it:

Memorand: that the Solemnization of the Marriage between Mr Andrew Hunt and Mrs Maria fferrers als Turner was this Ninth day of Januarie 1653 according to the Tend^{ce} of the Act of Parliam^t touching Marriages, was done before me
Robt Aldridge

('January 1653' here is old style, and hence after August 1653.)

The Barebones Assembly also enacted that the registration of births, marriages and deaths, and the custody of the register, should be undertaken by a new secular official, the parish register appointed by the justices and already mentioned. Sure enough, in the Fingest book we find (as noted above) registrations from October 1653 to April 1659 entered in a lay and cruder hand, with some confusion of dates. Over these years the writing though aspiring generally to a sort of Chancery hand is probably that of different persons acting as parish register; some used ruled lines to help inscription, while some verged on illiteracy. Since a fee of one shilling was legally chargeable for each registration, it is not surprising that compared with decades before and after, significantly fewer Fingest births, marriages and burials achieved registration in the parish book between 1651 and 1660.

The Ferrers Family Rent the Manor

We have seen (Chapter XVI) that in 1572 the prebendaries at Wells, with the cathedral chapter's approval, began leasing the manor of Fingest for an eighteen pound rent, the first tenant being a no doubt respectable cleric, the Register of the Archdeacon of Berkshire. In 1590, three years before this first tenancy expired and again with the chapter acquiescing, prebendary Whitelocke found a new tenant, a layman prepared to pay a twenty pounds rent, with 26s and 8d to the Master of the Fabric of Wells cathedral. As we know, this was Michael Farrar, alias Turner, yeoman of Great Marlow. The new lease was confirmed in 1598 by the Wells Bishop and chapter, a chapter member endorsing Turner as 'the tennant who hath spent his tyme and welth in the mayntenance of the right of our church to that prebend' (*Wells Chapter Library, Ledger F, fol. 154d, p.336*).

The 1598 confirmation of the lease, dropping 'yeoman', describes the tenant as 'Michael Farrar alias Turner of Fingest, gent.' and the manor as leased 'with all appurtenances'. We do not know if this Michael was still alive when the lease ran out in 1619, but whether he died before or after this he was not buried in Fingest churchyard, nor back in Marlow.

The next we hear of the Ferrers is that on 1st October, 1634, 'An indenture of the manor of Tingeherst alias Fingest co. Bucks, made by Dr Young to William Ferrar alias Turner of Cookeham co. Berks, for three lives, was ordered to be confirmed under the common or chapter seal' (*Calendar of MSS of Dean and Chapter of Wells, HMC*

1914, vol. ii, p.409). Dr John Young BD was Fingest prebendary at the time.

Fingest Manor: the Parliamentary Survey of 1650

William Ferrar of Cookham was probably either Michael's son, or his grandson. More about him emerges from a document (reference DD/CC 114098) in the Archives of the Somerset Record Office, a copy of which the County Archivist kindly sent me. It is a Parliamentary survey of the prebendal manor of Fingest that was taken in August 1650 by virtue of a Commission 'grounded upon an Act of the Comons of England assembled in Parliament for the abolishinge of deanes, deanes and chapters, Cannons Prebends and other Offices and Tytles of or belonging to any Cathedral or Collegiate Church or Chappell [.]' It describes (see below) the 'Mannor house' and the 'Warren house' (today called 'Manor Farm') and the lands going with them both, detailing for every field ('close') and wood a name, location and precise acreage. It also gives to a penny the annual quit-rents due, the rent rolls of freeholders and copyholders, all named; and the monies due from rents of Assize, court Silver, and courts Baron and Leet, the manor's whole annual worth adding up to £99.1s.10d.

Although the commissioners' survey does not explicitly say so, its evident purpose was the appropriation to Parliament of the manor's rent, although leaving its annual worth (at any rate for the time being) in the hands of the sitting tenant. A memorandum appended to the survey holds that the advowson of the parish church 'belongeth to the lord of the manor' – presumably the current tenant, not, as before, the Wells prebendary. It values the parsonage as worth forty pounds and notes that 'the present incumbent is Mr Willm Reeve'.

The Ferrers as Lords of the Manor

To their survey the commissioners usefully added a copy of the 1634 indenture of the manor by Dr Young for a twenty-two pound rent, with the conditions attached thereto. The indenture document tells more still of William Ferrar alias Turner. It is dated 27th March, 1634, in the tenth year of King Charles, and states that the manor was demised to William to hold for the several lives of himself, Thomasine his wife and Thomas, eldest son of Thomas Ferrar alias Turner of Lye alias Lee, Bucks, gentleman (Lee is in the neighbourhood of Great Missenden). Summarising, the commissioners note that in 1650 'two of the foresaid lives are in being viz.: Thomasine and Thomas and in the text they have written above Thomasine a small '55' and above Thomas '18' – presumably their respective ages then.

What then can we infer about the relationship of the eighteen year old Thomas to the William who rented the manor in 1634? The best I can suggest is: William, looking to the family's future hold on the Manor, named as the third life in the indenture not his son Thomas of Lee, but his grandson, another Thomas, who in 1634 was two years old. William must have died at Fingest quite soon afterwards, though the Parish Register at the time made no record of this or his burial. Thomas the elder, taking over his brother's tenancy, moved into the manor. The Ferrers' tenancy for three generations (at least) had by 1646 established him 'Lord of the Manor', as the inscription on his gravestone in the church confirms. His son Thomas held the lease in 1656 (*Feet of Fines*, Bucks, Mich., 1656), and a later Ferrers was holding the manor as late as 1737 (Lysons, *Magna Britannica*, vol. i(3), p.563). Meanwhile various Ferrers family baptisms, marriages and burials appear through the parish register for the intervening years.

Robert Gibbs in his *Worthies of Buckinghamshire* (1886) noting the name as connected with Fingest says that after the Conquest Henry de Ferrers, one of the compilers of the Domesday Survey, held Grendon Underwood (and two hundred and ten other manors) only for William de Ferrers to forfeit it in Richard I's time. The connection with the Fingest Ferrers seems exceedingly slim, the more so as the alias Turner was early dropped.

The Manor House and Lands in 1650

We get a good idea of the old Fingest Manor house as it then stood from its description in the Parliamentary survey:

> All that Capitall Messuage or Tenement commonly called the Mannour house with the Scite thereof, consistinge of a Hall a Parlour a Kitchen a Larder a Buttery a Celler, a milke house and ffive Chambers, Two Barnes, one Stable, one hay house and other outhouses, Two gardens, one orchard Two ffold yards and one Courtyard together with one little plot of ground called Greene garden (lyinge behynd one of the Barnes aforesaid) in all containing by estimacon ii Acres more or lesse.

Clearly, with its twelve rooms, including a dairy and a no doubt extensive cellar, it was by far the most sizeable house in the village; writing two hundred years later Lipscomb, in his *History of the County of Buckingham* calls it a 'plain old mansion'.

Apart from its deep well (until recently still in use) no trace of the old manor house is to be seen today, even on aerial photography. Its 'scite' is planted with conifers, and the new manor house built in the 1930s is fifty yards or more to the west. Nevertheless, it is likely that the cellars of the old house are still there to be explored, were present or future owners interested.

The old house itself, then – give or take additions and repairs – had by 1650 stoutly withstood the passage of mediaeval centuries. As to the manor's land, the reader will recall that just after the Conquest the manorial boundaries enclosed something like one thousand three hundred acres; so at first sight it is surprising that according to the survey the calculated extent of the manor's, closes and woods, including those of the 'warren house', had by 1650 shrunk to no more than two hundred and twenty-eight acres. It is plain however that then or later, the Ferrers may scarcely be classed as landed gentry, lords of the manor or not.

What we know of the manor's history in the intervening years explains a good deal of the discrepancy. Repeated demands on the value of their Fingest Manor estate were made by its fourteenth century episcopal lords, not least Bishops Burghersh, Gynwell and Buckingham. One after the other their bailiffs, managing the manor in the face of social disturbances resulting from park-making, and the Black Death, and after that the Peasants' Revolt, had no alternative but to meet episcopal claims by piecemeal sellings-off of arable plots to villeins then increasingly eager to cast off manorial shackles and become independent farmers. The absence of large open fields divided into strips in Chiltern valley husbandry encouraged this development, and at Fingest Manor this was especially the case at Bolter End and the north-east hamlets furthest from the manor house and the church.

Cadmore End

In a different category, however, was the hamlet of Cadmore End. By the thirteenth century the Scaccarios had added it, with the moorland around it, to the Abbefeld tenement in Lewknor parish they held by serjeanty of their exchequer office, knowing the long-established good arable land it contained (G.R. Elvey, Buckinghamshire in 1086, Rec. Bucks, vol. xvi, p.342). When he died in 1292 Simon de Scaccario held land in Cadmore End of the Bishop of Lincoln, the lord of Fingest Manor (Chapter IX again); so it seems the Scaccarios of Exchequers Manor (later Chequers Manor) in 'Little Abbefeld in Stokenchurch' still laid claim across the county border to Cadmore End land, later spoken for by 'Roger of Cademer' at the *Nonarum Inquistiones* of 1341.

By the Reformation, and, perhaps because of it, this same land had come into the possession of Thomas Umpton, gentleman, he who was named in Wolsey's 1522 muster roll for Fingest (see Chapter XV). The first mention to be found of Cadmore End 'Manor' is in its court rolls of the sixteenth century which recorded that Sir Edward Unton held it. The grandson of Thomas Umpton, he was knighted at the coronation of Elizabeth, and married in 1555 Anne, Countess of Warwick, the daughter of Edward Seymour, the egregious Duke of Somerset. This was her second marriage; her first, to Viscount Lisle son of the Duke of Northumberland – an attempt to bring together the houses of their two ducal fathers – had been a disastrous failure.

Manorial rolls from 1584 onwards (Oxford County Archives) show that Sir Edward held courts baron regularly at Aston Rowant and Chequers Manors. His wife's father had held Fingest for a while before exchanging it as prebend for a Wells parish, and this may have given him the notion of holding another court baron at Cadmore End 'Manor', thus distinguishing it from Fingest Manor and excluding its land from his father-in-law's exchange arrangement with Wells.

Sir Edward Unton died in 1582, and in his will directed that:

> my sonne Edwarde Unton shall have [...] the Mannour of Aston Rowant, and the mannor of Exchequer and my lands and tenements at Chisbecke and Cadmore End [...]

A glance at Figs. 15 and 16 (Chapter IX) makes it clear that at the time the Unton manors and lands mentioned were all thought of as in Oxfordshire, i.e. Exchequer Manor in the Little Abbefeld-in-Stokenchurch extension of Aston Rowant, Cadmore End in Lewknor Uphill, and Chisbecke (Chisbridge Cross) in Ackhamstead, the detached portion of Lewknor Uphill. Evidently 'Cadmore End' straddled from Oxon into Bucks with little regard for the county boundary.

This persisted thereafter when Exchequers Manor was alienated, via Unton family connections (J.G. Nichols, *The Unton Inventories*, p.xlv). With 'Cadmore End' it descended into the Tipping and Wroughton families (*Recov. R. East. 9 Geo. 1, m. 61, Mich. 30 Geo II, m. 47*). A Bartholomew Tipping held Exchequers (Chequers) Manor early in the seventeenth century, and was buried in the church at Stokenchurch. As schoolmaster there from 1725 Delafield saw Bartholomew Tipping's gravestone, five generations of Tippings having by then followed this first Bartholomew. Delafield says, that 'while the Family resided at Chequers there was a large capacious mansion place yet remembered, with a domestick Chappel lately demolished [...] in the yard adjoining to the present Farm House'. He adds with a sigh, 'But what is it that time will not bring to Desolation!'

Cadmore End Manor

Manorial rolls of 1613 onward in Oxford County Archives (Mis. Far. 1/4, T, 10) and 1641 and 1667 in Bucks County Archives (D/BASM 28A) name Bartholomew Tipping as the lord holding views of frankpledge and courts baron at both Exchequers Manor and Cadmore End Manor. The 1647 and 1667 rolls affirm that half of Fingest Lane (lengthways, evidently) with its trees belongs to Cadmore End Manor, and that the latter's tenants have a right to common pasturage for all their cattle on Bolter End Common as far as the adjacent land of Lane End.

The Tippings' rights hereabouts persisted up to and beyond 1839 when the 'Commutation of Tithes' lists were made. These show that in Fingest parish, though Cadmore End hamlet itself was by then in other hands, two hundred and thirty-five acres around it were still in the possession of a Tippings relative, Mrs Mary Ann Wroughton.

Not until 1844 did Oxfordshire relinquish the lands of Lewknor Uphill (Studdridge, Cadmore End and Ackhamstead) to Buckinghamshire. Then in 1855 Cadmore End was detached from Fingest parish to form with parts of Lewknor and Stokenchurch a separate consolidated chapel (Fig. 18), the extent of which mimics the Exchequers Manor–Cadmore End territory claimed by the Untons in the sixteenth century. The question where Cadmore End manor house was remains unanswered.

The twelve jury members sworn in at the manorial court were free tenants of Cadmore End Manor and are named in each roll. Most of the names appear again and again in the Fingest parish registers of the next hundred years and more. Though holding a manor court, Cadmore End had no church and was not a separate parish, so that free tenants of the manor, and the families of Bolter End and Cadmore End were still Fingest parishioners. As such they had no choice but the long walk down to and back from services at St Bartholomew's in Fingest; and their names and those of their descendants found their way into its register as baptised, married or buried there. For their dead, a bier would have been needed to carry the coffins over the long stony lane to the church and the churchyard. (At Radnage church, where many parishioners had a similar distance to cover for funerals, such a bier is still to be seen.)

A Village Green

Country parishes often had, or still have, a village green; but in Fingest's case the question that has puzzled us from the outset is – where?

We have already seen that from post-Conquest times the majority of Fingest's parishioners were soon to be found inhabiting the Cadmore End part of the parish, and from what Browne Willis writes (*Willis MS,* vol. xciv, p.78) it seems they became accustomed to using common land there for their green. Describing Fingest parish, he says: 'Here is in the extremity of the parish next Oxfordshire on the Sunday or Monday after St Bartholomew's a sort of a Fair or Revell called Cadmore End Fair'. He adds: 'This acct. sent me in 1739 by the Revd Mr Delafield curate of Thinghurst and schoolmaster of Stokenchurch'.

This leaves us to guess just where the 'fair or revell' might have been held. Cadmore End Common, perhaps, or Bolter End Common? Sadly, we cannot now tell; whichever it was, it is not difficult to imagine the general merrymaking and frolics that broke out there in celebration of the end of the Puritanical gloom of the Commonwealth and in expectation of a revival of religious tolerance; though hardly was the Restoration established than this proved to be out of the question.

Chapter XVIII
The Seven Bishops:
The 'Glorious Revolution'
(1660–1689)

Restored to the throne, Charles II prudently made no attempt to revive all the royal prerogatives formerly accepted without question; he relinquished the holding of land in chivalry, of courts and councils under royal control such as the Star Chamber, the High Commission, the Court of Wards and of the Regional Councils of the North and the Welsh marches. His sympathy for Catholicism and his Stuart conviction of his divine right did not prevent him, in matters of religious policy that had been central to the Civil War, sharing the hopes of the Convention Parliament that had restored him; both King and Parliament looked for peaceful reconciliation between Episcopalians and Presbyterians. But the gentry and the bishops had learnt to hate Puritan power, and the zeal of the 'Cavalier Parliament' of 1662 swept away all hopes of compromise in a tide of loyalty to King and Church – the Church of England. Bishops returned to their sees and ejected Episcopalian clergy entered again into their livings; Parson Richardson thought fit to return to Fingest a year before the Coronation.

A harsh blow to the Puritans was a new Act of Uniformity of Public Prayers enforcing use of the 1662 Book of

Common Prayer – amended by a revived Convocation – in all public worship, and the public assent of every minister of the Church to all that was contained in it. Under the Act none but episcopal ordination was valid, and all clergy, professors, heads of colleges, schoolmasters and tutors had to sign a declaration abhorring all claims to armed resistance to the King. Failure to comply by St Bartholomew's Day, 24th August, 1662, meant ministers being deprived of their livings, and if they preached thereafter being liable to three months' imprisonment – a penalty William Reeves apparently escaped.

The number of ministers ejected totalled one thousand seven hundred and sixty, according to *Calamy Revisited* (A.G. Matthews, Oxford Clarendon Press, 1933). In Bucks, twenty-nine ministers were ejected, one afterwards conforming. John Richardson was clearly not of their number. On resuming his rectory one of his first acts was to set about restoring the integrity of the churchyard, naming in the parish register parishioners obliged 'to make the churchyard mounds' – that is to make good the hedging, fencing and walls. On 2nd February, 1659, he listed twenty-seven of them, with the 'poles' and 'panes' of repair expected of each. (A pole is five and a half yards, but a pane merely 'a length of wall or fence'.) He himself as parson was to make good the gate (the only one mentioned in the list) in the east wall of the churchyard opposite the parsonage house. The listed parishioners include 'Mr Ferrers, Mr John Ferrers' and 'Mr Bartholomew Tipping' the three meriting, it seems, a 'Mr'.

Parson Richardson's Last Years

At the Restoration all acts and injunctions of the Interregnum were repealed. Accredited patronage of churches was recognised again and in 1660 Canon John

Piers, restored to the Wells chapter, resumed prebendary right to the advowson of the Fingest living and confirmed John Richardson as rector. The see of Lincoln regained a bishop, and the bishop his former rights of institution and induction. Newly appointed, ROBERT SANDERSON in July 1662 made his primary episcopal visitation to the archdeaconry of Buckingham, with the purpose of setting to right deplorable parish backslidings under Presbyterian rule. The Vicar General, Sir Edward Lake, was bishop's registrar and delivered to each deanery Articles of Enquiry which the churchwardens of each parish were required to study; in due course they had to make appropriate presentments at the Registrar's visitation. The Fingest churchwardens' presentments as agreed with and inscribed by the Registrar's clerk are in the Bodleian Library (*MS 'Archdeaconry Papers Bucks' c. 292, fol. 146*); with the rest of the Bucks county parish presentments they are to be found in *Buckinghamshire Dissent and Parish Life* (ed. J. Broad, *Bucks Rec. Soc., No. 28, 1993*). The presentments, each prefixed 'p', were:

Thomas Ferrers, Jeremiah Harman, gardiani, iurati

p   our church shall be sufficiently repaired after harvest. Noe cover to the chalice. A bible of the last traslacon wanting. Wee want a new Common Prayer booke. Noe table of degrees prohibited. Noe surplice. Noe booke to register strange preachers. Noe byer, noe herse-cloth.

p   We will take care that the churchyard be better fenced.

p   our parsonage house is not much out of repair and it shall be better repaired after harvest.

p   We have noe terrier but will make one.

p Thomas Ray and Anne his wife refuse to come to publique assemblies.

4 Dec 1662 periit, renovatur in prox

p Cicely Plumridge, widow, refuseth to come to publique assemblies

4 Dec 1662 periit

p Elizabeth Keane a papist

3 Mar 1662 qu. v.m. in prox

In the margin of the clerk's manuscript are named 'John Hunt, Robert Tiler gardiani 1662'; these were churchwardens when the December and March 1663 citations were added. Whether the backsliders were summoned by the judge's apparitor we do not know, but it comes through clearly that general neglect in the Puritan interregnum years had left the church itself in a shabby and uncared-for state.

Post-Restoration: Putting to Rights the Register

As well as dealing with the visitation presentments as best he could, Richardson had to restore the parish register to proper order. He made his new entries on coarse paper sheets unlike the parchment pages formerly used, writing on them in his good italic hand, with a legibility and accuracy of spelling much lacking in the Parish Registers' preceding efforts. Closely written, he recorded baptisms, marriages and burials as they occurred, husbanding the writing space available by not listing them separately as had been the earlier custom; one or two of his baptismal recordings he got out of order.

Towards the end of 1666 his writing becomes noticeably shaky, and the secretary hand he perhaps learnt as a schoolboy becomes more evident as the register moves into the early months of 1667. These were for him, we may judge, months of increasing infirmity, as well of increasing frustration with the register. He wrote:

> Memorand. because the Register book was ill kept by them who were entrusted with it I did (after the book came into my hands) in a confused way sett downe in paper the names of those that were married baptised and buried prefering to transcribe into a new parchment booke if the parish would provide one, which they have not done, that work I leave to be done by my successor. In witnes whereof I have subscribed my name. May ye 2nd 1667. John Richardson Rector.

He was able to carry on for the next couple of months, including an entry on the burial on 16th July of Mr Thomas Ferrers, one of the churchwardens who made presentments at the visitation. His last entry was 'William Newell sonne of Christofer & Susan bap. Aug 11th'. The next entries, mostly burials, are in the hand of Joseph Allen, parish clerk; his second reads 'Mr Jon Richardson parson of fingist was buried October the 4th'. In a list of 'Fingest rectores' in one of his volumes (*Willis MS,* vol. xciv, p.77) Browne Willis says he was buried in the church. There is no mention of Richardsons thereafter in the register; perhaps he was unmarried.

Dissenters

Approbation of the Restoration was acclaimed in its first years by the countrywide return of village maypoles, fairs, Christmas festivities and church celebrations of Easter. But years of adversity and national disquiet were in store. There was a final recrudescence of the plague in 1665, with upwards of seventy-five thousand dying in London; its virulence when it spread from there is still remembered in the Peak District village of Eyam where two out of every three inhabitants were victims. Of plague in Fingest at the time we have no note, except to remark that there were eight burials of parishioners in 1665/66; in the mid-years of the two previous decades there had been no more than one or two. Next, there was the great fire of London in 1666, and in 1667 the incursion of the Dutch fleet up the Medway and the Thames – calamities, for all we can tell, that caused little disquiet in Fingest.

More likely to have damaged parish cohesion was the waning of belief in an inexorable divine imperative that could not but bring godliness to the whole English nation; some thought through a return to the 'old religion' of Hooker and Laud, though for others it was through the solifidianism of Milton and Bunyan. The Reformation had severed Church of England worshippers irretrievably from a minority, somewhat over-represented among the gentry, still obedient to the papacy. The Act of Uniformity now severed the Anglican episcopal church from the general body of Protestant churches on the Continent, whether Lutheran or Reformed Communions. Even so, many of the ejected Puritan clergy of England, especially in London and the universities, were learned and active churchmen. Despite the Cavalier Parliament's Conventicle and Five Mile Acts which were intended to crush nonconformists the Quakers, Anabaptists and other 'field conventiclers' continued to hold their meetings, often out of doors, sometimes under the cover of large trees. 'Dissenters' acquired respectability in the eyes of many in the middle and lower ranks of society, quite the opposite of Catholics who were widely seen as subversive traitors.

John Cademan, the Next Rector (1667–1713)

Presented on the advowson of Wells prebendary John Piers, John Cademan was instituted in Fingest rectory on 11th November, 1667. At first he wrote in the register only irregularly, for on his induction he found that Joseph Allen the parish clerk, had taken it over from August 1667 when Richardson became unable to carry on. Allen continued to enter baptisms and burials as the occasion demanded for the next twelve months or so, though there are no entries of marriage in his hand; indeed between July 1667 and July 1670 there are no Fingest marriages at all in the register. An ordained priest was (and still is) requisite for the legality of a church marriage; and Joseph Allen being very likely by now an old man suspicious of a new parson, villagers proposing to get married may have had to resort to the secular services of a magistrate, as they had had to in the Interregnum.

Joseph Allen's entries, in irregular handwriting and irregularly spelt, fill up most of the space remaining on the paper pages Richardson added to make up the register into a book of sorts; in the last quarter of 1668 John Cademan was only able to find space at the bottom of one to enter four burials, though on another, following the parish clerk's last entry 'Sara Wite widowe was buered July the 2nd' he added:

Joseph Allen was buryed August the 26th 1669
Alice Allen his widdowe buryed August the 29th 1669

These were the last entries he made in the register he inherited (we can almost hear, reader, his sigh of relief).

What happened to the register next John Cademan explains (in anticipation, no doubt, of an impending bishop's visitation), writing on the same page Richardson had used to record his own difficulties:

June the 17th 1672
Memorandum, that this booke was kept by
Joseph Allen: parish clerke till the time of his death wch was about St Bartholomewes tide 1669 And being unfitt to set downe the burialls: christenings and marriages in by reason of its confusion and that there was no convenient place for them left I have ever since for my own memory gott them down in my Almanacks on the daies any of them happened on purpose to transcribe them into a new Register booke as soone as one can be procured. And that since my comeing to ffingest I have maried but two couples viz Jo:Tiler of this parish & Ellenour Towne daughter of Tho:Town of Henton in the parish of Chynner and County of Oxon on the 11th day of July 1670 And Richard Plomridge and Elizabeth Rickett both of this parish on the 7th day of May 1671 both of them haveing had the Banns of matrimony lawfully published between them.

Ita teste John Cademan Rector de ffingest

As it turned out, 'a new Register booke' was far from 'soon procured'.

Cademan entered no baptisms or burials in 1670 and 1671, and thereafter there is a long gap in the parish register's continuity from 1672 to 1689. Detail of this period would be lost but for 'bishops' transcripts' which the parish clerk was obliged to make for the episcopal authorities, presumably copying from the rector's almanac notes. These transcripts survive in the Bucks County Archives, giving baptisms, marriages and burials for the missing years.

Nonconformism Still to be Routed Out

Bishop Gilbert Sheldon succeeded to the see of Canterbury in 1663 an the death of William Juxon, who had been appointed at the Restoration. Archbishop for the next fourteen years, Sheldon worked hard to restore Laudian religious principles, and to bring back nonconformists into the Church of England by making life difficult for them as dissenters. Under his instruction the Bishop of Lincoln, WILLIAM FULLER, in 1669 sent out letters to every parish in his diocese asking about local nonconformism and dissenters' meetings; the inquiry was directed at clergy, not churchwardens. John Cademan, with his rector's right to the parish's parsonage house, glebe and tithes in mind, was apprehensive at the increase in numbers of nonconformists in nearby parishes such as Turville, Bradenham and High Wycombe, and took care to demonstrate Fingest's adherence to impeccable Anglicanism in his reply to the Bishop's officer:

> Fingest
> Honoured sir, to your directions for enquiry after conventicles and conventiculars, according to my Lord's Grace of Canterbury and my Lord of Lincoln's command, I return this (though not particular yet I hope both full and welcome answer) that there is not in my parish any one person who is either a keeper or follower of such unlawful meetings, nor any house, outhouse, barne or other place therein where any such are kept, but that all the inhabitants thereof doe resort unto the church in tyme of divine service as they are by law bound. In testimony whereof I have hereto sett my hand. John Cademan, Rector of Fingest. July 3. 1669.

Sheldon's enquiry was expedient, for in 1668 the House of Commons had rejected the King's 'Bill for Comprehension' of nonconformists, and in 1670 had passed a second more stringent Conventicle Act that fined attenders at nonconformist meetings ten shillings, and preachers at such meetings twenty pounds for the first offence.

Burial in Wool

By 1678 procurement of a new register book for Fingest could no longer be deferred. The House of Commons, nine out of ten of its members being landowners who were commercially interested as much in woollen cloth manufacture as in corn growing, forbade the import of foreign cloth and the export of raw wool, and ordained that everyone who died should be buried in a shroud of English woollen cloth. Parson Cademan had no choice but to procure and keep a register book confirming for every burial that it had been conducted according to law. In the new book the first entry on the left-hand page, is 'Joane the daughter of John and Joane Stacy buryed Oct 14th 1678'; and against it on the right-hand page: 'I received an affadavit; that she was wrapt & wound up according to Law made before Sir Humphry Winch Oct 18th'. Inscribed on its cover 'A Register Booke of the Buryalls that have been in the Parish since The Act for Burying in woolen was in force' the book was kept in this way until 1732.

Discord Over the Exclusion Bills

In 1672 the King's brother James, Duke of York and heir presumptive (Charles's queen Catherine was childless), caused public alarm and outrage by openly avowing his adherence to the Roman Catholic faith. Charles, always loyal to his brother and never doubting his right, thought to pour oil on troubled waters by proclaiming a Declaration of Indulgence that allowed religious toleration to all his subjects, whether nonconformist or Catholic. But Parliament, exercising its newly assumed power against the throne, compelled its withdrawal; indeed it went further with a contrary measure, the Test Act which required all subjects holding office under the Crown publicly to take the sacrament in the Church of England and to renounce the doctrine of transubstantiation.

A Second Test Act of 1678 excluded Catholics from sitting in the House of Commons. The next year the mendacious revelations by Titus Oates of a 'Popish Plot' to murder Charles and put James on the throne brought to fever heat disquiet about the succession, and the first of a series of Exclusion Bills debarring James from the throne was tabled. Before it reached a third reading, however, Charles prorogued and then dissolved Parliament.

Charles's Oxford Parliament

Thereafter, in the matter of James's right to succeed, things went Charles's way. Three further attempts to get an Exclusion Bill on the statute book failed either by the Lords throwing it out or the King dissolving Parliament. In 1681 most members of the House of Commons felt determined, if necessary at swordpoint, to pass an Exclusion Bill. But when the House met to this purpose, Charles took the wind out of its sails with a new proposal: that after his death William, the Protestant Prince of Orange, be appointed Regent to carry on government in James's name. William had married James's daughter Mary, also Protestant and next in the bloodline to succeed James. Rejecting this solution out of hand, Parliament voted a second reading of the Exclusion Bill, only to find itself again dissolved at the royal prerogative.

This fourth parliament of his reign Charles summoned to Oxford. Travelling from London with his court retinue to meet it, he stopped on the Oxford road for a night at Stokenchurch, the parish next to Fingest. Thomas Delafield mentions the occasion in his manuscript *The Antient and Present State of Stokenchurch* (Bodleian Library, *Gough MS, Oxon 47*, p.177) saying that he found 'some particulars in the old churchwardens' book' viz:

14th March 1680 Paid the Ringers when his Majesty came by £0.5s.0d.

He continues:

This Complement, paid by the Parish Bells, was to King Charles the 2nd in his Passage through this Place to Oxford in March this Year, to meet there his last Parliament, and which sat but Seven Days. On which occasion he did this little place the Honour of stopping at it and taking a Dinner at the sign of the George, now the King's Arms. A memorial of which was (and I suppose is still) preserved, in a painted Tablet, hung up in the chamber which he made his Dining Room, in these words

OUR GRACIOUS SOVERAIGNE
KING CHARLES THE SECOND
WAS PLEASED TO MAKE
THIS PLACE HIS DINEING
ROOM UPON THE
FOURTEENTH DAY OF MARCH
ANNO DOMINI 1681

Delafield notes:

> this daye is too backward; for it was indeed in 1680
> (following the computation of our church which
> begins the year at our Lady Day) as the
> churchwardens book truly sets it.

He goes on:

> His queen Catherine is said to have come with him,
> and to have been accommodated in a Tent pitched on
> the Common over against the Inne, while one of his
> Mistresses was admitted to the King's Appartment.
> For this I have only the constant tradition of the
> Common people here. But if it be true, these words
> of Ovid may be both asserted and denyed in
> Application to it:
> *Non bene conveniunt, nec in una sede movantur Majestas et*
> *amor.*

The tablet Delafield describes, doubtless familiar to Fingest
neighbours the time, is still to be seen at the King's Arms.
Delafield knew of it being master of Stokenchurch school
while curate at Fingest.

'Whig' and 'Tory'

For the rest of his reign Charles was constantly petitioned
to call a new Parliament to get the Exclusion Bill passed
into law, and repeatedly refused. Resolutely supporting the
King against such a bill, and politically opposed by
'petitioners' favouring it, were its 'abhorrers', upholding the
King's prerogative to rule as he thought fit. The petitioners'
views on the constitution earned them the nickname
'Whigs', originally applied to Scottish Covenanters;

abhorrers became 'Tories', as Irish peasants called royalists who had earlier fled to Ireland.

The Whigs' party was divided about who should take James's place as heir – Charles's eldest illegitimate son, the Duke of Monmouth, or Mary, James's Protestant daughter. A supposed conspiracy to assassinate both brothers and put Monmouth on the throne – 'The Rye House Plot' – led to the arrest and execution of two noble and respected petitioners, William Lord Russell and Algernon Sidney, both quite innocent of such treason. Laws against dissent were put into effect even more stringently; and the association of the Whigs with dissenters who favoured Monmouth weakened their political power. To a large majority of the people the Crown now seemed irresistible, and when Charles died in 1685 an overwhelmingly Tory-Anglican Parliament welcomed James II to the throne.

Non-Resistance Gives Way to Passive Disobedience – Four Momentous Years

Monmouth's foolhardy attempt only two months after James's coronation to lead a rising in the West Country and seize the Crown was routed at Sedgemoor by the royal army. His capture and execution on Tower Hill without trial was followed by Lord Chancellor Jeffreys's Bloody Assizes which hanged or transported hundreds of West country peasants.

At first the Tories rallied behind James, and with them the gentry and the Anglican church. But for the rest of his short reign James bent his whole effort to making Britain into a one-party Roman Catholic state, overriding the Protestant majority and always exercising his dispensing and suspending powers in favour of Catholics – in the Privy Council, in livings in the church and in offices in the universities.

When in April 1687 he issued by royal proclamation a second Declaration of Indulgence suspending on his own authority the Test Act which excluded Catholics and Nonconformists alike from public office, politicians, clergy and people became exasperated.

General discontent boiled over when in May the next year, 1688, he ordered the reading of his Declaration of Indulgence from every pulpit in the land. When the Archbishop of Canterbury, William Sancroft, and six other bishops (Thomas Ken of Bath and Wells was one of them) prayed to be excused this, James's angry response was to clap all seven in the Tower for seditious libel. Many of the clergy too would not read the Declaration while others complied but with various different reservations. One such, as Bishop Gilbert Burnet recounts in his *History of his Own Times*, told his congregation that though he was obliged to read it, they were not obliged to listen, so 'when they had all gone out he read it to the walls' (Mary Howarth, *A Plain Man's Guide to The Glorious Revolution 1688*, 1988). The reader may wonder whether John Cademan in Fingest dealt with the matter as ingeniously in the face of his congregation.

Even with his Declaration before them, Parliament, Tories and Whigs were prepared to tolerate James's continuing kingship, for they knew that when he died – and he was fifty-seven – the crown must pass to his Protestant daughter Princess Mary, married as she was to William of Orange, Charles I's grandson and thus himself a Stuart of the blood royal.

But no sooner were the seven bishops committed to the Tower, than on 10th June the Queen – Mary of Modena, James's second wife and a declared Catholic – gave birth to a healthy son. The totally unexpected arrival after fifteen years of fruitless marriage of a papist heir to the throne astounded everybody. The Palace announcement of the birth was universally declared a Catholic hoax, and tales of a warming-pan smuggled into the Queen's bedchamber to fake matters were everywhere believed.

The challenge of events to the Protestant succession of his wife was now urgently clear to the Prince of Orange.

A Declaration for Protestants and Parliament

The prosecution of the seven bishops had put the clergy in a great state of alarm, and the prospect of succession by a Catholic Prince of Wales had put an end to Parliament's loyalty to the Stuart monarchy, Whigs and Tories both. When the bishops' trial on 29th June by sixty noblemen at Westminster Hall delivered a verdict of 'Not Guilty' there was triumphant rejoicing throughout the country. Even before this, Parliamentarians and gentry, encouraged on all sides to abandon non-resistance, had begun to consider rebellion. On the very day of the bishops' acquittal, 30th June, seven high-ranking conspirators – with extreme secrecy, for it was high treason – sent a letter, signed with their marks only, to William of Orange, urging him to oust James and secure for Britain the Protestant religion and a free Parliament. The letter, carried across to the Hague by Admiral Herbert in the dress of a common seaman, came as no surprise to William. His cautiously worded reply took the form of a 'Declaration to the British people of the Reasons Inducing him to Appear in Armes in the Kingdom of England for Preserving of the Protestant Religion and for Restoring the Lawes and Liberties of England, Scotland and Ireland'.

Already well prepared to act, William was wary of arousing suspicion of his intentions in the States-General of the Dutch United Provinces, and still more of engaging the enmity of Louis XIV's France and the Catholic states of Europe. He did not move until he was sure that Louis's pretensions against the Archbishop of Cologne in the Rhine valley were diverting French forces from threatening his own Flanders frontier. Meanwhile he had organised embarkation of an army of four thousand cavalrymen with their horses and nine thousand footsoldiers in a large fleet of ships with nine thousand seamen assembled in the Zuyder Zee. Soon after its sailing on 19th October a violent north-west gale drove the ships back to harbour, and it was not until ten days later that he was able to make sail north-westerly, intending a landfall at the Humber. But the wind veered north-east, and carried the fleet south-west through the straights of Dover and down the Channel. He made land at Torbay, auspiciously on 5th November, anniversary of the Gunpowder Plot.

With his cavalry safely ashore at Brixham, William paraded his full force and marched for Exeter under the banner 'For the Protestant Religion and Liberty'. His arrival there on 9th November was greeted by cheering crowds, though the Devonshire gentry, remembering the local outcome of Monmouth's failed invasion attempt, were reluctant with their support until they saw that the conspirators' originally secret plot was everywhere burgeoning in William's favour in cities, ports and counties. From Exeter he moved on 21st November to march his army to Salisbury, complete with artillery and baggage wagons.

Shown a copy of William's Declaration for the first time on 1st November, just before the Torbay landing, James had become seriously alarmed. He issued a proclamation forbidding under pain of dire punishment circulation of the Declaration, promised to recall Parliament and rescind his recent extreme pro-Catholic measures, and set watches on Thames crossings. On 17th November he set off to join his standing army at Salisbury. He arrived there to be invited by John Churchill, his commander-in-chief, to inspect his army's advance troops at Warminster, but attacks of violent nose-bleeding he was subject to put him temporarily out of action (Mary Howarth, *A Plain Man's Guide to the Glorious Revolution 1688*, 1988). Recovered, he held a council of war on 24th November but with no battle contemplated he ordered a retreat to Reading, himself returning to Whitehall.

Support was now melting away. James had hardly left Salisbury to ride back to London to summon his Privy Council than John Churchill with leading men of the Royal Army and Royal Navy defected to William. On reaching Whitehall James found that his dearest daughter Anne had fled to join the insurgents at Nottingham. At Privy Council he named commissioners to treat with William, but now alone and his spirit broken by Anne's defection, his real resolve was flight. On 9th December Queen Mary and her infant son were taken from Whitehall Palace privily to Gravesend, where they boarded a sloop for France. Arriving though they did in bedraggled condition they were nevertheless received gallantly by Louis with the full splendour of the French Court. In the meantime James had made a botched attempt to get aboard a boat at Sheerness, and found himself at William's direction being escorted with due honour back to Whitehall again. He could only make a humbling offer to confer but his son-in-law, who had now reached Windsor, declined. At the Castle, William, as a foreigner in England, very correctly left it to James's envoy, Lord Halifax, to chair a meeting of the commissioners to settle their King's future. The inevitable upshot was that on 18th December James left Whitehall for the last time. Carried on the royal barge but escorted by Dutch soldiers, he was taken down river to the Medway and to Rochester. Even so late, the Lords sent him, as their still reigning King, a deputation begging him to return and parley, but James, at the end of his tether, refused. On 22nd December a fishing smack took him to France and on Christmas Day 1688 he was reunited with his queen and baby son at the Palace of St Germains, thereafter to be recognised by Louis – and by Jacobites at home – as the rightful King of Great Britain. His attempt in 1690 to regain the throne in Ireland with a French and Irish army failed at the battle of the Boyne. Still treated with all honours due to the King of Great Britain he died at St Germains in 1701.

William at Henley

We here return for a moment to 10th December. Before hearing of James's first attempt at flight, William, pressed by the Warden of All Souls to visit Oxford to dine at the University now pledged to his cause, had travelled as far as Abingdon. When news of the King's apparent abdication reached him there he immediately turned back for London taking the road via Wallingford, where he crossed the Thames on 12th December. He spent the next two nights at Phyllis Court, Sir William Whitelocke's house at Henley, where he received a hastily gathered deputation of peers, bishops and Aldermen of the City of London, headed by Sir Robert Clayton. They were urgently concerned about what James's disbanded army might now do, and they authorised William to issue an order 'from his court at Henley to all Colonels and Commanders-in-chief to call together by beat of drum or otherwise the officers and soldiers at convenient rendezvous, and there to keep them in good order and discipline' (*Clarendon's Diary*).

Meanwhile the City, discovering the King had fled, was in a state of such confusion that the Lord Mayor and Aldermen had called an ad hoc meeting of the Privy Council of peers and bishops at the Guildhall, which in the end agreed to request the Prince of Orange to take over government until a Parliament could meet. Complying without a flicker of an eyelid, William rode with his troops from Henley to Windsor Castle – again with cheering crowds – and then on to the Duke of Somerset's Syon House. On 18th December, while James was departing down the Thames to exile, William rode in a carriage to St James's Palace. He had completed with his troops the whole march from Torbay without bloodshed or battle, and politically without putting a foot wrong.

The Declaration of Rights

Although now in full military control and holding court in St James, William knew very well that the country was still without government, that it was the law of the country that only the King could summon Parliament, and that the exercise of government was with the King. With the Throne empty and Mary his wife its true successor, nothing in his successful campaign so far had given him a direct right to occupy it. He solved the problem by dealing with the Lords and the commoners separately. The peers he invited to convene in the House of Lords and discuss the possibilities for future government. As to commoners, members still available from the parliaments of Charles II he summoned to meet him at St James's along with the Aldermen and members of the Common Council of the City of London. Thus assembled on 26th December they proceeded to thank him for preserving 'our Religion, Laws and Liberties', and requested him to assume forthwith administrative and executive power. On 29th December the mainly Whig Parliamentary members, meeting in St Stephen's Chapel, agreed that the Throne was vacant, and asked him to call a Convention on 22nd January, 1689 of members elected by lawfully qualified vote. The Tory Lords were meanwhile struggling with scruples about renouncing their oath of allegiance to James while he was still alive; and further, if they were to renounce their oath, about giving it to William when, if the Throne were truly vacant, Princess Mary as heiress presumptive should already have been accepted as its occupant. At much length the Lords at least agreed with the interim Commons (though by a very narrow vote) that the Throne was indeed vacant.

William and Mary as Joint Sovereigns

The elected Convention Parliament met on 22nd January and for two weeks argument ran strong in both Houses about whether James had abdicated, or had deserted his kingdom. That settled – i.e. he had deserted the kingdom and abdicated its government, leaving the Throne thereby vacant – the question remained by whom was the Throne to be filled?

William, in St James's Palace, kept his peace, well knowing what the peers were arguing about. Some wanted William made Regent for James, with Mary no more than his wife; others the opposite – Mary as Queen Regnant in her own right, with the Prince of Orange her consort. When they finally voted the latter, and told him, William at last made it crystal clear he would be neither Regent nor his wife's 'gentleman-usher'. Mary was equally sure that she would not accept the crown save in conjunction with her husband. This put an end to uncertainty. Parliament agreed that William and Mary be offered the crown as joint sovereigns, the administration resting with William alone.

The conditions upon which the offer was made were set out in The Declaration of Right presented to William and Mary on 13th February in the banqueting room at White-hall. It was accepted by both; the Bill of Rights was later enacted, entrenching in statute law the 'Glorious Revolution', overriding the royal prerogative and replacing it by 'the will of the nation' expressed through Parliament.

And the Church?

For our purposes, the events of these momentous four years have demanded description here in almost day-to-day detail, for this is how John Cademan would have perceived and thought about them in these middle years of his Fingest incumbency. We shall be seeing next that he kept a constant if timid ear to the ecclesiastical ground, fearing a threat to village rectories such as his.

Chapter XIX
The Last Domiciled Rector – The Curacy of Thomas Delafield (1690–1755)

John Cademan held the living for rather more than four decades – twenty-one years till the 1688 Revolution, and then another twenty-five after. Considering the see-saw of constitutional power that the country was meanwhile undergoing, we can scarcely wonder that Cademan's incumbency at Fingest so felicitously mirrors that of the immortal Vicar at Bray:

> In good King Charles's golden days, When loyalty no
>   harm meant,
> A zealous High Church man was I, And so I got
>   preferment;
> To teach my flock I never missed Kings were by God
>   appointed,
> And damn'd are those that do resist, Or touch the
>   Lord's annointed.
>
> When royal James obtained the crown, And Pop'ry
>   came in fashion,
> The penal laws I hooted down, And read the
>   Declaration;

> The church of Rome I found would fit Full well my
> constitution;
> And had become a Jesuit, But for the Revolution.
>
> When William was our King declared To ease the
> nation's grievance,
> With this new wind about I steered And swore to
> him allegiance;
> Old principles I did revoke, Set conscience at a
> distance;
> Passive obedience was joke, A jest was non-resis-
> tance.

Indeed, to unite all Protestants under William III and against the deposed Roman Catholic James, the new Parliament of 1689 passed an Act (the 'Toleration' Act) specifically allowing nonconformists who believed in the Trinity their own places of worship. Toleration, of course, did not extend to Catholics who were barred from the same right, while both they and dissenters were excluded from civil office.

Non-Jurors

As the rhyme tells, at the constitutional settlement of the Revolution most of the clergy – including a perplexed John Cademan, no doubt – were prepared to tolerate allegiance to William and Mary even while acknowledging Parliament as the seat of authority. There persisted, however, a division in the Church of England. High Church Anglicans were uneasy, since their former belief in the King's divine right to authority had led them to swear fealty to James; as a matter of religious principle therefore, some – the non-jurors – refused to forswear that oath in favour of the allegiance to William that Parliament required. Four hundred or so clerics were of like mind, among them five of the seven bishops who had the year before refused James's Declaration of Indulgence. These five included Thomas Ken, consecrated Bishop of Bath and Wells in 1684. Declining to take the oath to William, in August 1689 he and his fellow Non-juring bishops were deprived of their sees. Continuing to dispute the ecclesiastical legality of their deprivation, and indeed, with the *congé d'élire* (royal permission) of the exiled James, they secretly named bishops of their own. Thereupon Parliament ordered conforming bishops to be consecrated in their place, and the schism was perpetuated.

However the thinning ranks of Non-jurors, high-principled to a man, in the end came to be seen by both High Church Tories and Low Church Whigs as political Jacobites, Roman in religion. Their stand proved no match for the next century's favouring of Anglican toleration, limited as it was.

'The grass withereth, and the flower thereof falleth away' (Peter 1:24)

As you may well judge, reader, for Fingest's rector developments in Church matters were less glorious than unsettling. The parish's prebendary being a member of the Bath and Wells chapter whose bishop had been marked as a Non-juror and deposed, Cademan began to give closer attention to the parochial duties he owed to the see of Lincoln. At last he persuaded himself of the propriety of starting a new register of baptisms and marriages to be kept in the church vestry (no doubt in the iron strong box still there), along with the burials register he had been obliged to keep since 1678. (Both of these books later acquired vellum covers tied with tapes, the burials in 1732 and the baptisms and marriages in 1764, as inscriptions on their covers show.) Baptism entries started at one end of the book and marriages were entered in the reversed aspect at the other. Entries for both continued until 1746 when their pages met.

In such registers, not in content only but as much in manner, almost three centuries later we savour, as if yesterday, the vicissitudes of a country rector's province. John Cademan's recognisable hand is evident in both books up to and including 1705. In 1695 he began to follow the date of each baptism with the date of the infant's birth, as had been the Puritan custom of the Commonwealth years. It is improbable, I think, that all the parents concerned practised 'occasional conformity', that is, as dissenters made their communion in the parish church occasionally in order to qualify as conformists. It is more likely that Cademan, inveterately weathering the political climate, thought it wise to put birth dates for all, in case the parents of some turned out to be closet nonconformists. His lists of baptismal entries for 1697–1705 were each year formally endorsed 'Inspected' – by the archdeacon's registrar, presumably.

In the Steps of the Legendary Vicar

For the year of Anne's succession, 1702, the Fingest baptism list looks unusual. Only eight names are entered, all of adults, identified as such by occupation viz. labourer, farmer, carpenter, shoemaker, collector; five women and three men. This surely suggests that despite 'toleration' being much in the air, with Queen Anne now on the throne the careful Cademan thought it contingent to see that a Church of England baptism was offered to adult villagers whose nonconformist parents had rejected it for their infants. As the traditional rhyme reminds us:

When gracious Anne became our Queen, The
Church of England's glory,
Another face of things was seen, And I become a
Tory;
Occasional Conformists base I damn'd their
moderation,
And thought the Church in danger was By such
prevarication.

Nevertheless, whatever the case so far as John Cademan
was concerned, it is hard to explain the absence of infant
baptisms in Fingest throughout the year 1702.

Cademan dropped entering dates of infants' births from
1703 and resumed customary form under all three headings
until 1706, though in a thickening hand less closely spaced
than before. Thereafter the registers were kept in a clearly
different hand until 1716, then in another. In 1726, drawing
firm double lines under his predecessors' efforts, 'Thomas
Delafield, curate' takes over.

John Cademan's Last Years at Fingest

Following up Bishop Fuller's 1669 inquiries, Bishop Wake
of Lincoln resumed visitations; Wycombe deanery was
visited in 1706, 1709 and 1712. Cademan's brief reports
from Fingest on each occasion survive and may be seen in
Buckinghamshire Dissent and Parish Life 1669–1712 (ed. J.
Broad, *Bucks Rec. Soc., No. 28*). For 1706, he reiterates that
the patronage belongs to a prebendary of the Chapter of
Wells, gives the parish's extent and its population (fifty-six
families), and disclaims there being any dissenters, papists
or reputed papists in the parish, nor any meeting house,
school, almshouse or endowed hospital. The Rectory, he
says, is valued at fifty pound per annum; and two

gentlemen live in the parish, Mr John Ferrers senior and junior.

His report for 1709 surprises us by beginning with the following:

Ordination Thomas Ardfert 6 June 1660
Institution 11 Nov, Induction 15, 1667

This Ardfert, not mentioned by name hitherto or indeed hereafter, was evidently ordained very soon after John Richardson's reinstatement as rector, but was only in-ducted, presumably at Fingest, when John Cademan appeared on the scene seven years later; a shadowy figure indeed. Nevertheless Cademan does indeed speak of a curate in his 1712 report to the bishop, six years after he gave up making his own entries in the parish register:

The Rector resides in his parsonage house. He has a Curate duly qualified to assist him salary £18 a year. Divine service once every Lord's Day. The Rector not able to do it and the Curate employed elsewhere in the afternoon, No catechising by reason of the Curate's absence. Communions 3 times a year, about 30 receive. Notice duly given. No penances or com-mutations since my last visitation.

It is possible that the curate in question was in fact the elusive Thomas Ardfert, but you will agree, reader, the evidence is thin. We can but guess that in these times of uncertainty Cademan inherited cure of souls outside Fingest that called for a curate.

Inspection of the burials register for the period 1706–1715 raises doubt, however, about whether Ardfert, or indeed any other curate, was then keeping it. The writing becomes less educated in form, and spelling errors are more frequent than might be expected of a curate; it seems rather the work of the parish clerk. A dated list of parish clerks in the seventeenth and eighteenth centuries on the cover of the baptism register shows that between 1706 and 1739 one John Rider (a descendant of rector Peter Rider, perhaps) held the office. Whether he or another, the scribe recording burials at the time was observant, if not critical; one entry reads:

> Mrs Mary Willmot of the parish of Hambelton rich widow was buried April:10:1709.

This describes her accurately, as the *Bucks Probate Inventory* confirms:

> William Willmott gent: Fingest 17 May 1690: house at Fingest, house at Ibston. Sum total ready money & debts due £1842-14-0; sum total of goods, loans, ready money & debts £2733-17-1.

Cademan's visitation reports are those of a man who, having secured his hold on the living for so long, was by 1706 in failing health; but he persisted, and it was not until 1713 he died. The parish clerk's entry in the burial register is simply:

> Mr John Cademan Rector of this parish was buryed ffebruary:5:-1713

Browne Willis, in a list of 'Finghurst Rectores' (*Willis MS*, vol. xciv, pp.77–78) also notes the burial:

> John Cadman pr.Oct 11 1667 by the Prebendary of Dultincolt in Wells Cathedral. He died and was buried in the chancell Febr. 5 1713 with a stone laid

over him but the inscription is hid and not to be made out.

Of his family, bishops' transcripts show the baptism of a daughter Anne on 17th November, 1677, and on 13th December of the same year the burial of another daughter, Margaret. Mary Cademan, his wife, was buried at Fingest on 30th December, 1722.

Parsonage Terriers

After Peter Rider's brief effort of 1601, (Linc. Arch. Office, *Ter. 15/61*) no further terriers are discoverable until John Cademan became incumbent. No less than five then appeared; in 1674, 1680, 1690, 1697 and 1706, and a sixth in 1707.

The County Archivist at Aylesbury kindly allowed me to examine those for the years 1674 to 1706. They agree pretty closely in their descriptions of the parsonage house, enlarged as it had been after Christopher Edwards's 'benefaction'. It comprises four bays with seven rooms, i.e. 'A Hall and a Chamber within it, a Roome over that chamber, A Kitchen A Buttery and two Roomes over them. There is adjoining to the house on the South & East a Great Garden & a little one on the West side of the Hall and chamber'.

Again, these five terriers give similar descriptions of the parsonage's backyards, gates and outbuildings, which include the thatched great barn with a stable and hogsty, the little barn also thatched, with its attached hovel and a carthouse. Set out also are the precise boundaries and areas of the five parcels of land that together make up the glebe, totalling twenty-four and a half acres, twice as much as in Peter Rider's day.

The original of the 1707 sixth terrier has not survived, but in 1745 curate Thomas Delafield (finding it in the parish chest, no doubt) made an attested copy which is now in the Lincoln Archives, where I saw it. It repeats its predecessors practically word for word, but differs in going on to enumerate the customary tithes, other dues to the rector for offerings, the customary dues to the parish clerk, and the (scanty) furniture of the church. Like the other five, it is duly signed by John Cademan, rector, and witnessed by the churchwardens.

Why so many terriers, so frequently? The long-perceived threat of local nonconformism may have been what induced the timorous Cademan to update the terrier repeatedly to counter dissenting dispute that might arise about his entitlement as rector to revenues from the glebe and parish. Further, by detailing tithes and dues, he may have helped to attract augmentation of the living by Queen Anne's Bounty since 'its tenths (annates or first-fruits), being 13s.9½d, had been discharged in 1706, and its clear annual value returned to the Bounty's Governors as £45 per annum' (Thomas Delafield, Bodleian Library, *Gough MS, Bucks 2*). In fact nothing materialised from this source until well into the next rector's incumbency, as we shall see.

John Cademan – The Last Domiciled Rector

Queen Anne's sudden demise in 1714 and the unopposed accession of the Hanoverian George I ended any support by the Church of Tory non-resistance and of the divine right that Dr Sacheverell had been preaching so furiously. Under a Whig ministry with its repeal of the Occasional Conformity Act and the Schism Act, bishops were so taken up with proclaiming civil and religious liberty that they had no time for preaching the gospel, and religious activity sank to a low ebb.

Finding himself in a quiet parish such as Fingest, the next parson was inclined to look for something more suited to his supposed breeding. When Cademan died the Wells prebendary of 'Dultincote alias Fingest' had since 1670 been Canon Gabriel Thistlethwaite, a fellow of New College, Oxford. As patron he put in motion the institution at Fingest of another member of New College, the Revd Francis Edmonds AM, and in 1714 he was duly inducted as *Alumni Oxoniensis*, Oxford, records.

With the temporalities of the living in his hands, it is possible that Francis Edmonds may for a time have actually resided in the Fingest parsonage house, since proper discharge of the cure of souls had, hitherto at any rate, required a resident priest. Plain evidence that he did is lacking, however, and inference is against it.

Firstly, the script of the parish registers indicates that after 1707 it was Rider, the parish clerk, who went on making the entries until 1716. Only then did another clearly more educated hand take over until the advent in 1726 of curate Thomas Delafield.

A second pointer is that in one of his manuscript essays Delafield (referring to himself in the third person) tells us:

At Ladyday 1726 he entred on the curacy of Fingest, under the Rector Mr Francis Edmonds, and in the place of the Revd Mr John Bachler Rector of Radnage and Vicar of Hitchenden in the County of Bucks.

(*An Attempt towards an Account of the Parish of Great Milton*, T. Delafield, Bodleian Library, *Gough MS, Oxon 48*, p.303.)

We can only conclude that the 1716–1726 entries in the Fingest register were those of the Revd Bachler. Under the authority of rector Francis Edmond maybe, it was Bachler who was then administering the curacy of Fingest, operating from his own rector in Radnage, four miles away.

A further doubt regarding Edmonds's personal involvement in the cure of Fingest emerges from another of Delafield's manuscripts, *The Ancient and Present State of Stokenchurch* (Bodleian Library, *Gough MS, Oxon 47*, p.131). Here he says that his predecessor as Stokenchurch's schoolmaster, the Revd William King, had 'never any ecclesiastical preferment of his own, but was occasionally curate at Radnage, Moorchappel, Fingest, Emmington, Stokenchurch and Chinnor'.

So it is clear that from Cademan's incumbency onwards the curacy of Fingest was regularly shared out to clergy, even rectors, from neighbouring parishes, on top of their own parochial duties. Delafield likewise makes it plain that while he was living at Stokenchurch as master of the school there, he thought nothing of taking on as well the curacy of Fingest, at least a three and a half mile ride away.

A development in Edmonds's clerical career later put him on more equal terms with the local gentry. In 1720 he was presented (by the archdeacon of Buckingham, pre-sumably) to the rectory of Tingwick, near Buckingham (*Registrum Custodum, Sociorum & Scholarum Collegii Novi*), and there is no doubt that thereafter he held the Tingwick living in tandem with that of Fingest. Indeed he resided there, and when he died in 1759 was buried there. It was another century or more before the Pluralities Act was passed forbidding clergymen simultaneously to hold more than one benefice with cure of souls; this was to be permissible only if the travelling distance between the churches was less than ten miles and the joint annual income less than one thousand pounds. Tingwick and Fingest are a good forty miles apart.

As we have hinted, Edmonds's New College fellowship and his appointment to and preference for the Tingwick living, reflect the rising cultural and social scale of parsons in Georgian times. His interest was not pecuniary, for he was not a poor man. He owned parcels of land in the parish of Buckingham and the manor of the prebend of Buckingham which brought him considerable annuities and rents, as is apparent in his lengthy will (*New College Archive 131*) which details how they are to be distributed to his relations and their spouses living in parishes neighbouring on Tingwick. Nevertheless, in keeping with the benevolent latitudinarianism of the time, he kept Fingest's fortunes in mind, for in 1721, as soon as he had moved to Tingwick, he made it a private benefaction of two hundred pounds which the governors of Queen Anne's Bounty matched with an equal augmentation; these two acquisitions increased the worth of Fingest rectory to one hundred and twenty pounds a year (Lipscomb, *History & Antiquities of the County of Buckingham*, 1847, vol. iii, p.566). At the practical level this improvement no doubt encouraged Thomas Delafield to accept the curacy.

Edmonds' Charities

During Anne's reign the Church of England had begun to react to the increasing numbers of nonconformist schools by establishing as many of its own charity schools as could be funded. The intention was to educate the poor, not only in reading and writing, but in moral discipline and the principles of the Anglican faith. Thomas Delafield, who had been born in 1690, tell us he was early put to such a free school in his native parish, Great Haseley (*Gough MS, Oxon 19,* vol. 1, pp.47, 133). As its curate later, it was he who brought the idea to Fingest; for we find, interleaved in the parish's contemporary marriage register, an agreement dated 21st April, 1740, signed by Delafield, two church-wardens, two overseers of the poor and eleven parishioners of Fingest, consenting that the church house (the parish clerk's habitation):

> shall be converted to a Schooll-house for the Parish clerke to teach the Poor Children of this Parish: on condition the Revd Francis Edmonds our Rector do put the said House into good Repair and keep it so: and further settle the Yearly sum of Five Pounds for ever as a salary for Teaching the said Children.

By 1751 arrangements by Francis Edmonds further to endow schools in both Tingwick and Fingest had been completed. In an entry book of the trustees for the church trust property and charity trusts of Fingest parish, begun in 1848, there is a copy of a trust deed furnished by the Warden of New College Oxford. It details how annuities or rent-charges amounting to thirty pounds a year on lands in the parish of Buckingham belonging to Francis Edmonds:

> are assigned by the latter to the Warden and Scholars of St Mary Winchester College in Oxford (New College) upon trust to pay one moiety to the Rector of Tingwick and the other moiety to the Rector of Fingest, towards the Education and Clothing of twelve poor children in each of these Parishes. Each of the rectors may apply one pound yearly, if he pleases, to his own use as a remuneration for his trouble.

All the deeds relating to this annuity are in a small wooden box, and with them now is Edmonds's letter to the Warden, the Revd Dr Purnell, asking him to keep the box with its content of deeds in the New College muniment house (tower). They are still there to be consulted.

In both parishes the schooling endowed by the Edmonds charities continued into the first decades of the present century. The Fingest registers and churchwardens' minutes give a detailed account of how the charity money was spent each year on school teachers' fees and providing clothing, boots, shoes and Bibles for six poor boys and six poor girls of the parish throughout the nineteenth century. In 1839 the then rector, Henry Tufnell Young, offered 'to give the girls turned out of the Charity School in the Parish of Fingest Ten Shillings each provided they do get them a Situation at Survis within six months'.

Thereafter the development of schooling in the parish and in villages once part of Fingest is traceable up to the present day. The large junior school quite recently built in nearby Lane End and named after him, keeps alive the memory of Francis Edmonds MA, Fellow of New College Oxford and Rector of Tingwick and of Fingest in the county of Bucks.

Three smaller charitable donations were also given to the parish at about this time. Thomas Picket in 1690 gave a cottage and two acres at land value of 40s per annum for the use of the poor to be distributed on St Thomas's Day annually; Mr Bartholomew Tipping gave also 40s per annum out of his farm at Cadmer End for the same purpose; and Mrs Mary Mole in 1734 gave three pounds per annum payable out of The Vinings to eight poor widows annually. A board in the church records the Picket and Mole charities.

Thomas Delafield, Curate 1726–1755

The modes of education of the rector of Tingwick and of his curate at Fingest demonstrate how wide the gulf was between rich and poor clergy of the times. In each of his manuscript accounts of the parishes of Haseley,

Stokenchurch and Great Milton we have already quoted from (*Gough MS, Oxon 19, 41, 47, 48*) Delafield reiterates the story of his life before his Fingest curacy. Born in Little Haseley of, he says, the meanest of parents as to worldly circumstances but of the first consideration for their integrity, morality and care of the duties of religion, he was put to the free school there with the rest of the poor children of the parish. There being no schoolhouse, the master taught in Great Haseley church, which gave young Thomas an opportunity to pore over the inscriptions, some in English, on the flatstone graves. On the church brasses too he found writing

> in the old English letter chiefly in Latin, and by a Key of the Numeral Letters could take the Date of the Year of them all. And then it was an agreeable Amusement to me to find out by Arithmetick the Antiquity of each. So early as this began my Inclination to these sort of studies.

He goes on to say that the master at the time was but an English scholar, and to remedy this in 1702 he left Haseley school for a private grammar school that the vicar of Great Milton, the Revd John Hinton, kept in his own house there. Delafield came and returned every day from Little Haseley for five years, receiving, in addition to Latin:

> the far best part of my narrow education which he gratuitously gave me. In 1707, disappointed in expectation and dependence on a friend to assist in putting me to the University of Oxford, and upon an unhappy turn in my father's circumstances, in obedience to his commands I followed him and the rest of our family to Putney in Surrey [...] being forced to leave school (with a small stock of learning

and, great want of friends) and to betake myself to a no dishonorable employment for subsistence.

About the next ten years of his life Delafield is silent. By 1717 he was back, applying for the mastership of Great Haseley school; but despite a petition signed, he says, by every housekeeper in the parish, his application was rejected. Nothing loth, and determined as ever to pull himself up by his bootstraps, he opened his own private school there. This proved a success and, by now married, he was able to support himself and his family 'in no contemptible condition'.

Next, events began to move for the Delafields. In 1724 the Revd Hinton died and in his place Delafield, having just received holy orders from Dr Richard Reynolds, the Lord Bishop of Lincoln, was admitted and inducted to the Great Milton vicarage. A year later, on the decease of the Revd Mr William King, he was appointed to the headmastership of Stokenchurch school, and moved his family there to live in the school house (which in 1728 he enlarged, mostly at his own expense). Then, as we know, on the very next Ladyday, 1726, he entered on the Fingest curacy at rector Francis Edmonds's behest and at an unstated but doubtless adequate stipend. He resigned the Milton living in the August, though as it turned out he was presented to it again in 1737 for two years while still settled at Stokenchurch. It was in 1745–46 that he produced the three volumes (a fourth is missing) of his *Essay towards an Account of Fingest* to which my efforts here owe much, as the reader well knows.

Delafield gave as much attention to parochial duties as was expected of a rural priest. He kept the registers, in 1737 gave one of Dr Busby's Catachetical Lectures for the county of Bucks (fee £4.10s), and saw that parishioners had proper religious instruction. On the back of a printed Notice of

Confirmation from the Bishop of Lincoln (included in his *Notes on Bucks (Gough MS, Oxon 6, p.34v)* he noted:

> N.B. On April the 29, 1745. In Obedience to this order recd from Dr John Thomas, some little time before made Bp. of Lincoln in the room of Dr Richard Reynolds deceased I (living then at Stokenchurch where I was Schoolmaster) being curate of Fingherst for Mr Francis Edmonds the Rector, did bring about 25 persons of that Parish to the Bishop at High Wycombe, and having before publickly and privately instructed them, gave them each a Certificate as prescribed of them being duly Qualified for Confirmation
>
> Thos. Delafield, Curate of Fingherst.

Another memorandum in the register records:

> That on Holy Thursday 1753 there was a Procession or parochial Perambulation round the Bounds of this Parish of Fingest.
>
> Thomas Delafield, Curate.

His free school and parsonical education brought to life in Thomas Delafield an antiquarian chronicler who liked nothing better than dating past parish incumbencies, and ordering the sequences of parish registers and church authorities over the centuries as well as he could by studying them. He was content to commit all his findings to manuscript in a remarkable sequence of papers that few could then have had opportunity to read. His rural schooling of narrow learning and Latin tags had little chance to blossom in the age of philosophical reasoning that was then dawning on the clerical world of the eighteenth century.

Nevertheless, his writing, uncritical and deferential to higher authority as it invariably is, has an appealing freshness that brings alive the parochial Buckinghamshire world he knew so well.

By his wife Mary (of whom he says little) he had six children. In 1737 he named them (*Gough MS, Oxon 47*, pp.141–2):

> viz: Nicholas, Cooper of a Man Of war in his Majesties service in the Mediterranean in the fleet under Admiral Haddock; Mary; Thomas, a Book-binder in London; William a Painter there; Elizabeth and Esther.

His son Thomas became apprentice clerk to an attorney in St Giles, Cripplegate.

There is an echo of his daughters' lives in a letter the reverse side of which their father used to add notes to his *Account of Great Milton (Gough MS, Oxon 48, Appendices p.45)*; it is addressed to Mrs Esther Delafield at Stokenchurch (Esther was his third daughter) and reads:

> Dear Sister,
>   I receved yours but I dont thinke it Worth my Wiell to go Bradname to Make a gown and if it is i donte care to Staey so Longe from home to plesure aney boddey neither will i do it Pray ower Duty to Father and Mother and a maney thankes and love to Sister and except of the same Your Self.
>   from your Loving Sister
>   Eliza Nash

> Wee shall be verey
> glad to see Mother
> or aney of you here

Throughout his time at Fingest, Delafield kept the parish registers meticulously, each entry in proper order and written to look well, as he felt befitted the curacy of so ancient a benefice. To account for a year's gap in the burial register suffered during his curacy he was obliged to insert an explanatory note:

> N.B. This Vacancy of One Year and eighteen Days, viz. from Oct:29.1743 to November 16, 1744 is not owing to the Omission or want of […] to the Register. For, though […]

Sadly, we shall never know want of what, for vestry dampness (or other wetting) has rendered the rest illegible. He thought it important enough to add a signature – 'Thos. Delafield, curate' – which he rarely did elsewhere in the registers. The last time we find him signing an entry is after the burial of a Lewknor parishioner at Fingest on Trinity Sunday 1755.

In the June and July that followed he added two more entries (unsigned as usual) for baptisms; evidently he was then still travelling from Stokenchurch, though this was less than a month before he died. On 17th August, 1755, he was buried in the churchyard at Great Haseley, the parish of his birth. His wife Mary, who died in 1784, was buried in the same grave.

Chapter XX

Barren the Ground… and Thorny… (1759 onwards)

Thomas Delafield, living four miles away in his school-house at Stokenchurch, gave conscientious attention to his parochial duties in Fingest, and took pains, moreover, to preserve amongst his parishioners a degree of piety and reverence for the cloth. But, by the time he died, in the middle of the eighteenth century, a general decline in God-fearing in the country was being echoed in Fingest, and we begin to lose the scent of pastoral continuity in the parish. Two other things contributed to this: the continuing use of curates to serve pluralist rectors as parish priests, and the ending of the Ferrers family as lords of the manor.

To consider pluralism first. At the Restoration all acts and injunctions of the Protectorate had been repealed, and the advowson of Fingest rectory, which in 1650 the Puritan parliamentary survey had assigned to the lord of the manor, had been restored to the appropriate prebendaries of Wells chapter. In 1667 John Cademan had been presented to the living by John Piers, *'generosus literatus'*, prebendary for Dulcote, otherwise Fingest (*Le Neve, Fasti Ecclesiae V. Bath and Wells Diocese*, ed. J.M. Horn, 1979). Likewise Francis Edmonds had then been presented by Canon Gabriel Thistlethwaite, and in 1714 inducted; but when in 1716 preferment had brought him the superior rectory of Tingwick, finding himself now a pluralist incumbent, he was accordingly obliged to arrange that John Bachler, rector or vicar in other local parishes, should for a small stipend undertake cure of Fingest souls as well. Thus began a series of curacies serving rectors in one way or another pluralistic that continued until well into the next century.

The Fingest Curates

On Delafield's demise, Rector Edmonds at Tingwick, by then habituated to relegating the cure of souls in his Fingest parish, continued the practice and in September 1755 John Clarke briefly took up the curacy. In his first month he officiated at a marriage, two burials and a baptism and duly entered them in the registers; thereafter till May 1756 the only other parish records he kept were of four baptisms. By July his hand in the registers can be seen to be giving place to that of Henry Brown, curate, who for the next eight years kept the registers in due form.

Halfway through Brown's curacy, Edmonds died. Pluralism and nepotism were now making inroads into English clerical life, and the barren officialism that resulted was manifest locally with the collation at Wells as prebendary of Dulcote (or Fingest) of Philip Bearcroft DD.

Secure in his Wells canon's stall, in 1759 he presented 'Philip Bearcroft' as the next Fingest incumbent (Lipscomb, *Hist. and Antiq. Bucks.,* vol. iii, 1847). It seems more than likely that in fact he was presenting himself to the living, no doubt intent on garnering from afar its now augmented proceeds of one hundred and twenty pounds a year at the expense of a curate's stipend. A kinder interpretation is that this 'Philip Bearcroft' was a son or family member presented to the living; indeed soon after, in 1761, prebendary Bearcroft himself died (*Le Neve, Fasti Ecclesiae Anglicanae*, ed. J.M. Horn, 1969), and the next Fingest rector, William Perkins, was not presented until 1776. Whatever the truth of the matter, the handwritings in the registers (with marriage entries signed by the officiating priests) show Henry Brown regularly performing his parish curate duties until December 1764, when Howell Powell took office; so from 1761 to 1776 these two between them served a rector either non-existent or a shadowy absentee.

Howell Powell continued to make entries in the registers as 'curate' until 1793; on his death the burial register records that:

> The Revd Howell Powell died at Turville Dec.15th and was buried under the Communion Table at Fingest Dec.18th 1793. Aged 56 years. He was 23 years Vicar of Turville and 30 years Curate of Fingest, where he was buried at his own Request.

We may note in passing that the mediaeval incongruity of appointing a vicar of Turville to office in Fingest – and, what is more, dual office – had been long forgotten; but, more relevantly, at this point doubts arise about exactly who was rector and who curate, and when.

The record is confusing. The sequence of pamphlets on 'The Parish Church of St Bartholomew, Fingest' which since 1932 the church has provided for visitors, all include lists of rectors since 1217. For the eighteenth and nineteenth century years we are at present concerned with, the 1932 edition reads:

1776 William Perkins, M.A.
1780 Howell Powell, B.A.
       also Vicar of Turville
1793 Thomas Powell
1797 Joseph Harris
1819 Peter Piercy, M.A.
1841 George Augustus Baker, M.A.

Subsequent editions of the pamphlet (as well as the brass plate on the north wall of the nave) list the rectors for this period as:

1776   William Perkins, M.A.
1780   Howell Powell, B.A.
        also Vicar of Turville
1793   Thomas Powell
1797   Joseph Harris
1813   Jas. Price, M.A.
1820   Henry Drury
1841   George Augustus Baker, M.A.

Lipscomb, in his 1847 account of the parish, tells a different story. He agrees that William Perkins A.M. presented by Prebendary Charles Willes on 9th July, 1776, was Fingest rector until 1780. But next, says Lipscomb, Thomas Powell A.B. was presented by the same Charles Willes, and went on to hold the incumbency as rector for forty years until 1820. What relationship, nepotistic or otherwise, there may have been between Howell Powell and Thomas Powell he does not say, but if he is right it seems that Thomas as rector employed Howell (a much older man) as his curate, and when Howell died approved his burial under the Fingest communion table.

To verify matters, we have to refer to the independent contemporary record in the Fingest marriage register, where each entry for marriage was customarily signed by the officiating priest. From 8th December, 1764 to 21st October, 1793, the fifty-six Fingest marriage entries carry Howell Powell's signature as curate. Then he died, and the next two in November 1793 are signed 'Thomas Powell', as is the first entry in 1794 which has 'Rector' added; but thereafter the signature 'Thomas Powell' is no more to be seen in the rest of the register.

To get nearer the truth, then, about what was going on in the Fingest curacy at this time, we have to look at the signed names of the clergy officiating at marriages right up to 1820. (The reader may well choose to pass over the next listings.)

The names in question, with dates, are as follows:

```
1794, Nov 17;  George Berkeley, curate
1795, Sep 6;       ditto
1796, Jun 18;  N. Williams B.A., curate
1797, Apr 18;  Jos. Harris, minister
      Oct 30;      ditto
      Nov 8;   Jas. Price, vicar of High Wycombe
1799, May 13;  Jos. Harris, minister
      Sep 2;   Jas. Price, vicar of Wycombe
      Oct 28;  Jos. Harris, minister
1800, Jun 4;   Jas. Price A.M., vicar of High Wycombe
1801, Oct 1;   N. Williams, curate
1802, May 13;  Jos. Harris, minister
      Aug 16;  N. Williams, minister
1803, May 8;       ditto, curate
      Sep 17;  Jos. Harris, minister
1804, Jan 19;      ditto
1805, Jun 5;   W.J. Fennell, curate
      Aug 3;   Jos. Harris, minister
      Nov 7;       ditto
1806, Feb 15;  W.J. Fennell, curate
      May 31;      ditto
      Sep 22;  Jas. Price A.M.
      Sep 25;  Isaac King LLB
1807, Oct 5;   Jas. Price, curate
      Oct 8;   Jos. Harris, minister
      Dec 26;      ditto
```

```
1808, Jan 2;    Jas. Price A.M., curate
      Apr 18;   ditto
1810, Apr 15;   Jos. Harris, minister
      Jun 21;   ditto
      Aug 2;    ditto
1811, Apr 13;   ditto
      Jun 4;    Jas. Price A.M., curate
1812, May 16;   Jas. Price, curate
      Sep 28;   Jas. Price A.M., curate.
```

In 1813, pursuant to an 1812 Act of Parliament, printed marriage register forms took the place of the written register, although banns still had a handwritten book. The signatures of the officiating priests on the printed marriage forms till 1820 are:

```
1813, Oct 29;   Jas. Price A.M., curate
1814, May 21;   ditto
      Jun 13;   ditto
1815, Apr 15;   Isaac King LLB
      Nov 23;   Jas. Price A.M., curate
1817, Jul 10;   W. Hughes, Rector of Bradenham
      Oct 23;   Jas. Price A.M., curate
1819, May 24;   Peter Piercy A.M., curate
      Jun 1;    ditto
      Dec 27;   ditto
1820, Jan 1;    ditto
      Jan 29;   ditto
      Jul 29;   ditto
      Aug 13;   ditto
```

The upshot of these tedious listings is that throughout the years from 1780 to 1820, while the signature 'Thomas Powell, Rector' appears but once, marriages were otherwise attested by signatures of a variety of curates, some appearing often, some only once or twice, and a couple being rectors or vicars elsewhere. With this contemporary evidence before us, we have to conclude that the pamphlets and the brass plate in the church for these years contain errors in rectors' names and dates; indeed it seems that: (1) Thomas Powell, like his forbears, was a pluralist rector who employed curates, though operating from heaven knows where – Wells? Tingwick? (2) Howell Powell became not rector in 1780 but curate in 1764; (3) James Price was, as he describes himself, 'curate', and at times also 'vicar of High Wycombe'; and (4) Joseph Harris, 'minister', whose signature alternates with those of a variety of self-described curates, was in fact a curate himself.

The Last of the Ferrers at the Manor

Leaving for a moment our perusal of the marriage register for truths it contains, we come to another cause of disruption of parish continuity at this time – changes at the manor. For centuries Fingest Manor, being one of the numerous diocesan properties of Lincoln, had been used as living quarters by the Bishop when it suited him, and more lately as the dwelling of his bailiff. Then in 1548 Bishop Holbeach had no sooner alienated the manor to Somerset than the Duke granted it on to William Thynne, prebendary at Wells. By 1598 Prebendary Whitlock, continuing to lease the manor, took a new tenant, 'Michael Farrar, gent', and his descendants established themselves there. After three generations of tenancy, having adopted the more elegant 'Ferrers', they assumed the lordship though of a manor of reduced extent. Deeds and records in the muniment room of the Aylesbury museum (*Bucks Archeol. Soc. 339/22/1, 2, 3*) show some of the sub-leases they assigned to improve their land's yield.

Delafield devoted a separate page of the burial register he took over to recording burials of the members of the Ferrers family for whose interment he had 'broken ground' in the chancel, presumably at the grave of Thomas Ferrers bearing his 1646 epitaph as 'lord of the manor'. Delafield thus buried in the chancel six members of the family who died between 1728 and 1751 (at a fee for five of them of 13s and 4d each), two of them, father and son, again described as 'Lord of this Manour'.

The sixth he names as 'Mr John Ferrers of Gt Marlow being an Outparishioner' (his fee here was £1.1s.0d). This, with the fact that thereafter the name appears no more in the burial register, strongly suggests that by 1751 the manor had passed out of the Ferrers family's hands, although the Lysons (*Magna Britannica*) say the family was still holding the manor in 1737. Browne Willis, in his description of the epitaph on the Ferrers grave in the chancel of Fingest church (*Willis MS,* vol. x) has a marginal note: 'I presume Mr Ferrers demesnes and manor here now, Ao 1750, belong to Bartholomew Tipping, Esq.'.

The Manor; From Prebendaries to Ecclesiastical Commissioners

The Ferrers, though maybe lords of the manor, were not landowners, but lessee tenants of Wells canons, and this too was the case for those that followed them; in turn, Bartholomew Tipping (according to Willis), then Thomas Dorell in 1780 (according to the Lysons (*Magna Britannica*)) and next Thomas Williams, MP for Marlow, in 1797 according to Lipscomb. In his 1847 *History*, Lipscomb describes the manor house as 'a plain old mansion'.

In 1840 the Cathedral Act made all prebends honorary and vested their revenues in the Ecclesiastical Commission; and then in 1850 an Order in Council substituted a money payment to the prebendary of Dultincote for the property of his prebend. Thus Thomas Williams's grandson, Thomas Piers Williams, also MP for Marlow, became by inheritance lessee of the Ecclesiastical Commissioners. By 1861 the manor house was in ruins (J.J. Sheahan, *History and Topography of Bucks*, 1861, p.883). Today, as we know, all trace of it above ground has gone though the cellars doubtless remain, and might repay a dig.

After 1820: Rectors, Curates, Parish, and the Advowson

To return to incumbents of the benefice. Lipscomb (*Hist. Antiq. Bucks., 1847*), the pamphlets in the church and the brass plate on the north wall of the nave all agree that in 1820 the next rector was Henry Joseph Thomas Drury. He came of a family of classicists, had been educated at Eton and King's College, Cambridge, and became undermaster and afterwards master at Harrow School. His father was Joseph Drury, headmaster of Harrow, who had been instituted prebendary of Dultincote in 1812, and presented his son to the Fingest rectory in 1820. At Harrow, Henry Joseph Thomas Drury had Byron as a pupil, and had acquired a reputation as a classical scholar, forming a library of Greek classics at the school. All this being said, although as a schoolmaster he was also an ordained priest, as Fingest's rector he never set foot in the place. Diocesan records (*Linc. Archiv. Cttee. Rep, 1959–60*) show that he was granted a non-residence licence because he was assistant master at Harrow. In the Tithe Commissioners' assessment of 1840 the apportionment of rent-charges in lieu of tithes agreed for their commutation stipulated that as rector Drury should be paid £188.16s.0d. The next year he died. During his incumbency, curates signing Fingest marriage forms were George Isherwood until 1828, George Scobell until 1834 and in 1838 Henry Tufnell Young, owner of Mallard's Court in Stokenchurch parish.

Fingest-with-Ibstone

For the last year of his non-resident incumbency Drury had arranged for George Augustus Baker, officiating curate at Ibstone, to take on the Fingest curacy as well. When Drury died, Baker, still living at Ibstone, was appointed rector of Fingest. The parish then had a population of two hundred and ninety-five (Lipscomb, *Hist. Antiq. Bucks, 1847*). Ten years later, incorporation of a sizeable area of the parish into the new chapelry of Cadmore End (Fig. 18) removed one hundred and twenty from Fingest's then population of three hundred and eighty-seven (*Order in Council, 24th October, 1853*). In 1852 what remained of the parish was attached to Ibstone, Baker now becoming rector of the new benefice of Fingest-with-Ibstone. This had required certification by the Archbishop of Canterbury of the necessary transfer of the advowson of Fingest from the Wells prebendary of Dultincote, Fingest being a Buckinghamshire parish and Ibstone an Oxfordshire one. The advowson of this double parish was given to two patrons alternately, the Bishop of Oxford and the Warden and scholars of Merton College, Oxford.

In 1848, with disruption of the parish impending, rector Baker and Thomas Sewell, his curate at Fingest, discovered themselves to be legal trustees of its church trust and charity trust property. Sewell prudently started an entry book setting out month by month sums received from rents of church land and from the Picket and Mole charities and how expended; he also entered the names of boys and girls provided with clothing and attending Lane End school under the terms of the Edmonds Charity, most of them from families of parishioners in the new Cadmore End chapelry. The entry book was intermittently kept up until in 1921 the church property was sold and the proceeds invested, and the Edmonds Charity charge was redeemed and also invested, remitting fifteen pounds per annum to the 'Fingest Foundation of the Revd Francis Edmonds'.

How much George Baker and Thomas Sewell contributed to renovation of the Fingest chancel over and above Emily Gowland's reopening of its north windows is unclear, despite the brass plate with their names on it. However, Baker's returns to the *Buckingham Religious Census* of 1851 attest the increasing unfruitfulness of his Fingest rectory; he remarks that 'The Parish Church of Fingest is situated so inconveniently for the Population that the great Major[it]y of the Parishioners attend Public Worship in the District Church at Lane End'.

A church had been consecrated at Lane End in 1832 through the efforts of rector Ridley of Hambleden who had taken his family there to escape a cholera epidemic in his own parish. An *Order in Council* of 1867 establishing Lane End Ecclesiastical District as a Consolidated chapelry depleted Fingest parish even further.

That George Baker was buried in Fingest churchyard in 1866 (along with his curate Sewell and the benefactress Emily Gowland) hints that despite the diminishing trend in the parish's area and numbers, the church building itself was increasingly adducing Victorian veneration. Baker's sister Georgiana, and his successor as rector of Fingest-with-Ibstone, Richard Philip Goldsworth Tiddeman, between them found the funds to put in hand Street's restoration work, which closed the church for two years.

At Ibstone the Revd Tiddeman, making claims against the Revd Baker's estate for dilapidations at Ibstone rectory, and certain payments due to him including sums for timber felled and a sizeable heap of dung, found himself in a legal battle with his predecessor's son, H.S. Baker. In a box-file at Oxford County Archives (*MS Oxf. Dioc, papers, c.1492*) is preserved a thick roll of letters exchanged over a year between lawyers acting for H.S. Baker and for Tiddeman, between their clients themselves and between their clients and the bishop's office; but also, gilding so dull a brief, lengthy indignant protests from Mrs Tiddeman defending her husband's rights, disparaging the Baker camp, and bringing alive to our ears her spoken contempt for their penny-pinching attitude. In the end, to her great satisfaction, Baker paid off most of what he owed.

After Tiddeman, in 1878 Henry Joscelyne M.A. was instituted rector of the double benefice. He was buried in Ibstone churchyard in 1906, to be succeeded by John Stratton Davis M.A. That neither Tiddeman, Joscelyne nor Stratton Davis, living at Ibstone, felt need of, or at any rate were not given curates, underlines how inconsiderable and insignificant Fingest parish had become, yielding ground to its growing neighbours at Cadmore End and Lane End with their relatively new churches which, despite its Victorian restoration, it could not hope to outdo. It fell to Stratton Davis in 1913 to perform the penultimate truncation of the old parish by selling the 'ancient glebe', house and all.

Bernard William Mackie (1931–65) was the last rector of Fingest-with-Ibstone. When my wife and I came to The Old Rectory in 1969 one of the old villagers we came to know, George Harman, told us he remembered the Rev. Mackie coming from Ibstone to Fingest and holding services in a church with no congregation.

In 1965 the parish of Fingest became part of the Hambleden valley group of churches under a group rector, Wilfred E. Watts. In 1976 an *Order in Council* performed the ultimate ablation, creating a new 'benefice of Fingest' of starveling size (Fig. 2).

The Parsonage House

Rector Francis Edmonds never lived in it, and whether any curate did then or after is doubtful. It is more than likely that even in Edmonds' time the house with its outbuildings and glebe land was let as a farmhouse, the rent it produced going to the shadowy 'Bearcroft secundus' and then Perkins as 'rectors'. What is more, apart from the marriage register signatures, the only further mention we hear of Thomas Powell's name is through Queen Anne's Bounty Office Governors, of Deans Yard, Westminster; they certify, with Revd Thos. Powell as witness, that they

> acquired for the living of Fingest in the year 1793 a property [...] containing 15 a.2r.26p. and situate in the parish of Hambleden [...] The Title deeds are in this office.

The reader may recall that 1793 was the year before Thomas Powell described himself as 'rector'; the bounty land in question is 'Great Murridge', opposite Fingest House; in Powell's favour, doubtless, it increased the area of Fingest glebe land available to let to farming tenants. Whatever the effect, the parsonage house and land was known thereafter as 'Glebe Farm'; only recently was the house gentrified as The Old Rectory.

The indenture of its sale as 'Glebe Farm' names as vendor the Revd John Stratton Davis of the first part, the Ecclesiastical Commissioners of the second part, Charles Bishop of Oxford and the Warden and scholars of Merton College, patrons, and Thomas Ellis Collier of the third part purchaser for the sum of eight hundred pounds to be paid to the Ecclesiastical Commissioners. What was sold was the farm house, its outbuildings and forty acres of pasture, arable and woodland, with a tithe rent charge of £6.11s.5d

324

payable part to the rector of Fingest and part to the rector of Hambleden (for the 'Murridge' fields).

Author's Tail-piece

Here ends a fumblingly pieced-together patchwork of parish history, stretched here, distorted there, and ever more threadbare in its shadowy representment of the tangled patterns of the country's history. Pictured, however sketchily, are first the budding Chiltern parish, 'Fingest-with-Skirmett'; then with the loss of Skirmett prompting parish growth to the Oxfordshire county border, we more clearly perceive the evergreen mediaeval Fingest, flowering under the favouring rule of abbots, then bishops. Sadly then, reader, with the end of the Middle Ages, a slow withering of the flower, more apparent with each passing century. By the mid-nineteen hundreds, just 'Fingest-with-Ibstone'; and finally the 1976 Order, enshrouding Fingest village in a parish withered to almost nothing.

And now...?

Bibliography: Important Sources

Bond, Francis, *Dedications and Patron Saints of English Churches*, Oxford University Press, 1914

Darby, H.C. and Campbell E.M.J., *The Domesday Geography of S.E. England*, Cambridge, 1962

Lipscomb, George, *The History and Antiquities of the County of Buckinghamshire*, 1847, vol. iii

Maitland, F.W., *Domesday Book and Beyond*, Cambridge University Press, 1897

Mawer, A. and Stenton, F.M., *The Place Names of Buckinghamshire*, Cambridge University Press, 1969

Momigliano, Arnaldo, *Studies in Historiography*, London, Weidenfeld & Nicholson, 1966

Shean, J.J., *History and Topography of Buckinghamshire*, 1861

Taylor, H.M. & J., *Anglo-Saxon Architecture*, Cambridge University Press, 1965

Delafield, Thomas, Bodleian Library, Gough MS, Oxford:

———, *'Notes on Bucks', Oxon 6*

———, *'Notitia Haseliana', Oxon 19*

———, *'History of Haseley', Oxon 41*

———, *'History of Stokenchurch', Oxon 47*

———, *'History of Great Milton', Oxon 48*

———, *'Account of Fingest', Bucks 2*

Records of Buckinghamshire, Bucks Archaeological Society, vols. vi–xxxvi (1900–1996)

Victoria County History of Buckinghamshire, vols. i–iii

Willis, Browne, *MSS, Bodleian Library, Oxford, vols. i, xii, xiii, xiv, xvii, xl, liv, xciv*